A READER'S GUIDE

For Parents of Children with Mental, Physical, or Emotional Disabilities

By Cory Moore

WOODBINE HOUSE • 1990

Published by:
Woodbine House
5615 Fishers Lane
Rockville, MD 20852
301/468–8800; Toll Free 800/843–7323

Library of Congress Cataloging-in-Publication Data

Moore, Cory.
    A Reader's guide for parents of children with mental, physical, or
emotional disabilities / Cory Moore. — 3rd ed.
      p. cm.
    ISBN 0–933149–27–1 : $14.95
    1. Handicapped children—Bibliography. 2. Mentally handicapped children—Bibliography.
3. Physically handicapped children—Bibliography. 4. Mentally ill children—Bibliography. I. Title.
Z5814.C52M67 1990
[HV888]
016.3624'083–dc20
                                        89–40590
                                            CIP

Manufactured in the United States of America
1 2 3 4 5 6 7 8 9 10

DEDICATION

A **Reader's Guide** is dedicated to the memory of Peg (Kathryn A.) Morton who originated its idea and co-authored its first two editions.

Peg's daughter Beckie was the youngest of her five children. Profoundly retarded, her needs directed Peg's all-too-few years in ways that have touched and shaped the lives and thoughts of parents and professionals throughout the community of developmental disability.

Peg was tireless in the quest that went far beyond her own. She accepted all challenges. Where there were no services, she created them. She listened and acted; she wrote and shared. Peg was a leader. She was also a warm, caring human being who strengthened all of us who knew her, a woman of unique intelligence and talent, a loving daughter, sister, aunt, a devoted wife and mother, a rare and special friend. I measure what I do every day by what Peg might have done. I so wish we could have shared this venture.

A Message to Our Readers

If you have an idea for a special-needs book, we would like to hear from you. Woodbine House is committed to publishing books that help children with disabilities, their families, and the professionals who work with them. We are always looking for fresh ideas for books about specific disabilities and about issues that affect all people with disabilities. We welcome suggestions and manuscripts from parents, teachers, librarians, medical specialists, and others who care about special-needs children and their future.

To submit a manuscript or propose a book idea for our special-needs collection, please write to us at this address:

Special-Needs Editor
Woodbine House
5615 Fishers Lane
Rockville, MD 20852

If you would like a personal reply, please enclose a self-addressed, stamped envelope with your letter.

TABLE OF CONTENTS

PART III
Specific Topics of Interest

PART IV
Books for the Younger Reader

PART V
Journals, Magazines, Newsletters, and Directories

PART VI
Appendix and Indexes

Introduction

Many new parents approach the raising of their children with no special preparation, yet advice, assistance, models to emulate, and other parents to talk with are abundant—usually no further away than the house next door. Parents of children with disabilities are also unprepared to raise their children, but advice, assistance, models to emulate, and other parents to talk with who have similar problems and concerns may well be far more difficult to find. And these parents unquestionably need specific knowledge, awareness, and understanding in order to help their children grow up as physically and emotionally healthy as possible.

Raising a child with a disability requires more knowledge and understanding—of that child, of oneself, and of others—than is required in raising a typical child. And since parents are the monitors of their child's well-being throughout life, they would do well to prepare themselves the best they can to meet this challenge. Reading about the experiences of others, learning about sources of information, and becoming familiar with what professionals are advising are activities that can provide a bewildered parent with some of the tools that will make child-rearing more successful and satisfying.

As the parent of a child with multiple disabilities, now grown to adulthood, I have long recognized the value of information. I have learned from talking with other parents of children and adults with disabilities, I have drawn on my experiences, and I have read extensively. I have found reading helpful in my own effort to grow with my daughter. I hope this **Reader's Guide** will provide others with the kinds of information that will simplify the tasks of surveying the current literature, selecting what is of particular interest, locating it in libraries, or ordering it from publishers, organizations, or agencies.

Books in Part I are relevant to all disabilities. They are divided into six categories: (1) Basic Reading—books about persons with disabilities and their families; (2) Your Child at Home—books that tell how parents can teach, train, and play with their child; (3) Your Child at School—books that concentrate primarily on educational experiences; (4) Your Child Grows Up—books about the transitioning and adult years; (5) Personal Accounts—From Those Who Have Lived It—books written by persons with disabilities about their own lives or by parents and others describing their experiences in living or working with children or adults with disabilities; and (6) Where to Write for Information—private and public associations, government agencies, and other organizations that distribute books, pamphlets, newsletters, and resources that parents can send for.

Part II contains selections about specific disabilities—autism, chronic conditions or illnesses (such as dwarfism, cystic fibrosis, diabetes, and hemophilia), cleft palate, epilepsy, hearing impairment, learning disabilities, hyperactivity, and/or attention deficit disorder, mental illness and behavior disorders, mental retardation, multiple disabilities, physical disabilities, speech and language disabilities, and visual disabilities. Again, books within each section are divided, whenever possible, into the six categories outlined above.

Part III annotates selections under specific topics of interest to parents, to persons with disabilities, and to those who work with them. Some are relevant to all disabilities, some are more specific. Be sure to check the subjects for ones of interest to you.

Part IV contains Books for the Younger Reader, both fiction and nonfiction written for typical children and teenagers about their peers with disabilities. Books for the younger reader with a disability are also included.

Part V contains listings of journals, magazines, newsletters, and directories helpful to people with disabilities, their families, and the professionals who work with them.

Part VI includes an appendix of publishers' addresses and indexes of organizations and agencies, authors and editors, titles, and subjects.

While all the books listed are supposedly in print, it may not be possible to find them in your local bookstore and sometimes bookstores will not place special orders. For that reason, the listing of publishers' addresses is included. Prices given are subject to change and publishers have different shipping and handling charges, so do write or call for current costs before ordering. There are also specialty bookstores to write to for help in securing a particular book you want. Some mail-order resources with especially comprehensive inventories are:

- BOSC—Books on Special Children. P.O. Box 305, Congers, New York 10920.

- Disabilities Bookshelf, Sandy Creek Children's Bookstore. 1914 Perry Street, Durham, North Carolina 27705.

- The Disability Bookshop. P.O. Box 129, Vancouver, Washington 98666.

- The Exceptional Parent Library. Boston University Bookstore, 660 Beacon Street, Boston, Massachusetts 02215.

- The Spinal Network Bookstore. P.O. Box 4162, Boulder, Colorado 80306.

Recent years have seen an amazing outpouring of literature on the subject of disabilities. The **Guide** is not all-inclusive. It represents what *this* reader judges to be the most relevant and helpful works, those that subscribe to up-to-date theories and approaches, and are readable and interesting. The **Guide** was compiled for parents and should be useful to the professionals who work with families, as well. In an attempt to make acquisition of the books as easy as possible, I have included only those still reputed to be in print. As I write and as you read, new books are being published and others have become unavailable. I apologize for any inconvenience. I would be delighted to hear from you with recommendations for books I may have missed for future editions of the **Guide.** Please write to me c/o Woodbine House, 5616 Fishers Lane, Rockville, Maryland 20852.

*   *   *

I should like to express my sincere appreciation and thanks to Sue Nichols of the Montgomery County, Maryland, Library System for helping me locate and evaluate books; Cindy Love for her librarian skills; Bobbi Stettner-Eaton for her organizational skills; Ken Moore and Lissa Kahn for their important behind-the-scenes work; Nancy Bonomo for deciphering my cut-and-paste text and putting it together; the Association for Retarded Citizens/Montgomery County for allowing me to use the time and energy to make the **Guide** possible; and Susan Stokes and the other good people at Woodbine House for making it all happen.

Cory Moore

ALL DISABILITIES

PART 1

Basic Reading

Batshaw, Mark L.; Perret, Yvonne M. **Children with Handicaps: A Medical Primer.** 2d ed. Baltimore: Paul H. Brookes, 1986. 473 pp. $26.00 (Paper).

> This fine textbook—an expansion of the 1981 first edition—helps to answer questions about what might have happened before, during, or after birth to cause a developmental disability. Beginning with an introduction to genes, chromosomes, and heredity, the growth of a human being is traced. Mental retardation, visual impairments, hearing, speech and language problems, autism, attention deficit disorder and hyperactivity, learning disabilities, cerebral palsy, and epilepsy are described. The emotional impact on families, some ethical dilemmas, public benefits, legal services, and estate planning are included. Sensitive discussions, clear illustrations, case studies, and a readable style provide both basic information and insights about children with disabilities.

Dickman, Irving; with Gordon, Sol. **One Miracle at a Time: How to Get Help for Your Disabled Child—From the Experience of Other Parents.** New York: Simon & Schuster, 1985. 351 pp. $17.95. Fayetteville, N.Y.: Ed-U Press. $8.95 (Paper).

> Irving Dickman, a veteran parent, has written a book that could serve as a well-organized support group: it offers personal experiences, solid advice, and fine resource information from parents "who have been there"; it covers all the areas affecting parents raising a child with a disability—early experiences, dealing with doctors and schools, becoming an advocate, family relationships, support systems, and a host more. It is "a book about how things *are*, not how they're supposed to be." Sol Gordon has contributed a chapter in his special expertise, sexuality education, as well as a pertinent "Word to Professionals."

Featherstone, Helen. **A Difference in the Family: Life with a Disabled Child.** New York: Penguin, 1982. 288 pp. $6.95 (Paper).

> This is an honest, remarkable book; the definitive work about how it really feels to raise a child with a severe disability. By "speaking publicly about private matters," Featherstone, both a parent and educator, has produced an important consciousness-raising guide that should help parents feel less alone and assist professionals to appreciate the problems and pleasures of those who live with and love a child who is different.

Glidden, Laraine Masters. **Parents for Children, Children for Parents: The Adoption Alternative.** Washington, D.C.: American Association on Mental Retardation, 1989. 209 pp. $21.00 (Paper).

> This interesting monograph explores why people choose to adopt children with special needs, how adoption occurs, and why people who adopt find it a rich and rewarding experience. The anecdotal material makes the study of forty-two families in Great Britain both understandable and fascinating reading.

Goldfarb, Lori A.; Brotherson, Mary Jane; Summers, Jean Ann; Turnbull, Ann P. **Meeting the Challenge of Disability or Chronic Illness: A Family Guide.** Baltimore: Paul H. Brookes, 1986. 181 pp. $16.00 (Paper).

The authors of this wonderfully helpful and refreshing guidebook recognize the strengths in all families and believe in their capacity to survive even the most challenging circumstances. Part I, *Taking Stock,* is designed to help each family discover its own values, resources, and coping methods. Part II, *Problem Solving,* offers a step-by-step method to find solutions to unresolved problems. Ideas and examples abound. Thought-provoking exercises are sprinkled throughout as "flexible tools for self-discovery." There is, in addition, a good resource list of readings and organizations.

Good, Julia Darnell; Reis, Joyce Good. **A Special Kind of Parenting: Meeting the Needs of Handicapped Children.** Franklin Park, Ill.: La Leche League International, 1985. 172 pp. $8.95 (Paper).

One of the authors parented two children with disabilities. She shares the truths she learned from her experience and from a questionnaire answered by a number of other parents. Topics range from learning about the disability, grief, coping and acceptance, strengthening a marriage, family needs, the child with special needs from preschool age through the teen years, medical emergencies, hospitalization, and communicating with medical professionals. The tone of the book is friendly; its advice is wise.

Levy, Joel M.; Levy, Philip H.; Nivin, Ben, eds. **Strengthening Families: New Directions in Providing Services to People with Developmental Disabilities and Their Families.** New York: Young Adult Institute Press, 1989. 354 pp. $29.95 (Paper).

A number of parents and professionals contributed to this interesting compilation of articles based on presentations made at a national conference. Topics address family support services; the parent/professional partnership; models, strategies, and approaches for empowering families; models and strategies for addressing early childhood needs; and social, legal, political, and policy issues.

Lindemann, James E.; Lindemann, Sally J. **Growing Up Proud: A Parents' Guide to the Psychological Care of Children with Disabilities.** New York: Warner Books, 1988. 208 pp. $9.95 (Paper).

Writing for parents of children with all kinds of disabilities and spanning the years from infancy to young adulthood, a psychologist husband-and-wife team provides guidelines and principles that will maximize the possibilities for children to "grow up proud." Attitudes to help parents develop optimal expectations are gently and clearly encouraged. Concrete and interesting, the book's pages are filled with sensible counsel, suggestions, and illustrative examples.

Paterson, George W. **Helping Your Handicapped Child.** Minneapolis: Augsburg, 1975. 103 pp. $3.50 (Paper).

For parents of children with disabilities "who seek to interpret their experience within a framework of religion," this small book should prove helpful. While it suffers from archaic language ("afflicted with") and out-of-date information, its tone is sensitive to parents' reactions and children's needs.

Perske, Robert. **Hope for the Families: New Directions for Parents of Persons with Retardation or Other Disabilities.** Nashville: Abingdon, 1981. 96 pp. $9.95 (Paper).

Written "for families who are trying to turn a tough situation into a rich experience," this helpful, hopeful book deals simply and honestly with parents' feelings, fears, and wishes. Optimism, humor, and sound advice abound. Martha Perske's remarkable drawings add a special appeal.

Prensky, Arthur; Palkes, Helen. **Care of the Neurologically Handicapped Child.** New York: Oxford University Press, 1982. 331 pp. $28.95.

This book describes normal and abnormal development, what to expect from the various specialists parents may consult, and seven of the most common neurological disorders: epilepsy, cerebral palsy, birth defects, mental retardation, neuromuscular disease, learning disabilities and language disorders, and hyperactivity. It is intended to help parents be informed, ask the right questions, and define where to best apply their energies and efforts in helping their children.

Pueschel, Siegfried M.; Bernier, James C.; Weidenman, Leslie E. **The Special Child: A Source Book for Parents of Children with Developmental Disabilities.** Baltimore: Paul H. Brookes, 1988. 368 pp. $22.00 (Paper).

The authors and contributors were all on staff at the Child Development Center at Rhode Island Hospital. Information starts with the discovery of a disability and covers family issues, working with professionals, the various common problems in children with special needs, inherited and acquired developmental disabilities, special care, tests and procedures, adaptive equipment, medical and surgical treatments, psychological tests and procedures, education, legal issues, and resources. The book is both comprehensive and helpful.

Routberg, Marcia. **On Becoming a Special Parent: A Mini-Support Group in a Book.** Chicago: Parent/Professional Publications, 1986. 131 pp. $8.00 (including postage) (Paper).

The author is a mother who shares a potpourri of hints, thoughts, and strategies on a number of topics—from "keeping your cool" to paying the bills, from special education to professional jargon. She writes from her experience and from her heart to help support parents new to the arena of developmental disability. Her recommendations are sound; her information is reliable.

Schleifer, Maxwell J.; Klein, Stanley D., eds. **The Disabled Child & the Family: An Exceptional Parent Reader.** Boston: The Exceptional Parent Press, 1985. 183 pp. $15.95 (plus $2.50 handling) (Paper).

The Exceptional Parent magazine has long been a respected source of information and guidance for families. This anthology of sixty-two articles explores family reactions, looks at the challenges faced as a child with a disability grows up, examines technology, and provides names and addresses of organizations and agencies.

Segal, Marilyn. **In Time and with Love: Caring for the Special Needs Baby.** New York: Newmarket Press, 1988. 191 pp. $21.95; $12.95 (Paper).

> The author is both a psychologist and the mother of a daughter with disabilities. Her book is sensitive, useful, honest, and filled with charming photographs. Source material grew out of an early intervention program for families of infants with special needs who asked that a guidebook present perspectives on feelings, accurate information, and practical suggestions. The book's subjects include coping skills for all family members, daily interactions and routines, learning games and activities, decision-making, and a resource guide containing a listing of organizations, publications, toys, and equipment.

Simons, Robin. **After the Tears: Parents Talk about Raising a Child with a Disability.** Orlando, Fla.: Harcourt Brace Jovanovich, 1987. 89 pp. $4.95 (Paper).

> Only another parent of a child with a disability can truly understand the early "nothingness," the slow recovery, and the growth and strength of "a whole new way of life" that can come after the tears. Parents share their feelings, their solace, and their suggestions in this attractive and important booklet that will be read in a sitting and pondered for a long time. Throughout this honest work is the message to talk, to share, to follow your instincts, to recognize your own needs, and to do what you know is best and most realistic for your family and your child.

Smith, Barbara Gosline. **Although . . . Those Who Overcame.** Pismo Beach, Calif.: Padre Productions, 1981. 168 pp. $9.95 (Paper).

> This unique compilation of hundreds of mini-biographies of people who have not let a handicapping condition thwart their abilities is indexed by specific disabilities.

Weiner, Florence. **No Apologies: A Guide to Living with a Disability, Written by the Real Authorities—People with Disabilities, Their Families, and Friends.** New York: St. Martin's, 1986. 188 pp. $13.95 (Paper).

> This fine collection of essays offers practical advice, lists of resources, and personal observations on a variety of subjects, including "living/making it with a disability," medical care, education, work and money, and organizing. The author is a disability rights activist and a sibling; her hard-hitting, honest book is enlightening, encouraging, and empowering.

Your Child at Home

Allen, Anne and George. **Everyone Can Win: Opportunities and Programs in the Arts for the Disabled.** McLean, Va.: EPM Publications, 1988. 272 pp. $11.95 (Paper).

Art programs nationwide are described to illustrate the ways in which the arts can enrich the lives of people with disabilities, by liberating self-expression and providing successful experiences. Examples range from dance, drama, puppetry, and the visual arts, to poetry, prose, and music. All disabilities are represented. Black-and-white photographs appear throughout. The authors contend that when art is used for enjoyment rather than therapy, therapeutic results often occur.

Baker, Bruce L.; Brightman, Alan J.; Blacher, Jan B.; Heifetz, Louis J.; Hinshaw, Stephen P.; Murphy, Diane M. **Steps to Independence: A Skills Training Guide for Parents and Teachers of Children with Special Needs.** 2d ed. Baltimore: Paul H. Brookes, 1989. 323 pp. $24.00 (Paper).

This is parent-child interaction at its best—attractively presented, easy to follow, almost guaranteed to work. Updated, revised, and packaged in one comprehensive volume, the subjects still cover the essentials: get-ready skills, self-help, toilet training, play, independent living, self-care, home care, information skills, and behavior problem management. The *Basics of Teaching* section is clearly written to help parents translate training to the home environment.

Bratt, Berneen. **No Time for Jello: One Family's Experiences with the Doman-Delacato Patterning Program.** Cambridge, Mass.: Brookline Books, 1989. 210 pp. $17.95 (Paper).

For almost thirty years, the controversial Doman-Delacato "patterning" therapy, introduced at the Institutes for the Achievement of Human Potential in Philadelphia, has encouraged hope for parents of children with brain injury and interest by professionals. Berneen Bratt has now detailed the experiences of a family involved in the program, which eventually proved, for the most part, ineffective. Later, as a graduate student in Early Childhood Special Needs, Bratt investigated professional and popular literature concerning the Institutes and its founder; an appendix summarizes both supportive and critical writings.

Butler, Dorothy. **Cushla and Her Books.** Boston: The Horn Book, 1981. 128 pp. $12.95 (Paper).

Born with hearing and visual impairments, poor motor control, and suspected mental retardation, Cushla progressed to above average intellect. Books were read to her daily from the time she was four months old and are credited for her progress. This fascinating account suggests an approach for parents to use with young children with disabilities.

Caldwell, Bettye; Stedman, Donald, eds. **Infant Education: A Guide for Helping Handicapped Children in the First Three Years.** New York: Walker, 1977. 167 pp. $8.95 (Paper).

This collection of articles will be useful to parents who want to learn about early work done throughout the country by infant educators.

Crump, Iris M. **Nutrition and Feeding of the Handicapped Child.** Boston: Little, Brown, 1987. 163 pp. $22.50 (Paper).

Intended for school staff, this book contains practical information that should help parents of children with a variety of disabilities who wish to have more knowledge about nutrition and information on handling feeding problems.

Goldberg, Sally. **Teaching with Toys: Making Your Own Educational Toys.** Ann Arbor: University of Michigan, 1981. 91 pp. $8.95 (Paper).

The author is a former teacher, an editor of children's educational programs, and a creator of baby toys. She is also the mother of a child with a learning difficulty. Her book presents both ideas about educating with toys and instructions for making and using specific toys to teach self-awareness, colors, letters, numbers, shapes, and reading. The book has a pleasant format with sketches and photographs.

Gordon, Ira J. **Baby Learning through Baby Play: A Parent's Guide for the First Two Years.** New York: St. Martin's, 1970. 121 pp. $6.95 (Paper).
Gordon, Ira J.; Guinagh, Barry; Jester, R. Emile. **Child Learning through Child Play: Learning Activities for Two and Three Year Olds.** New York: St. Martin's, 1972. 128 pp. $8.95; $6.95 (Paper).

These two guides describe games to enhance development while providing fun for child and parent. Although directed to the typical child, both books are easily adapted to the child with a disability.

Hartman, Harriet. **Let's Play and Learn: An Activity Book for Parents and Young Children.** New York: Human Sciences Press, 1976. 138 pp. $12.95 (Paper).

This is a collection of teaching games for parents to play with their young children, with or without disabilities.

Healy, Alfred; Keesee, Patricia D.; Smith, Barbara S. **Early Services for Children with Special Needs: Transactions for Family Support.** Baltimore: Paul H. Brookes, 1989. 233 pp. $20.00 (Paper).

In highly readable style, with quotes from parents and professionals, the authors look at the mission and the mandates of P.L. 99–457, the early intervention legislation that focuses on "support for the family as a means of enhancing the development of the child" identified as "different." Their book speaks to the need for true and meaningful family and professional collaboration, suggests action steps, and provides a lengthy annotated bibliography for those who wish to explore issues in depth.

Harnes, Merle B. **Creative Games for Learning.** Reston, Va.: Council for Exceptional Children, 1977. 152 pp. $8.50 (Paper).

This notebook gives directions for fifty games to make and play with young children and suggestions for their adaption for use with children with disabilities. Clear instructions and illustrations show how to construct each game from simple materials, how to use the game, what learning purpose it serves, variations to promote learning in other areas, and suggestions for easy storage. The book should prove useful for teachers and parents.

Koch, Jaroslav. **Total Baby Development.** New York: Pocket Books, 1978. 351 pp. $8.95 (Paper).

Three hundred and thirty-three exercises and games suitable for use during the first year of a baby's life are shared. For parents who can't squeeze it all in, the author provides a mini-program.

Lévy, Janine. **The Baby Exercise Book: The First Fifteen Months.** New York: Pantheon, 1974. 111 pp. $6.95 (Paper).

A well-written manual, illustrated with photographs, describes simple exercises to use with babies at various developmental stages spanning the first fifteen months.

McConkey, Roy; Jeffree, Dorothy. **Making Toys for Handicapped Children: A Guide for Parents and Teachers.** Rev. ed. New York: Prentice Hall, 1983. 198 pp. $10.95 (Paper).

Detailed and clear instructions for making fifteen toys to stimulate spontaneous play in children with disabilities are accompanied by photographs and illustrations. The helpful text explains how to use the toys to best advantage in fostering the following of directions, imitation, pretending, use of language, and interaction.

Millman, Joan; Behrmann, Polly. **Parents as Playmates: A Games Approach to Preschool Years.** New York: Human Sciences Press, 1979. 139 pp. $14.95 (Paper).

This imaginative collection of activities is planned to help parents turn "ticklish times into enriching ones" for themselves and their preschoolers.

Mollan, Renée. **Yes They Can! A Handbook for Effectively Parenting the Handicapped.** Buena Park, Calif.: Reality Productions, 1981. 104 pp. $12.95 (Paper).

The aim of this engaging and informal handbook is to give parents some keys to guide a child with a disability toward independence and responsibility. The author is a speech pathologist who has worked with children and their families; her message is a good one.

Morris, Lisa Rappaport; Schulz, Linda. **Creative Play Activities for Children with Disabilities: A Resource Book for Teachers and Parents.** 2d ed. Champaign, Ill.: Human Kinetics Publishers, 1989. 215 pp. $12.95 (Paper).

The two hundred and fifty games and activities in this delightful compilation are an outgrowth of the "Let's Play to Grow" program developed by the Joseph P. Kennedy, Jr., Foundation. They are designed to promote the development of infants to eight year olds with disabilities. Activities focus on the senses, movement, water play, outdoors, make-believe, arts and crafts, music and rhythm, and group activities. Directions and information on necessary equipment and special adaptations when needed for children with physical, visual, hearing, emotional, and developmental disabilities accompany the descriptions. A good resource section of organizations, books, toys, records, and equipment is included.

Rogovin, Anne; Cataldo, Christine Z. **What's the Hurry? Developmental Activities for Able and Handicapped Children.** Austin: Pro-Ed, 1983. 208 pp. $19.00.

Eighty-eight activities involving materials that can be made easily and inexpensively are organized into physical, personal, and intellectual areas of development. Photographs of each device accompany the description.

Rubin, Judith Aron. **Child Art Therapy: Understanding and Helping Children Grow through Art.** 2d ed. New York: Van Nostrand Reinhold, 1984. 304 pp. $22.95 (Paper).

This survey of art therapy techniques used with children who are labeled emotionally disturbed and disabled includes sections on family, mother-child, and group therapy, and emphasizes the healing and self-knowledge gained through art under the guidance of a sensitive and well-trained therapist. Many case histories are included.

Sparling, Joseph; Lewis, Isabelle. **Learningames for the First Three Years: A Guide to Parent-Child Play.** New York: Walker, 1979. 226 pp. $12.95; $8.95 (Paper). New York: Berkley Publishing, 1986. $3.95 (Paper).

The authors point out that since the real beginning of learning starts very early and since parents are natural teachers of their children, knowing how to make more learning occur becomes essential. Activities for building trust, showing feelings, making sounds, and playing games with words and toys are prescribed for each age level. Plentiful photographs illustrate the activities.

Sparling, Joseph; Lewis, Isabelle. **Learningames for Threes and Fours: A Guide to Adult-Child Play.** New York: Walker, 1984. 217 pp. $16.95.

This is a sequel to **Learningames for the First Three Years.** One hundred games are described; both how to play and why to play each game are attractively discussed with text and illustrative photographs. Children with developmental disabilities, somewhat older than the prescribed ages, will profit from these pleasant parent/child activities.

Sternlicht, Manny; Hurwitz, Abraham. **Games Children Play: Instructive and Creative Play Activities for the Mentally Retarded and Developmentally Disabled Child.** New York: Van Nostrand Reinhold, 1981. 117 pp. $18.95.

This sourcebook of games designed to stimulate the senses, improve abilities, and foster the development of logical reasoning and judgment, as well as encourage a sense of humor, creativity, and imagination, offers valuable and pleasant encouragement for parent interaction with children.

Your Child at School

The following books concentrate on educational experiences, for the most part. Please refer to Part III: *Specific Topics of Interest* for works dealing with advocacy, integration, parent-professional partnerships, and public policy.

Bizer, Linda; Markel, Geraldine. **The ABC's of the SAT: A Parent's Guide to College Entrance Examinations.** New York: Arco, 1983. 150 pp. $4.95 (Paper).
    In this guide for parents to help teenagers through the college admission process is a short but useful chapter, "The SAT and Handicapped Teenagers." It outlines the availability of special testing arrangements and a few specific advocacy strategies.

Blatt, Burton; Morris, Richard J., eds. **Perspectives in Special Education: Personal Orientations.** Glenview, Ill.: Scott, Foresman, 1984. 324 pp. $24.95.
    In this highly interesting and unusual volume, ten prominent individuals in the field of special education share their very personal reflections on how they became involved, their careers, and what they see as future directions. The chapter authors are Seymour Sarason, Samuel Kirk, Herbert Goldstein, William Morse, Robert Edgerton, Robert Guthrie, Edward Zigler, James Gallagher, Richard Schiefelbusch, and Burton Blatt.

Borba, Michele; Borba, Craig. **Self-Esteem: A Classroom Affair.** New York: Harper & Row, 1978, 1982. 2 vols. Vol. 1: 148 pp. $8.95 (Paper). Vol. 2: 144 pp. $9.95 (Paper).
    These charming, helpful books were written to show teachers how to build a child's sense of achievement in the classroom.

Brolin, Donn E.; Kokaska, Charles J. **Career Education for Handicapped Individuals.** 2d ed. Columbus, Ohio: Merrill, 1985. 464 pp. $32.95.
    The authors view career education as a "whole life process." They describe the concept and its development, and present competencies in daily living skills, personal-social skills, and occupation guidance and preparation that can be taught in the home, school, and community. This readable textbook contains much useful information for parents from a developing historical perspective as well as on a day-to-day practical basis.

Jordan, June B.; Gallagher, James H.; Hutinger, Patricia L.; Karnes, Merle B., eds. **Early Childhood Special Education: Birth to Three.** Reston, Va.: The Council for Exceptional Children and its Division for Early Childhood, 1988. 257 pp. $24.00 (Paper).
    This attractively formatted volume looks at the new issues and challenges of Public Law 99–457, which mandates services for infants and toddlers with disabilities and their families. It addresses issues of leadership for the program at the state and local level, how to find the children who need services, how to maximize parent involvement through the individualized family service plan, who the program providers should be, interdisciplinary teaming, effective evaluation, and public policy. Examples of existing model demonstration programs are detailed. This is a book for professionals; topic summary lines in the margins help to make it accessible to the general reader as well.

Morris, G.S. Don; Stiehl, Jim. **Changing Kids' Games.** Champaign, Ill.: Human Kinetics Publishers, 1988. 143 pp. $10.00 (Paper).

Aimed at teachers and coaches, this book will also appeal to parents who see their child excluded from participation in physical education or recreational activities because of a physical disability. It suggests modifications for basic movement, ball, net, and active academic games. Perhaps more important, **Changing Kids' Games** offers a good discussion of why games are played and how they can be designed, evaluated, and presented for everyone.

Nordoff, Paul; Robbins, Clive. **Therapy in Music for Handicapped Children**. London: Gollancz; distributed by David & Charles, 1985. 191 pp. $13.95 (Paper).

Through descriptions of their experiences in England, Europe, and America, working with children spanning all degrees of mental, emotional, and physical disabilities, the authors lead the reader to appreciate the role music can play in the growth and enrichment of every child. First published in 1971, this fine book has been reissued in paperback form.

Wodrich, David L. **Children's Psychological Testing: A Guide for Nonpsychologists.** Baltimore: Paul H. Brookes, 1984. 196 pp. $19.95 (Paper).

The "nonpsychologists" referred to in the title are expected to be doctors, lawyers, and teachers; parents, too, will find much of helpful interest in this description of what psychological tests actually measure, how they are organized, and what test scores mean. Over fifty of the tests most frequently used to evaluate children with learning disabilities, mental retardation, and emotional problems are described in nontechnical language.

Your Child Grows Up

Jones, Marilyn. **Exploring Computer Careers for the Handicapped.** New York: Rosen Publishing Group, 1985. 149 pp. $9.95.

> For people with visual, hearing, and orthopedic disabilities who want to learn about the education needed to get into computer careers, this small book offers information, descriptions, and a listing of training programs as of 1985. Technology is not its focus.

Stearner, S. Phyllis. **Able Scientists—Disabled Persons: Careers in the Sciences.** Oak Brook, Ill.: John Racila Associates, 1984. 65 pp. $12.95 (Paper).

> This compilation of brief biographies of scientists and engineers illustrates a number of career options open to students with vision, hearing, and physical impairments.

Summers, Jean Ann, ed. **The Right to Grow Up: An Introduction to Adults with Developmental Disabilities.** Baltimore: Paul H. Brookes, 1986. 336 pp. $21.95 (Paper).

> This textbook should prove of interest to parents looking ahead. It explores the needs of adults with developmental disabilities, what services are necessary to meet those needs, and the self-advocacy, federal laws, and policies that will ensure that all needs will be met. Chapters include sexuality, marriage and parenthood, maintaining dignity in later years, residential and vocational options and issues, leisure and religious experiences, and independent living programs.

Personal Accounts—From Those Who Have Lived It

Anderson, Peggy. **Children's Hospital.** New York: Harper & Row, 1985. 532 pp. $18.95.

Anderson has written an absorbing account of six children who were patients at a prominent American hospital. In the beginning, their ages ranged from nine days to fifteen years; their reasons for being in the hospital ranged from cystic fibrosis to facial deformity, prematurity to leukemia, birth defects to injuries sustained in a car crash. This is compelling real life drama that explores the responses of the children, their families, and the hospital staff to the intolerable situation of children living or dying with serious illness or injury.

Bernstein, Jane. **Loving Rachel: A Family's Journey from Grief.** Boston: Little, Brown, 1988. 279 pp. $17.95.

Bernstein is a writer. With a novelist's attention to language and detail, she shares the birth of her second child, the discovery of that child's disabilities—optic nerve hypoplasia and infantile spasms—the seesawing of emotions as she and her husband Paul react to the events of Rachel's first four years. **Loving Rachel** makes painfully real the day-by-day feelings, the changed relationships with family and friends, the strains on a marriage, the different grieving styles of two people. This is an important book; its intensely personal story chronicles feelings and thoughts that are universal.

Bowe, Frank. **Comeback.** New York: Harper & Row, 1981. 172 pp. $13.45.

Comeback introduces the reader to "six people with varying disabilities whose lives . . . exemplify the simple but remarkable fact that disabled people *can*." The six are a political activist, a sex counselor, a poet/director of community relations, a busboy, a theoretical physicist, and a neurochemist. Their disabilities are loss of vision, childhood polio, deaf-blindness, mental retardation, amyotrophic lateral sclerosis, and loss of hearing.

Brightman, Alan J., ed. **Ordinary Moments: The Disabled Experience.** Syracuse, N.Y.: Human Policy Press, 1985. 160 pp. $10.95.

This extraordinary book is about people who share what it means to be "a magnet for whispers." Read it slowly and step for a moment into the shoes of another. **Ordinary Moments** uses words and photographs to make the experiences and feelings of eight individuals with physical disabilities intensely real. "First impressions aside," says one, "I'm a lot more like you than you probably imagine." Brightman also includes brief samplings from his favorite books about disability.

Campling, Jo, ed. **Images of Ourselves: Women with Disabilities Talking.** New York: Routledge & Kegan Paul, 1981. 140 pp. $9.95 (Paper).

This is a collection of thoughts and personal insights from twenty-five English women, ranging in age from seventeen to seventy-five, from a variety of backgrounds, with many different disabilities. They talk about their experiences, relationships, sexuality, motherhood, education, employment, and, most significantly, their own attitudes and the attitudes of others toward disability.

Cassie, Dhyan. **So Who's Perfect!** Scottdale, Pa.: Herald Press, 1984. 148 pp. $12.95 (Paper).

    The author has interviewed "people with visible and physical differences" under the broad categories of movement, cosmetic, hearing, sight, speech, and size. Each person interviewed talks about childhood, school, social life, work, and religious beliefs; many also answer the request to share a message with society.

Jones, Ron. **The Acorn People.** New York: Bantam, 1977. 76 pp. $2.75 (Paper).

    Ron Jones relates the experiences of his group of children with disabilities at a summer camp. The children grow together, give themselves a name, conquer a mountain, participate in a water extravaganza, and captivate the reader. It is a touching, funny, and inspiring account.

Roth, William. **The Handicapped Speak.** Jefferson, N.C.: McFarland, 1981. 211 pp. $18.95.

    In question-and-answer format, the author interviews thirteen people with different disabilities. All of them are articulate and perceptive in sharing their thoughts about themselves, their lives, their reactions, and, in some instances, more global perspectives arising from their experience. The author's comments, indicating the pressing need for changes in public policy, are direct and thoughtful.

Rousso, Harilyn; O'Malley, Susan Gushee; Severance, Mary. **Disabled, Female, and Proud!** Boston: Exceptional Parent Press, 1988. 136 pp. $9.95 (Paper).

    Ten women with a variety of disabilities who are leading interesting and satisfying lives share their stories. This book is designed to help counter societal stereotypes and encourage young women with disabilities to make their own choices. Parents will find much to think about.

Where to Write for Information

The associations, organizations, and agencies listed distribute booklets, pamphlets, newsletters, and other materials about disabilities in general. Parents will find information about organizations that distribute information on specific disabilities and topics elsewhere in the **Guide.**

American Alliance for Health, Physical Education, Recreation, and Dance (AAHPERD). P.O. Box 10375, Alexandria, VA 22310.

AAHPERD's publications occasionally are specific to people with disabilities; it is possible to place a standing order to receive all future "publications for the handicapped." **Focus on Dance IX: Dance for the Handicapped** is $5.95; it addresses different approaches, techniques, and philosophies for providing dance experiences for people with hearing impairment, visual impairment, emotional disturbance, learning disability, and other physical and mental disabilities.

American Association of University Affiliated Programs for Persons with Developmental Disabilities (AAUAP). 8605 Cameron Street, Suite 406, Silver Spring, MD 20910.

The AAUAP is a national organization representing University Affiliated Programs throughout the United States. The mission of the UAPs is to support the independence, productivity, and integration into the community of all citizens who are developmentally disabled. Write for information on a UAP in your area.

The Association for the Care of Children's Health (ACCH). 3615 Wisconsin Avenue, N.W., Washington, DC 20016.

Long recognized for its advocacy in promoting health care policies, programs, and environments that are responsive to the unique emotional and developmental needs of children, ACCH has a resource catalog filled with wonderful materials; do send for it. An excellent booklet for a family coping with the daily concerns of a child with chronic illness, a disability, multiple disabilities, or other serious health problems is called **The Chronically Ill Child and Family in the Community.** The ACCH's bimonthly newsletter is called **ACCH News; Children's Health Care** is the quarterly journal.

Association for Persons in Supported Employment (APSE). P.O. Box 27523, Richmond, VA 23261–7523.

APSE was formed to promote the concept of paid integrated employment and full community participation for all individuals. Parent membership is welcomed. A newsletter, **The Advance,** is published quarterly. Regular membership is $35.00; $20.00 for a person with a disability.

Beach Center on Families and Disability. The University of Kansas, Bureau of Child Research, 4138 Haworth Hall, Lawrence, KS 66045.

Beach Center is the first federally funded national rehabilitation research and training center on families and disabilities. Directed by Ann and Rud Turnbull and Jean Ann Summers, its philosophy is based on six values developed through research and experience as professionals and members of families in which there is a person with a disability: positive contributions, great expectations, full citizenship, choices, relationships, and inherent strengths. The first issue of the **Families and Disability Newsletter** was published in the spring of 1989. It will appear three times a year; there is no charge. Get on their mailing list.

Channing L. Bete Company. 200 State Road, South Deerfield, MA 01373–0200.

The booklet, **What Everyone Should Know about Children with Special Needs,** is 79 cents; a minimum of 25 must be ordered. It encourages seeking early diagnosis in an attractive, easy-to-read format.

The Brown University Child Behavior and Development Letter. P.O. Box 3352, Providence, RI 02906.

This monthly newsletter focuses on the many aspects of normal development in young children and often includes articles on disabilities and health issues. Write for ordering information and a sample copy.

Center on Human Policy. Syracuse University, 200 Huntington Hall, Second Floor, Syracuse, NY 13244.

The Center provides basic information regarding legal rights, strategies for change, and community programs and services. It also issues publications, films, slide shows, and posters, with a strong emphasis on the integration of people with disabilities into the mainstream. Send for their resource list.

Centering Corporation. P.O. Box 3367, Omaha, NE 68103–0367.

The Rubber Band Syndrome: Family Life with a Child with a Disability, is a monograph based on interviews with eight families, designed to help educators understand the adjustment cycle. It sells for $2.00.

Centre for Research and Education in Human Services. P.O. Box 3036, Kitchener, Ontario, Canada N2G 4R5.

This Canadian resource publishes several monographs and papers of interest to parents. Send for the order form; it includes **Reuniting Families: A Resource Guide for Family Involvement in the Closing of Institutions; Special Education: Implications for Children; Parents and School Boards;** and **Listening to People Who Have Directly Experienced the Mental Health System.**

Council for Exceptional Children (CEC). 1920 Association Drive, Reston, VA 22091–1589.

CEC is a professional organization "dedicated to advancing the quality of education for *all* exceptional children and improving the conditions under which special educators work." Members receive **Exceptional Children,** the research journal, **Teaching Exceptional Children,** a practical, classroom-oriented magazine, and a newsletter called **Exceptional Times.** CEC publishes extensively; be sure to ask for its publication list. Among its titles is a useful reference called **P.L. 94–142, Section 504, and P.L. 99–457—Understanding What They Are and Are Not** ($5.00). CEC is the home of the Educational Resources Information Center Clearinghouse on Handicapped and Gifted Children (ERIC) described below.

Educational Resources Information Center (ERIC). U.S. Department of Education.
　　ERIC is a national information system; its goal is to identify, select, process, and disseminate information on education through a network of clearinghouses. Publications include bulletins, resource lists on topics of current interest, major publications, and digests that summarize information on selected topics. Two clearinghouses that distribute information of special interest to parents of children with disabilities are:

　　ERIC Clearinghouse on Adult, Career, and Vocational Education. Ohio State University, Center on Education and Training for Employment, 1960 Kenny Road, Columbus, OH 43210–1090.
　　　　ERIC/ACVE makes available written materials on all aspects of adult, career, and vocational education. Their publications include no-cost resources such as **Parent Involvement in Career Education,** and two-page digests such as **Family Influences on Employment and Education** and **Parents' Role in Transition for Handicapped Youth.** Longer documents have varying prices. **The ERIC File** is issued twice a year and is sent to anyone who requests material from the Clearinghouse.

　　ERIC Clearinghouse on Handicapped and Gifted Children. Council for Exceptional Children, 1920 Association Drive, Reston, VA 22091–1589.
　　　　Send for their Product Flyer; it lists many two-page digests that provide general information on specific topics, practices and research, ERIC/OSEP Research and Resource Summaries, Directories of Ongoing Research funded by the Office of Special Education Programs of the U.S. Department of Education, syntheses of research projects called **Issue Briefs,** and bibliographies. Examples of the digests ($1.00 each) are **Being at Ease with Handicapped Children,** and **Disabilities: An Overview.** One ERIC/OSEP Research and Resource Summary ($1.00) is **Early Childhood Education for the Handicapped.** Directories at $5.00 include **Parents, Technology,** and **Social Skills.**

The Exceptional Parent. 1170 Commonwealth Avenue, Third Floor, Boston, MA 02134.
　　Published eight times a year, **The Exceptional Parent** magazine is an extremely helpful resource for any parent of a child with a disability; besides good information and articles by and about families, it offers opportunities to network with other parents through its "Letters to the Editor" column. Subscriptions are $18.00 a year. Their bookstore offers a good selection of publications of interest to parents.

Family Resource Coalition. 230 North Michigan Avenue, Suite 1625, Chicago, IL 60601.
　　The Family Coalition is "a national grassroots federation of individuals and organizations, promoting the development of prevention-oriented, community-based programs to strengthen families." The **FRC Connection** newsletter is published every other month; the **FRC Report** appears three times a year. A single theme issue of the **FRC Report** (volume 7, number 2, 1988) was devoted entirely to families with special needs and contains a broad array of topics by professionals and parent/professionals. Send for a free copy.

Federation for Children with Special Needs. 312 Stuart Street, Boston, MA 02116.

This Federation is a coalition of parent groups representing children with a variety of disabilities. It operates and coordinates information, advocacy, and training projects. One of their manuals is **After School. . . Then What? The Transition to Adulthood** ($5.00). Ask for their publications list and a description of their activities.

The Governor's Planning Council on Developmental Disabilities. State Planning Agency, 201 Capitol Square Building, 550 Cedar Street, St. Paul, MN 55101.

Send for a free copy of **A New Way of Thinking;** it suggests that having a home, learning, working, and developing and sustaining relationships should govern the way in which service systems are set up for people with developmental disabilities.

HEATH Resource Center. American Council on Education, One Dupont Circle, N.W., Washington, DC 20036–1193.

HEATH (Higher Education and Adult Training for People with Handicaps) is the national clearinghouse on postsecondary education and training for people with disabilities. HEATH publishes a newsletter twice a year called **Information from HEATH;** it is free to subscribers. So are resource papers and information packets. One helpful booklet, **How to Choose a College: Guide for the Student with a Disability,** will aid in organizing the college search and decision-making. The current issue of the **HEATH Resource Directory** is an impressive collection of over one hundred and fifty annotated references to organizations and directories which can provide information on access and awareness, disability specific resources, community integration, technology, funding, and legal assistance. Laws and regulations are also described. Single copies are free.

The Institute for the Study of Developmental Disabilities. Indiana University, 2853 East Tenth Street, Bloomington, IN 47405.

The Institute's catalog includes several titles regarding early childhood, including **Individual Educational Programming for Infants and Toddlers** and **Sensory and Art Experiences for Infants and Toddlers.**

International Exchange of Experts and Information in Rehabilitation. 400 East 34th Street, New York, NY 10016.

Monographs available from experts around the world address a number of topics relating to disability. Write for their list.

Mainstream, Inc. 1030 15th Street, N.W., Washington, DC 20005.

Mainstream promotes the mainstreaming of people with disabilities in employment by ensuring that service providers and employers have access to "the tools and rules." Send for a publications list.

March of Dimes. Public Health Education and Community Services Department, 1275 Mamaroneck Avenue, White Plains, NY 10605.

The purpose of March of Dimes is the prevention of birth defects. Single copies of their current brochures and pamphlets are free while supplies last. They include **Birth Defects: Tragedy**

and Hope; Your Special Child; Genetic Counseling; and easy-to-read public health education information sheets on a number of birth defects.

Maryland State Department of Education. Division of Special Education, 200 West Baltimore Street, Baltimore, MD 21201.

A pleasant series, called **Parent Helper: Handicapped Children Birth to Five,** provides general concepts of child development and suggests activities that can be used by parents to help sponsor learning. Separate booklets deal with cognition, communications, motor development, and socialization.

Montana University Affiliated Program. 33 Corbin Hall, University of Montana, Missoula, MT 59812.

The mission of the Montana University Affiliated Program is to support and enhance services to persons with developmental disabilities. For $4.45 you can order an excellent forty-four-page booklet called **Acceptance Is Only the First Battle: How Some Parents of Young Handicapped Children Have Coped with Common Problems.** Mothers write on a variety of topics, including being a "detective in the medical community," choosing from conflicting advice, support groups, becoming political, dealing with professionals, and surviving the first three years. Several publications have been developed by the staff of the Educational Home Model Project for early intervention specialists and day care providers. A title of particular interest to parents is **Selecting a Day Care . . . When Your Child Has a Handicap** ($1.65). Write for the Product Materials List.

National Association for the Education of Young Children (NAEYC). 1834 Connecticut Avenue, N.W., Washington, DC 20009–5786.

NAEYC is a professional association "working to improve program environments" for young children. It offers information and publications. Send for the **Early Childhood Resources Catalog;** one helpful title is **Toys: Tools for Learning**.

National Association of State Directors of Special Education (NASDSE). 2021 K Street, N.W., Washington, DC 20006.

Some of NASDSE's publications will be of interest to parents. Their quarterly newsletter, **Counterpoint,** contains articles for parents and professionals; it is distributed free of charge by many State Departments of Education/Divisions of Special Education.

National Center for Clinical Infant Programs. 733 15th Street, N.W., Suite 912, Washington, DC 20005.

A brochure addressed to professionals will be endorsed by all parents. It is titled **Four Critical Junctures: Support for Parents of Children with Special Needs.** Ask also for **Zero to Three.**

National Center for Youth with Disabilities. Adolescent Health Program, University of Minnesota, Box 72–UMHC, Harvard Street at East River Road, Minneapolis, MN 55455.

The Center provides information and technical assistance relating to the health and social functioning of adolescents. **Connections** is published quarterly.

National Committee for Citizens in Education (NCCE). Suite 410, Wilde Lake Village Green, Columbia, MD 21044.

NCCE is an education-advocacy organization committed to improving education for all children by increasing parent-citizen participation in the public schools. The national newsletter is called **Network,** and every issue contains some item of interest to parents of children with disabilities. Send for the list of publications. Some of the most popular titles include **The Rights of Parents in the Education of Their Children; Parents Organizing to Improve Schools; Parents Can Understand Testing;** and **The School Budget: It's Your Money, It's Your Business.**

National Easter Seal Society. 70 East Lake Street, Chicago, IL 60601.

The National Easter Seal Society is a community-based health agency with centers across the country that offer direct services, screening, advocacy, and public education to children and adults with disabilities and their families. The Society has a variety of booklets and pamphlets of interest. Write for their order forms that list titles pertaining to attitudes/awareness, independent living, prevention/safety, speech-language-hearing, adult care, and child care. The free, twice-a-year official newsletter is called **The National Easter Seal Communicator.**

National Information Center for Children and Youth with Handicaps (NICHCY). P.O. Box 1492, Washington, DC 20013.

NICHCY provides fact sheets, article reprints, resource information, specialized packets, and bibliographies on topics of interest to parents. It will also send addresses and toll-free numbers of parent organizations and disability-related groups on a national, state, and local level, free of charge. Its newsletter is called **News Digest** and is published three times a year. Its publications are all "parent friendly"; if you are a parent new to the world of developmental disability, request a copy of **You Are Not Alone: For Parents When They Learn That Their Child Has a Handicap** by Patty McGill Smith.

National Library Service for the Blind and Physically Handicapped. Library of Congress, Washington, DC 20542.

Ask for the publications list of reference circulars on a variety of subjects and the listing of regional libraries. The library distributes "talking books" (books recorded on tape), playback machines, and braille and large print materials to people with visual impairments or with other disabilities that impede ability to learn from the printed word.

National Organization for Rare Disorders (NORD). P.O. Box 8923, New Fairfield, CT 06812.

NORD acts as both a clearinghouse for information and a family network system. Articles cover a general description, the symptoms, causes, treatments, and resources for disorders affecting fewer than 200,000 people. Send for the order form.

National Organization on Disability (NOD). 910 16th Street, N.W., Suite 600, Washington, DC 20006.

NOD is the only independent federal agency appointed by the President that makes recommendations on issues of public policy affecting Americans with disabilities. Get on its mailing list to receive copies of position papers and its free quarterly newsletter, **Focus.** Request the January 1988 report to the President and the Congress of the United States, **On the Threshold of**

Independence, and the September 1989 report, **The Education of Students with Disabilities: Where Do We Stand?**

National Rehabilitation Association (NRA). 633 South Washington Street, Alexandria, VA 22314–4193.

NRA is for professionals and persons with disabilities; it is active in advocacy, legislative design, and developing training programs. Send for general information on rehabilitation services. The Association's quarterly journal is called **Journal of Rehabilitation.** The **NRA Newsletter** is published eight times a year.

National Rehabilitation Information Center (NARIC). 8455 Colesville Road, Suite 935, Silver Spring, MD 20910–3319.

NARIC offers services including database searches, library research, and referrals on disability and rehabilitation-related issues. **NARIC Quarterly: A Newsletter of Disability and Rehabilitation Research and Resources** is free. The **Guide to Periodicals on Disability and Rehabilitation** is available for $15.00. Request a listing of the **Rehabilitation Research Review** monograph series. One volume, by Ann Turnbull, is titled **Stress and Coping in Families Having a Member with a Developmental Disability.** The charge for each Review is five cents a page with a five dollar minimum.

National Rural Development Institute. Western Washington University, Miller Hall 359, Bellingham, WA 98225.

The Rural Institute offers several publications of interest to both educators and parents, such as **Images: Issues and Trends in Rural Special Education** ($9.00), and a special edition of the **Rural Special Education Quarterly** on "Rural Family-Professional Relationships," Fall, 1984 ($6.00).

PACER (Parent Advocacy Coalition for Educational Rights) Center. 4876 Chicago Avenue South, Minneapolis, MN 55417–1055.

This parent organization provides a variety of resources, including a long list of fine booklets, information handouts, and newsletters. One title of interest is **Opportunity Knocking: The Story of Supported Employment** ($6.00); there are many others. **The Pacesetter,** a news magazine, is packed with information and items of interest that go far beyond the borders of Minnesota.

Parent Resources on Disabilities (PROD). P.O. Box 14391, Portland, OR 97214.

PROD is a parent-run organization devoted primarily to advocacy on medical issues for parents of children with disabilities. Its topnotch quarterly publication is called **The Bridge** and covers subjects of interest in depth. Recent issues have dealt with "sorting out" how SSI works, surviving stress, family support services, paying medical bills, and understanding the ethical questions involved when participating in medical research. A year's subscription costs ten dollars.

PEAK (Parent Education and Assistance for Kids) Parent Center. 6055 Lehman Drive, Suite 101, Colorado Springs, CO 80918.

Speak Out is published three times a year and is free to parents of children with disabilities. It covers many subjects of current interest to families. PEAK's fine curriculum on integration is annotated on page 144.

Pediatric Projects, Inc. P.O. Box 1880, Santa Monica, CA 90406–9920.

A Buyer's Guide to Medical Toys and Books for Toddlers through Teens is written for people who provide services to children. It is a delightful way for parents to keep informed about safe and appropriate resources. $12.00 for a one-year subscription.

Pilot Parents. Greater Omaha Association for Retarded Citizens (GO/ARC), 3610 Dodge, Omaha, NE 68131.

An excellent manual called **A Design for Developing a Program for Parents of Handicapped Children** is available for $10.50. It outlines a systematic approach for veteran parents to reach out and be available to parents who are new to the arena of disability. Everything needed to set up a program is included in its one hundred and five pages, from philosophy to publicity, from training to matching parents.

The Portage Project. Cooperative Educational Service Agency, 626 East Slifer Street, P.O. Box 564, Portage, WI 53901.

The Portage Project has long been recognized as a leader in involving parents in the education of their children with special needs. **A Parent's Guide to Early Education** sets out activities for teaching children, from birth through five, skills in the areas of socialization, language development, self-help, cognitive, and motor development. The **Guide** costs $15.00 plus $2.00 handling charges. The **Parent Readings,** designed to help parents learn to be better managers of their child's behavior, uses real-life examples, practical suggestions, and amusing cartoons that make some points better than words could. Included with the **Parent Readings** is an **Instructor's Manual** which describes how to help parents work with the skills listed in a **Parental Behavior Inventory.** The three items are called an *Instructor Set* and cost $12.00 plus $2.00 handling charge.

President's Committee on Employment of People with Disabilities. 1111 20th Street, N.W., Suite 636, Washington, DC 20036–3470.

The President's Committee is a national source of information and assistance concerning employment of people with disabilities. Write for their publications list; it contains a number of items of interest about employment, affirmative action, and accommodations. **Tips and Trends** is a monthly publication; **Worklife** is a quarterly magazine. Both are free.

Public Affairs Committee. 381 Park Avenue South, New York, NY 10016.

Public Affairs pamphlets have been a source of basic information on widely varied topics for many years. Titles of interest to parents of children with disabilities include **Getting Help for a Disabled Child—Advice from Parents; Helping the Slow Learner; Jobs for Disabled People;** and **Independent Living: New Goal for Disabled Persons.** Each pamphlet costs one dollar.

Research and Training Center on Rural Rehabilitation Services. University of Montana, Missoula, MT 59812.

Ｗ RTC-Rural is the only one of a national network of federally funded Research and Training Centers to focus on "improving the daily lives and enhancing the independence of people with disabilities who live, work, and recreate in rural America." Send for information.

St. Clares-Riverside Medical Center. Pocono Road, Denville, NJ 07834.

Ｗ Their **Self-Help Sourcebook: Finding and Forming Mutual Aid Self-Help Groups** provides valuable information on identifying self-help support networks. It is available for $9.00. The Center also circulates a directory of national groups.

Special Parent/Special Child. Lindell Press, P.O. Box 462, South Salem, NY 10590.

Ｗ Parents of young children will find this newsletter particularly helpful; its focus is on different developmental skills and how parents can understand and help their child (with any disability) in the learning of those skills. Six issues a year cost $18.00.

United Cerebral Palsy Associations (UCP). Community Services Division, 1522 K Street, N.W., Washington, DC 20005–1202.

Ｗ UCP is a nationwide direct-service organization with affiliates providing an array of services ranging from preschool to adult work programs. Write for a free subscription to **Family Support Bulletin;** it is filled with items of interest to people concerned with any disability.

United States Government.

Ｗ For general information about U.S. Government programs serving people with disabilities, write: Clearinghouse on Disability Information, U.S. Department of Education, Office of Special Education and Rehabilitative Services, Washington, DC 20202. The Government also has within its vast structure a number of sources of information of interest to parents of children with disabilities. Write to any of the following agencies and request publications lists. Generally, single copies of pamphlets, reports, and monographs are free.

U.S. Department of Education, Office of Special Education and Rehabilitative Services (OSERS), Clearinghouse on Disability Information. Room 3132, 330 C Street, S.W., Washington, DC 20202–2524.

Ｗ Publications available from the Clearinghouse are **OSERS News in Print,** a periodic newsletter which focuses on Federal activities affecting people with disabilities and new developments in the information field, **Pocket Guide to Federal Help for Individuals with Disabilities; A Summary of Existing Legislation Affecting Persons with Disabilities;** and **Educating Students with Learning Problems: A Shared Responsibility** by former Assistant Secretary Madeleine Will. Send for the Clearinghouse's fine annotated listing called **Selected Federal Publications Relating to Disability.**

U.S. Department of Education, Rehabilitation Services Administration (RSA). Room 3414, 330 C Street, S.W., Washington, DC 20202–2524.

RSA provides general information on rehabilitation programs and a listing of state Vocational Rehabilitation offices. It also publishes the quarterly, **American Rehabilitation,** available from Superintendent of Documents, U.S. Government Printing Office, Washington, DC 20402 for five dollars a year.

U.S. Department of Health and Human Services, National Center for Education in Maternal and Child Health. 38th & R Streets, N.W., Washington, DC 20057.

Starting Early: A Guide to Federal Resources in Maternal and Child Health, is a most valuable resource for identifying the agencies of the U.S. Government and Federally operated or funded information centers dealing with issues in maternal and child health. An extensive bibliography of publications and audio-visual materials is included. **Comprehensive Clinical Genetic Services Centers—A National Listing** is available.

U.S. Department of Health and Human Services, National Maternal and Child Health Clearinghouse (NMCHC). 38th & R Streets, N.W., Washington, DC 20057.

NMCHC has a number of resource directories, topical bibliographies, information packets, and other educational materials on health-related issues available; most of them are free. Send for their catalog, published jointly with the National Center for Education in Maternal and Child Health. Titles include **Equals in This Partnership: Parents of Disabled and At-Risk Infants and Toddlers Speak to Professionals** and **Learning Together: A Guide for Families with Genetic Disorders.** Pamphlets include **Developmental Dyslexia and Related Reading Disorders** and **Facts about Down Syndrome.** An important new addition is **The Intent and Spirit of P.L. 99–457: A Sourcebook,** which discusses the law that mandates services to infants and toddlers with disabilities and their families.

U.S. Department of Health and Human Services, Office of Human Development Services, Administration for Children, Youth, and Families (ACYF). Room 2070, 330 C Street, S.W., Washington, DC 20202–2524.

Children Today, a bimonthly magazine for parents and people who work with children, publishes articles about children with disabilities and their families; it is available from the Superintendent of Documents, U.S. Government Printing Office, Washington, DC 20402 for $7.50 a year. Other ACYF publications discuss many aspects of child development and topics of concern to parents, such as **Child Development in the Home; A Handicapped Child in Your Home;** and **Young Children and Accidents in the Home.** Two Head Start series, available only through the U.S. Government Printing Office, offer useful information to parents: **Mainstreaming Preschoolers,** about young children with disabilities, and **Caring for Children,** directed to staff of child care facilities.

U.S. Department of Health and Human Services, Office of Human Development Services, Administration on Developmental Disabilities. 330 Independence Avenue, S.W., Washington, DC 20202.

Upon request, the Administration provides a listing of state agencies and state protection and advocacy services that offer legal advocacy to persons with disabilities and their families.

U.S. Department of Health and Human Services, Public Health Service, Alcohol, Drug, Abuse, and Mental Health Administration, Information Resources Inquiries Branch. 5600 Fishers Lane, Rockville, MD 20857.

Available publications include the **Caring about Kids** series: **Dyslexia; Helping the Hyperactive Child;** and **Stimulating Baby Senses;** and the **Plain Talk** series: **Plain Talk About—Dealing with the Angry Child; Raising Children;** and **Stress.** Single copies can be ordered, free of charge. An information packet is also available on autism, as well as a bibliography on learning disabilities.

U.S. Department of Health and Human Services, Public Health Service, National Institute of Neurological and Communicative Disorders and Stroke, Office of Scientific and Health Reports. 9000 Rockville Pike, Building 31, Bethesda, MD 20892.

Publications include the **Hope through Research** series: **Autism; Cerebral Palsy; Epilepsy; Hearing Loss; Spina Bifida;** and **Tourette Syndrome.**

U.S. Government Printing Office (GPO). Superintendent of Documents, 710 North Capitol Street, Washington, DC 20402.

The GPO has developed an index of over two hundred and seventy subject bibliographies that list publications on a single subject or field of interest, such as **Children and Youth; Elementary and Secondary Education;** and **Mental Health.** Write for a free copy of **New Catalog** which tells about the most popular books sold by the Government from virtually every Government agency. Titles of interest include **Dozen Dangers to Your Baby's Brain and How to Reduce Those Dangers** (Stock Number 017–092–00100–2; $1.00), **Curricula for High-Risk and Handicapped Infants** (Stock Number 065–000–00208–6; $3.00), and **Characteristics of High School Students Who Identify Themselves as Handicapped** (Stock Number 065–00233–7; $2.00). A Head Start series, called **Mainstreaming Preschoolers,** is currently being revised. These guides for teachers, parents, and others who work with preschoolers with a variety of disabilities were exceedingly well-done; inquire about their current status.

Very Special Arts. 1825 Connecticut Avenue, N.W., Suite 417, Washington, DC 20009.

Send for information about curricula and instruction in the arts for children and adults with disabilities.

SPECIFIC
DISABILITIES

PART II

Autism

Basic Reading

Donnellan, Anne M., ed. **Classic Readings in Autism.** New York: Teachers College, 1985. 440 pp. $29.95.

    With the help of a panel of international experts, Anne Donnellan has selected twenty-one samples of "noteworthy medical, educational, psychological, and linguistic papers," beginning with Leo Kanner's first description of eleven children with autism. Each article is followed by a commentary designed to place the paper in historical perspective. Sophisticated readers will find much of interest in this significant volume.

Morgan, Sam B. **The Unreachable Child: An Introduction to Early Childhood Autism.** Memphis: Memphis State University Press, 1981. 197 pp. $7.95.

    The Unreachable Child is an intelligent, lucid, and fascinating review of autism—its symptoms, the psychogenic hypotheses and biogenic theories advanced up to 1981 and the author's "inferences and insights" regarding its cause, differing treatment techniques, and research on the adjustment of children with autism in their adult years. Morgan is highly sensitive to parents.

Murphy, Judy. **Home Care of Handicapped Children: A Guide. Autism.** Lyons, Colo.: Carol L. Lutey Publishing, 1982. 85 pp. $6.50 (Paper).

    One of a series intended for potential caregivers of a child between the ages of three and twelve, this practical and helpful guide has good information to share with families, as well. Part I offers general guidelines concerning child health, self-help activities, social behavior, communication, play, and safety and protective measures. The second section, specific to autism, discusses signs of autism, theories regarding causes (including one no longer regarded as acceptable), guidelines for helping the child, understanding the child with autism, and appropriate activities.

Paluszny, Maria J. **Autism: A Practical Guide for Parents and Professionals.** Syracuse, N.Y.: Syracuse University Press, 1980. 200 pp. $11.95 (Paper).

    This is a clearly written description of the autistic syndrome, its possible causes, treatments and remedies, an overview of educational responsibilities under current law, and how to plan for the future. A chapter on the importance of parent involvement is included.

Powers, Michael D., ed. **Children with Autism: A Parents' Guide**. Rockville, Md.: Woodbine House, 1989. 368 pp. $12.95 (Paper).

    From Bernard Rimland's fascinating introduction in which he describes how his 1962 book revolutionized thinking about autism and how that book came to be written, through the jargon-free, sensitive chapters describing current thinking about a "puzzling and painful disorder," **Children with Autism** should prove a helpful guide to parents. It explains what autism is, describes its treatment, discusses the effect of the condition on family life, offers suggestions and strategies for adjusting and teaching, working with professionals, finding programs and making legal decisions, and outlines ideas for advocacy. It lists local, state, and national resources. A chapter on the years ahead focuses on adults with autism. Parent statements share feelings, advice, and experiences.

Rutter, Michael; Schopler, Eric. **Autism: A Reappraisal of Concepts and Treatment.** New York: Plenum, 1978. 552 pp. $37.50.

Dr. Rutter presents a comprehensive overview of knowledge of the autistic syndrome as of 1978. Sections include contributions on social and psychological characteristics, psychological studies, biological investigations, family characteristics, psychotherapy, biological and behavioral treatments, education, and follow-up.

Treffert, Darold A. **Extraordinary People: Understanding "Idiot Savants."** New York: Harper & Row, 1989. 291 pp. $17.95.

For more than twenty-five years, psychiatrist Treffert has been intrigued by Savant syndrome—"an exceedingly rare condition in which persons with serious mental handicaps . . . or major mental illness . . . have spectacular islands of ability or brilliance which stand in stark, markedly incongruous contrast to the handicaps." His book tells some remarkable stories of savants of yesterday and today, their caring families, teachers, and caregivers, and the new theories and research advanced to explain an intriguing paradox. Dr. Treffert gently guides the reader to a greater "appreciation, admiration and awe for these special people and their equally special families."

Wing, Lorna M. **Autistic Children: A Guide for Parents and Professionals.** 2d ed. New York: Brunner-Mazel, 1985. 176 pp. $20.00. Secaucus, N.J.: Citadel, 1974. 157 pp. $5.95 (Paper).

This is a clear, sympathetic guide, by a world-renowned authority, to the condition of autism in children. Behaviors are described and autism is compared with and distinguished from other childhood handicaps and problems. A wealth of practical suggestions is offered to parents in the areas of management and education.

Your Child at Home

Bachrach, Ann W.; Mosley, Ada R.; Swindle, Faye L.; Wood, Mary M. **Developmental Therapy for Young Children with Autistic Characteristics.** Austin: Pro-Ed, 1978. 185 pp. $19.00.

The authors lay out by specific areas a curriculum for teaching and managing children with autism. Classroom and at-home activities are outlined, and explicit directions are given for parents to help their preschoolers. Parent involvement is strongly recommended and educational strategies are clearly described.

Kozloff, Martin A. **Reaching the Autistic Child: A Parent Training Program.** Cambridge, Mass.: Brookline Books, 1983. 245 pp. $14.95 (Paper).

The author reviews theories and therapies and presents in detail a parent training program employing behavior modification. Four case histories are delineated.

Luce, Stephen C.; Christian, Walter P. **How to Reduce Autistic and Severely Maladaptive Behaviors.** Austin: Pro-Ed, 1981. 37 pp. $6.00 (Paper).

    The manual identifies procedures that can be used to reduce a variety of maladaptive child behaviors with examples for readers to analyze.

Your Child at School

Furneaux, Barbara; Roberts, Brian, eds. **Autistic Children: Teaching, Community, and Research Approaches.** New York: Routledge, Chapman and Hall, 1977. 193 pp. $19.95.

    British authors write about the problems of training and educating children who have autism. Schools and educational practices in Britain and America are described.

Oppenheim, Rosalind C. **Effective Teaching Methods for Autistic Children.** Springfield, Ill.: Charles C. Thomas, 1977. 124 pp. $19.25.

    The author, a director of the Rimland School for Autistic Children, presents teaching ideas and techniques gleaned from years of working with children who were initially nonverbal and children with autism. The book was written for teachers, and is highly recommended for parents, too, because of its clear and usable approach.

Simons, Jeanne; Oishi, Sabine. **The Hidden Child: The Linwood Method for Reaching the Autistic Child.** Rockville, Md.: Woodbine House, 1987. 256 pp. $17.95 (Paper).

    With many illustrative case studies and anecdotes, a view of autism and the "kind and firm" treatment techniques practiced at the Linwood Children's Center are presented. Therapy is structured around accepting and observing the child, establishing a relationship, and changing behavior based on each child's individual direction.

Your Child Grows Up

Schopler, Eric; Mesibov, Gary B., eds. **Autism in Adolescents and Adults.** New York: Plenum, 1983. 438 pp. $39.50.

    A number of respected experts in the field of autism have contributed chapters to this comprehensive volume that focuses on autism in adolescents and adults. Many subjects are covered, including needs in the areas of language and communication, education, recreation and leisure, vocational options, medical care, sex education, legal rights, and management of aggressive behavior. Social and community programs are described. The section on family perspectives includes two insightful commentaries by mothers of adults with autism.

Personal Accounts—From Those Who Have Lived It

Christopher, William and Barbara. **Mixed Blessings.** Nashville: Abingdon, 1989. 224 pp. $15.95.

    William Christopher is "Father Mulcahy" of television's "M*A*S*H" series. He is also the father of Ned, now a young man, identified as having autism after a long search for answers to his puzzling childhood behaviors. Christopher and his wife explore in their book what it has been like to raise Ned. Their story will be familiar to many parents.

Grandin, Temple; Scariano, Margaret M. **Emergence: Labelled Autistic.** Novato, Calif.: Arena, 1986. 184 pp. $8.95 (Paper).

Bernard Rimland's Foreword speaks of reading this book as "an adventure" in which the story is "breathtakingly unusual." What makes this book so truly special is that the author is "a recovered autistic individual." She shares her history, from childhood memories to her success as an expert in the design and construction of livestock handling facilities, her feelings, her fears, and her insights into the world of autism; she includes her own helpful suggestions for parents and professionals.

Greenfeld, Josh. **A Child Called Noah: A Family Journey.** Orlando, Fla.: Harcourt Brace Jovanovich, 1988. 204 pp. $7.95 (Paper).

The first six years of "a family journey" is shared by a writer-father who allows us to read his diary entries. They are real, gripping, intensely personal, often staggering. The book was originally published in 1970.

Greenfeld, Josh. **A Place for Noah.** Orlando, Fla.: Harcourt Brace Jovanovich, 1988. 324 pp. $7.95 (Paper).

This is a continuation of the painfully honest, often angry, diary of Josh Greenfeld's life with Noah, his son with autism, begun in his previous book, **A Child Called Noah.** The compelling account covers Noah's life from age five through eleven.

Greenfeld, Josh. **A Client Called Noah.** New York: Henry Holt and Company, 1986. 369 pp. $18.95. Orlando, Fla.: Harcourt Brace Jovanovich, 1988. $7.95 (Paper).

In his third book about the life of a family which includes a member with severe brain damage, Josh Greenfeld again provides journal extracts. A final chapter updates their story to the year 1985 when Noah is nineteen and living in a group home. Greenfeld sums up his first book, **A Child Called Noah,** in the word "denial," and **A Place for Noah** as "rage." He would characterize this latest work as "acceptance" or "resignation." His love for his son remains clear. And so does his profound anguish at living with and without Noah.

Hart, Charles. **Without Reason: A Family Copes with Two Generations of Autism.** New York: Harper & Row, 1989. 292 pp. $18.95.

Without Reason spans two generations. Fifty years divide Charles Hart's much older brother and Hart's first-born son. In time, the author learns that both have autism. Hart copes with attempts to understand his son's world and improve his skills. He must also assume responsibility for his brother when their mother is no longer able to care for him. Hart is an activist and an advocate who has lived with and researched autism, and, in this book, helps to explain part of its mystery.

Park, Clara Claiborne. **The Siege: The First Eight Years of an Autistic Child with an Epilogue, Fifteen Years After.** Boston: Atlantic-Little, Brown, 1982. 328 pp. $14.95; $8.95 (Paper).

This is a mother's compelling, absorbing, and inspiring account of her family's attempt to lay siege to the invisible fortress surrounding their daughter. Elly has autism. This edition includes an epilogue written from the perspective of a parent who has helped her child grow to adulthood and has learned much in the process.

Pinney, Rachel; Schlachter, Mimi. **Bobby: Breakthrough of a Special Child.** New York: McGraw-Hill, 1986. 248 pp. $4.95 (Paper).

The unorthodox treatment of a therapist over less than a year yielded dramatic results in transforming Bobby, a four-year-old child with autism, from an impossibly difficult little boy to a child who began to reach out to other people. Pinney's "hours" with Bobby were spent exploring New York City and vacation spots, where the child was given total freedom, undivided attention, and nonjudgmental observation. Pinney sets out her observations; Bobby's parents and the companion trained by Pinney share theirs, as well.

Where to Write for Information

Autism Services Center (ASC). Douglass Education Building, Tenth Avenue and Bruce Street, Huntington, WV 25701.

ASC is a private, nonprofit agency directed by a parent-professional and established to offer information, technical assistance, advocacy, and professional training through a roster of associates and consultants who are educators, therapists, researchers, and parent-professionals. Write for their helpful reprints and information on services.

Autism Society of America (ASA). Suite 1017, 1234 Massachusetts Avenue, N.W., Washington, DC 20005.

The Society is dedicated to the education and welfare of persons with severe disorders of communication and behavior. Write for information about activities and publications. Articles on family life, professional information, governmental affairs, publications, and chapter activities appear in the quarterly publication, the **Advocate.** Subscription is by membership in the Society. Dues are $30.00 for families, $20.00 for individuals, and $12.50 for students.

ERIC Clearinghouse on Handicapped and Gifted Children. Council for Exceptional Children, 1920 Association Drive, Reston, VA 22091–1589.

Send for their complete Product Flyer. **Peer Tutoring and Small-Group Instruction for Students with Autism and Developmental Delays** costs one dollar.

Institute for Child Behavior Research (ICBR). 4182 Adams Avenue, San Diego, CA 92116.

ICBR conducts research on methods of preventing, diagnosing, and treating autism and other severe behavioral disorders of childhood. Through its quarterly newsletter, **Autism Research Review International,** it disseminates research findings. Write for its publications and book list; there is much interesting and important reading here. Dr. Bernard Rimland is the director of ICBR.

The Institute for the Study of Developmental Disabilities. Indiana University, 2853 East Tenth Street, Bloomington, IN 47405.

The catalog includes a number of publications concerning children and adults with autism; one of them, **Learning Together,** introduces preschool and early elementary school children to a classmate who has autism.

Minneapolis Children's Medical Center. Exceptional Children with Communication and Interaction Disorders, 2525 Chicago Avenue South, Minneapolis, MN 55404.

Having a Brother Like David is a booklet to share with young children who have a sibling with autism. In simple language, a young boy shares the difficulties and frustrations of not being able to meet David's special needs. There is genuine concern, as well.

U.S. Department of Health and Human Services. Public Health Service, Alcohol, Drug Abuse, and Mental Health Administration, Information Resources Inquiries Branch, 5600 Fishers Lane, Rockville, MD 20857.

An information packet on autism is available.

U.S. Department of Health and Human Services. Public Health Service, National Institute of Neurological and Communicative Disorders and Stroke, Office of Scientific and Health Reports, 9000 Rockville Pike, Building 31, Bethesda, MD 20892.

A single copy of **Hope through Research: Autism** is free. So is **Autism: Fact Sheet**.

Chronic Condition or Illness

Basic Reading

Ablon, Joan. **Little People in America: The Social Dimensions of Dwarfism.** New York: Praeger, 1984. 194 pp. $10.00 (Paper).

Through the perceptions of adults about their early life, marriage, children, education, employment, health, and dealing with the "larger world," and the impact on them of LPA (Little People of America), a highly successful self-help group, readers will learn about life experiences of people of profoundly short stature. The author of this study is a medical anthropologist; her book is unique.

Ablon, Joan. **Living with Difference: Families with Dwarf Children.** New York: Praeger, 1988. 194 pp. $15.00.

Ablon is a medical anthropologist. In this fascinating work, she explores the lives of families of children who are profoundly short from the time they first learn of their child's dwarfism through their early years together. Three case studies illustrate different reactions. Topics include physical development and health, the "logistic" problems, and school, social, and family life. The reporting families all belonged to Little People of America Parent Groups; a chapter on the history and organization of LPA also appears. Rounding out this fine presentation are photographs and appendices with an overview of the literature concerning the impact of child disability and physical difference on the family, the literature on children of short stature, and professional and organizational resources for dwarfism.

Court, John M. **Helping Your Diabetic Child.** New York: Taplinger, 1975. 223 pp. $8.95; $4.95 (Paper).

Specifically written for parents of children with diabetes, this most helpful, older book gives a broad, illustrated summary of information about the disorder, a detailed description of the treatment, and a final section answering questions commonly asked by children and adolescents with the condition. Appendices give information concerning foods, diets, and recipes.

Ducat, Lee; Cohen, Sherry Suib. **Diabetes: A New & Complete Guide to Healthier Living for Parents, Children & Young Adults Who Have Insulin-Dependent Diabetes.** New York: Harper & Row, Perennial Library, 1983. 253 pp. $7.95 (Paper).

Lee Ducat, founder of the Juvenile Diabetes Foundation, is the mother of a son who was diagnosed with diabetes at the age of nine. This "primer of coping" shares solid information, plus tips and ideas. In light, conversational style, the reader is guided through what he needs to know about "sugar babies," "sugar kids," "sugar teens," and "sugar grownups." A detailed resource list is included.

Goldfarb, Lori A.; Brotherson, Mary Jane; Summers, Jean Ann; Turnbull, Ann P. **Meeting the Challenge of Disability or Chronic Illness: A Family Guide.** Baltimore: Paul H. Brookes, 1986. 181 pp. $16.00 (Paper).

    The authors of this wonderfully helpful and refreshing guidebook recognize the strengths in all families and believe in their capacity to survive even the most challenging circumstances. Part I, *Taking Stock,* is designed to help each family discover its own values, resources, and coping methods. Part II, *Problem Solving,* offers a step-by-step method to find solutions to unresolved problems. Ideas and examples abound. Thought-provoking exercises are sprinkled throughout as "flexible tools for self-discovery." There is, in addition, a good resource list of readings and organizations.

Jeter, Katherine F. **These Special Children: The Ostomy Book for Parents of Children with Colostomies, Ileostomies, and Urostomies.** Palo Alto, Calif.: Bull Publishing, 1982. 193 pp. $19.95; $13.95 (Paper).

    This comprehensive resource explains ostomies and conditions that lead to ostomies and offers reassurance, advice, and information about resources for parents in the management of their children through the years. In addition to line drawings throughout the book, there are explanatory drawings for children to color as they learn.

Jones, Monica Loose. **Home Care for the Chronically Ill or Disabled Child: A Manual and Sourcebook for Parents and Professionals.** New York: Harper & Row, 1985. 306 pp. $25.00; $12.95 (Paper).

    This is an encyclopedia of useful information for parents caring for a child with acute chronic illness or disability. Comprehensive and practical, it covers issues from the time the problem is defined to coping with the last stages of terminal illness. Meeting a child's medical needs, daily physical needs, educational and social needs, as well as the needs of all family members are its subjects. The author's daughter Bronwyn died at the age of nine from Werdnig-Hoffman's syndrome (infantile spinal muscular atrophy); guided by her own experiences, Jones writes with realism and gentleness. Effective line drawings illustrate the text. Appendices include organizations and suggested readings.

McCollum, Audrey T. **The Chronically Ill Child.** New Haven, Conn.: Yale University Press, 1981. 273 pp. $10.95 (Paper).

    This sensitive guide for the family of a child with acute or chronic illness or disability offers sound practical advice and supportive insights into feelings and attitudes. Family relationships, methods of helping the child deal with the challenges of his illness at various ages, and sources of help are explored.

Moller, James H.; Neal, William, A.; Hoffman, William. **A Parent's Guide to Heart Disorders.** Minneapolis: University of Minnesota Press, 1988. 153 pp. $14.95.

    This small and helpful guidebook makes clear how the normal heart works, what can go wrong, how heart disease can be corrected or controlled, and the most successful ways parents can cope with a growing child. An important chapter deals with death, dying, and grieving; another with new horizons in prevention and research. Appendices identify medical and hospital staff, patient rights, less common congenital heart diseases, professional organizations, support groups, and readings.

Murphy, Judy. **Home Care of Handicapped Children: A Guide. Asthma.** Lyons, Colo.: Carol L. Lutey Publishing, 1982. 76 pp. $6.50 (Paper).

One of a series intended for potential caregivers of a child between the ages of three and twelve, this practical and helpful guide has good information to share with families, as well. Part I offers general guidelines concerning child health, self-help activities, social behavior, communication, play, and safety and protective measures. The short second section, specific to asthma, discusses the condition, its treatment, prevention and care, and understanding the child with asthma.

Murphy, Judy. **Home Care of Handicapped Children: A Guide. Cystic Fibrosis.** Lyons, Colo.: Carol L. Lutey Publishing, 1982. 74 pp. $6.50 (Paper).

One of a series intended for potential caregivers of a child between the ages of three and twelve, this practical and helpful guide has good information to share with families, as well. Part I offers general guidelines concerning child health, self-help activities, social behavior, communication, play, and safety and protective measures. The short second part, specific to cystic fibrosis, discusses the condition, nutrition, diet, lung care, and understanding the child with cystic fibrosis.

Murphy, Judy. **Home Care of Handicapped Children: A Guide. Diabetes.** Lyons, Colo.: Carol L. Lutey Publishing, 1982. 71 pp. $6.50 (Paper).

One of a series intended for potential caregivers of a child between the ages of three and twelve, this practical and helpful guide has good information to share with families, as well. Part I offers general guidelines concerning child health, self-help activities, social behavior, communication, play, and safety and protective measures. The short second section, specific to diabetes, discusses the condition, special care, signs and causes of blood sugar imbalance, and understanding the child with diabetes.

Murphy, Judy. **Home Care of Handicapped Children: A Guide. Hemophilia.** Lyons, Colo.: Carol L. Lutey Publishing, 1982. 78 pp. $6.50 (Paper).

One of a series intended for potential caregivers of a child between the ages of three and twelve, this practical and helpful guide has good information to share with families, as well. Part I offers general guidelines concerning child health, self-help activities, social behavior, communication, play, and safety and protective measures. The second part, specific to hemophilia, discusses causes, treatment, understanding the child with hemophilia, practical hints for the caregiver, and medications which should never be given to a child with hemophilia.

Saunders, Felicia M. **Your Diabetic Child: A Comprehensive, Compassionate Guide Written Especially for Parents.** New York: Bantam, 1987. 192 pp. $3.95 (Paper).

> The mother of two young children with diabetes talks about feelings, shares basic medical facts about diabetes and diabetic management, and offers some practical solutions to everyday problems.

Travis, Georgia. **Chronic Illness in Children: Its Impact on Child and Family.** Stanford, Calif.: Stanford University Press, 1976. 565 pp. $37.50.

> The author examines the effect of long-term illness on the child and the family and describes supports that families and professionals can use to deal with problems of stress, pain, separation, depression, prolonged hospitalization, and death.

Personal Accounts—From Those Who Have Lived It

Deford, Frank. **Alex: The Life of a Child.** New York: New American Library, 1984. 208 pp. $3.50 (Paper).

> A father starts and ends his book with the death of his daughter at age eight of cystic fibrosis. He writes of the charm and the joy of a most extraordinary child. And he writes of cystic fibrosis, a brutal disease, "a tyrant that rules everyone in the family," that can "destroy the hearts and the faith of all its members." He writes of loving, of missing, of anger. This is not grim writing; Deford is wonderfully gifted and there are moments of humor along with the anguish. **Alex** is deeply touching.

Krementz, Jill. **How It Feels to Fight for Your Life.** Boston: Little, Brown, 1989. 132 pp. $15.95.

> Fourteen children who have faced or are facing serious illnesses and disabilities speak candidly about their very real emotions. Some of the conditions with which they live are cystic fibrosis, diabetes, heart disease, juvenile rheumatoid arthritis, asthma, epilepsy, and spina bifida. Photographs of the young authors are included.

Massie, Robert; Massie, Suzanne. **Journey.** New York: Ballantine, 1975. 417 pp. $3.95 (Paper).

> Written specifically about hemophilia, the chronic, debilitating disease with which their son lives, these articulate, involved parents have much to say to families of children with any handicapping condition in this substantial, memorable book.

Miller, Robyn. **Robyn's Book: A True Diary.** New York: Scholastic, 1986. 179 pp. $2.75 (Paper).

> Robyn Miller was born with cystic fibrosis and, surprisingly, experienced good health for her first sixteen years. For the five years that remained to her, things were very different. Her remarkable journal shares her pain, the loss of friends, her feeling of being lucky "to have the day," her understanding of the magic that is life. **Robyn's Book** is powerful and extraordinary writing.

Murray, J.B.; Murray, Emily. **And Say What He Is: The Life of a Special Child.** Cambridge, Mass.: MIT Press, 1975. 304 pp. $16.50; $5.95 (Paper).

> Compelling and intensely real, this is the poignant story of the life and death of a child with an undefined degenerative disease told in diary and letter-excerpt form by his parents.

Where to Write for Information

American Diabetes Association. 1660 Duke Street, Alexandria, VA 22314.

An eighty-page guide written specifically to help the child with diabetes and all family members is called **Children with Diabetes.** The price to nonmembers is $9.45. Other publications include: **Your Child Has Diabetes . . . What You Should Know, Kid's Corner** (a booklet of puzzles and games), and a free quarterly newsletter.

American Juvenile Arthritis Organization. Arthritis Foundation, 1314 Spring Street, N.W., Atlanta, GA 30309.

The Foundation circulates an excellent guide for parents of children with arthritis called **We Can.**

American Liver Foundation (ALF). 998 Pompton Avenue, Cedar Grove, NJ 07009.

ALF provides a free nationwide referral service and network for parents of children with liver diseases. A newsletter is called **Sharing Cares and Hopes.** Pamphlets include **Liver Disease: A Problem for the Child** and **Biliary Atresia.**

Aplastic Anemia Foundation of America. P.O. Box 22689, Baltimore, MD 21203.

This organization, created to support research and clinical treatment of a serious disease, circulates a helpful booklet written by parents called **Aplastic Anemia and Other Blood Disorders: Families Coping with Hospital Life.**

The Association for the Care of Children's Health (ACCH). 3615 Wisconsin Avenue, N.W., Washington, DC 20016.

ACCH has long been known for its advocacy in promoting health care policies, programs, and environments that are responsive to the unique emotional and developmental needs of children. Its resource catalog is filled with wonderful materials including books for adults and children, brochures, bibliographies, directories, and position statements. An excellent booklet for a family coping with the daily concerns of a child with chronic illness is called **The Chronically Ill Child and Family in the Community.** Just a few of the many other titles that will be of interest to parents are **Activities for Children with Special Needs; Let's Play with Our Children; New Directions for Exceptional Parenting; Your Child with Special Needs at Home and in the Community;** and **Community Checklist for Care of Children with Special Needs.** Their bimonthly newsletter is called **ACCH News; Children's Health Care** is a quarterly journal.

Asthma and Allergy Foundation of America (AAFA). 1717 Massachusetts Avenue, N.W., Suite 305, Washington, DC 20036.

The AAFA distributes a number of basic brochures. Among them are **Allergy in Children** and **Tips for Teachers: The Allergic Child.** Ask them for information about a book called **Children with Asthma: A Manual for Parents.**

Beach Center on Families and Disability. The University of Kansas, Bureau of Child Research, 4138 Haworth Hall, Lawrence, KS 66045.

Beach Center is the first federally funded national rehabilitation research and training center on families and disabilities. A primary focus of the Center is technology-dependent children and the families that care for them. Write for information on their materials.

Channing L. Bete Company. 200 State Road, South Deerfield, MA 01373–0200.

The booklet, **What Everyone Should Know about Muscular Dystrophy,** is 79 cents; a minimum of 25 copies must be ordered. It covers basic information in an attractive, easy-to-read format.

Cystic Fibrosis Foundation. 6931 Arlington Road, Bethesda, MD 20814.

The organization distributes several publications: **Facts about Cystic Fibrosis; A Teacher's Guide to Cystic Fibrosis;** and **The Genetics of Cystic Fibrosis;** as well as a three-times-a-year newspaper called **Commitment.**

ERIC Clearinghouse on Handicapped and Gifted Children. Council for Exceptional Children, 1920 Association Drive, Reston, VA 2209–1589.

Send for their complete Product Flyer. A two-page digest, **Students with Specialized Health Care Needs,** costs one dollar. So does **Students with Physical Disabilities and Health Impairments.**

Human Growth Foundation. The Montgomery Building, 4720 Montgomery Lane, Bethesda, MD 20814.

The Human Growth Foundation provides parent education and support around the issue of abnormal growth. Publications include **Patterns of Growth Booklet** and **Growing Children: A Parents' Guide.**

International Rett Syndrome Association (IRSA). 8511 Rose Marie Drive, Fort Washington, MD 20744.

IRSA circulates several publications, including article reprints. Titles include **Parent Idea Book** ($3.00 to nonmembers), **Rett Syndrome: A View on Care and Management,** and **Share the Journey** (a collection of poems). Write for ordering information. The Association also publishes a quarterly newsletter with articles by family members and a professional page.

Juvenile Diabetes Foundation International. 432 Park Avenue South, Sixteenth Floor, New York, NY 10016.

The organization was founded in 1970 by parents of children with diabetes who were determined that a cure be found through research. Send for the pamphlet list; it includes **Parent to Parent: Your Baby Has Diabetes; Your Child Has Diabetes;** and **What You Should Know about Diabetes.**

Little People of America (LPA). P.O. Box 633, San Bruno, CA 94066.

This organization "provides fellowship, moral support, and helpful information to those in-dividuals accepting the unique challenges of being a little person." LPA publishes a national newsletter, called **LPA Today.** Send for their free booklet, **My Child Is a Dwarf.** The organiza-tion also circulates the two books by Joan Ablon, reviewed earlier.

Lowe's Syndrome Association. 222 Lincoln Street, West Lafayette, IN 47906.

Lowe's Syndrome is a rare disease involving the eye, brain, and kidney, and is found only in males. The Association circulates a fine booklet, free of charge, called **Living with Lowe's Syndrome: A Guide for Families, Friends, and Professionals,** which outlines medical and developmental information, including genetic research and effects on families. Their newsletter, published three times a year, is called **On the Beam.**

March of Dimes. Public Health Education and Community Services Department, 1275 Mamaroneck Avenue, White Plains, NY 10605.

Single copies of their current publications are available free of charge. They include **When Your Baby Needs Early Extra Care.** Easy-to-read Public Health Education Information Sheets include **Sickle Cell Anemia; Tay-Sachs Disease; PKU; Congenital Heart Defects;** and **Neurofibromatosis.**

Minerva Press. 6653 Andersonville Road, Waterford, MI 48095.

Send for **Understanding Childhood Asthma: Diagnosis, Treatment, and Environmental Control;** a single copy is 99 cents.

Muscular Dystrophy Association. 810 Seventh Avenue, New York, NY 10019.

MDA Services to the Patient, the Family, the Community will acquaint parents with the As-sociation. Of particular interest is the pamphlet, **Learning to Live with Neuromuscular Disease: A Message for Parents.**

National Arthritis and Musculoskeletal and Skin Diseases Information Clearinghouse. Box AMS, Bethesda, MD 20892.

Arthritis in Children: An Annotated Bibliography lists print and audiovisual materials for children, parents, and teachers.

National Association for Sickle Cell Disease (NASCD). 4221 Wilshire Boulevard, Los Angeles, CA 90010–3503.

The **Parent/Teacher Guide: How Parents and Teachers Can Work Together to Achieve School Success for Children with Sickle Cell Anemia** will help parents to help their children; general information on the disease and advice about school-related issues will be of interest to teachers. NASCD also publishes fact sheets, a home study kit for families, a booklet called **How to Help Your Child Take It in Stride,** and **Sickle Cell News.**

National Digestive Diseases Information Clearinghouse. 1255 23rd Street, N.W., Suite 275, Washington, DC 20037.

> A single copy of **Cystic Fibrosis: The Puzzle and the Promise** is free.

National Hemophilia Foundation. Soho Building, 110 Greene Street, Room 406, New York, NY 10012.

> Write to the foundation for **Your Child and Hemophilia; The Psychological Factors in Hemophilia;** and **What You Should Know about Hemophilia.**

National Kidney Foundation. 30 East 33rd Street, New York, NY 10016.

> The Kidney Foundation distributes a number of public education pamphlets and a newsletter. Titles include **What Everyone Should Know about Kidneys and Kidney Disease** and **A Note to Parents of Children with End-Stage Renal Disease.**

National Tay-Sachs Foundation and Allied Diseases Association. 385 Elliot Street, Newton, MA 02164.

> Titles include **What Every Family Should Know** and **One Day at a Time.**

Osteogenesis Imperfecta Foundation, Inc. (OIF). P.O. Box 14807, Clearwater, FL 34629–4807.

> OIF will send at no charge general materials, news articles, and medical articles; request their literature list. A quarterly publication is called **Breakthrough.**

Parent Resources on Disabilities (PROD). P.O. Box 14391, Portland, OR 97214.

> PROD is a parent-run organization devoted primarily to advocacy on medical issues for parents of children with disabilities. Its topnotch quarterly publication is called **The Bridge** and covers subjects of interest in depth. Recent issues have dealt with "sorting out" how SSI works, surviving stress, family support services, paying medical bills, and understanding the ethical questions involved when participating in medical research. A year's subscription costs ten dollars.

Prader-Willi Syndrome Association. 5515 Malibu Drive, Edina, MN 55436.

> Send for their publication list, which includes several titles of interest to parents: **Prader-Willi Syndrome: A Handbook for Parents; An Overview of the Prader-Willi Syndrome; Understanding Prader-Willi Syndrome: A Literature Review for Educators and Families;** and a book written by a sister called **Sometimes I'm Mad, Sometimes I'm Glad . . . On Being a Prader-Willi Family.** The organization publishes a bimonthly newsletter, **The Gathered View.**

President's Committee on Employment of People with Disabilities. 1111 20th Street, N.W., Suite 636, Washington, DC 20036.

> Write for their publications list; it contains a number of items of interest concerning the employment of people with chronic disabilities, affirmative action, and accommodations.

Public Affairs Committee. 381 Park Avenue South, New York, NY 10016.

> **Asthma—Episodes and Treatment** sells for one dollar.

U.S. Department of Health and Human Services. National Maternal and Child Health Clearinghouse, 38th & R Streets, N.W., Washington, DC 20057.

The Clearinghouse has a number of resource directories, topical bibliographies, information packets, and other educational materials on health-related issues available; most of them are free. One title is **The Open Door: Parent Participation in State Policy-making about Children with Special Health Care Needs.** Send for their catalog.

U.S. Department of Health and Human Services. Public Health Service, National Institute of Neurological and Communicative Disorders and Stroke, Office of Scientific and Health Reports, 9000 Rockville Pike, Building 31, Bethesda, MD 20892.

A single copy of **Hope through Research: Tourette Syndrome** is free.

Cleft Palate

Brookshire, Bonnie L.; Lynch, Joan I.; Fox, Donna R. **A Parent-Child Cleft Palate Curriculum.** Austin: Pro-Ed, 1984. 123 pp. $19.00.

    The authors developed this curriculum for clinicians to use in a pilot intervention program for infants and toddlers with cleft lip or palate and their parents. The language and activities can be understood by parents. A section on parent information discusses the professionals parents will meet, feeding considerations, surgery and other possible procedures and treatments, hearing, speech, language, and causes.

Murphy, Judy. **Home Care of Handicapped Children: A Guide. Cleft Palate and Cleft Lip.** Lyons, Colo.: Carol L. Lutey Publishing, 1982. 71 pp. $6.50 (Paper).

    One of a series intended for potential caregivers of a child between the ages of three and twelve, this practical and helpful guide has good information to share with families, as well. Part I offers general guidelines concerning child health, self-help activities, social behavior, communication, play, and safety and protective measures. The brief second section discusses cleft palate and cleft lip, including what the causes may be, and offers hints for the caregiver.

Wicka, Donna Konkel; Falk, Mervyn L. **Advice to Parents of a Cleft Palate Child.** 2d ed. Springfield, Ill.: Charles C Thomas, 1982. 68 pp. $14.25.

    Compact yet extensive, this manual concentrates on the incidence and causes of cleft palate, speech characteristics, feeding management, plastic and reconstructive surgery, dental management, emotional considerations, hearing problems, and techniques for speech and language development.

Wynn, Sidney K.; Miller, Alfred L. **A Practical Guide to Cleft Lip and Palate Birth Defects: Helpful, Practical Information and Answers for Parents, Physicians, Nurses, and Other Professionals.** Springfield, Ill.: Charles C Thomas, 1984. 129 pp. $20.50.

    The questions and answers in this friendly, informative book were developed by parents and professionals. Topics cover the description and treatment of cleft lip and palate, first attitudes and feelings, present and future handling of children, and associated problems involving hearing, dentistry, heredity, psychology, surgery, speech, and language. Parents and doctors share honestly and openly. Many drawings, illustrations, and photographs add to the book's value.

Where to Write for Information

American Cleft Palate-Craniofacial Association. 1218 Grandview Avenue, Pittsburgh, PA 15211.

    The Association provides information and referrals to cleft palate and palate/craniofacial treatment centers nationwide. The organization has both nominally priced pamphlets and free information. The booklet, **The Child from Birth to Three Years,** answers many basic questions. Booklet Two covers **The Child from Three to Twelve Years.** There is also **Information for the Teenager.** Free fact sheets include **Dental Care,** and a **Selected Bibliography for Parents of Children with Cleft Lip/Palate.**

March of Dimes. Public Health Education and Community Services Department, 1275 Mamaroneck Avenue, White Plains, NY 10605.

An easy-to-read information sheet on **Cleft Lip and Palate** is available free of charge.

National Easter Seal Society. 70 East Lake Street, Chicago, IL 60601.

A booklet called **Bright Promise . . . For Your Child with Cleft Lip and Cleft Palate** is available for $1.75.

Epilepsy

Cragg, Sheila. **Run Patty Run.** New York: Harper & Row, 1980. 175 pp. $12.00.

 Patty Wilson, who set a world distance record for women runners, has epilepsy. This biographical account describes her father's determination to make her famous, her running triumphs, and how her honesty in dealing with her own epilepsy has helped others.

Freeman, Stephen W. **The Epileptic in Home, School, and Society.** Springfield, Ill.: Charles C Thomas, 1979. 285 pp. $33.75.

 Written in question-and-answer style, this practical, older book covers questions raised about the psychological, educational, vocational, legal, and medical problems of epilepsy. Family adjustment, effective discipline, and management are addressed. The book includes an interesting look at biofeedback as the "hope of the future" in treating epilepsy.

Gadow, Kenneth D. **Children on Medication, Volume II: Epilepsy, Emotional Disturbance, and Adolescent Disorders.** San Diego: College-Hill Press, 1986. 282 pp. $19.95 (Paper).

 This work describes antiepileptic drug therapy for seizure disorders, childhood psychoses, a variety of adolescent psychiatric disorders, and, additionally, enuresis, cerebral palsy, school phobia, and Tourette syndrome. Its intent is "to provide . . . pharmacological information that will help caregivers better understand medical decisions."

Gumnit, Robert J. **Living Well with Epilepsy.** New York: Demos, 1990. 166 pp. $19.95; $11.95 (Paper).

 Dr. Gumnit has designed his book to give information and encourage the outlook necessary to live successfully with epilepsy; its audience is both people with seizures and "others who share the adventure of life with them." It covers many subjects, from causes and treatment to diagnosis, medications, and first aid, and spans ages and concerns from seizures in newborns and infants to epilepsy in the workplace. Its tone is friendly and compassionate; its contents are comprehensive and informative.

Jan, James E.; Ziegler, Robert G.; Erba, Giuseppe. **Does Your Child Have Epilepsy?** Austin: Pro-Ed, 1983. 231 pp. $19.00 (Paper).

 Complex medical issues, what epilepsy is (and isn't), its treatment, and its impact on children and families through the years are translated into everyday language in this sensitive, comprehensive, common-sensical work. The authors are neurologists. Case histories, photographs, illustrations, and parent observations add to its usefulness.

Murphy, Judy. **Home Care of Handicapped Children: A Guide. Epilepsy.** Lyons, Colo.: Carol L. Lutey Publishing, 1982. 125 pp. $6.50 (Paper).

 One of a series intended for potential caregivers of a child between the ages of three and twelve, this practical and helpful guide has good information to share with families, as well. Part I offers general guidelines concerning child health, self-help activities, social behavior, communication, play, and safety and protective measures. The second part, specific to epilepsy, includes a discussion of causes, care of a child before, during, and after a seizure, equipment, medication, and diet.

Reisner, Helen, ed. **Children with Epilepsy: A Parents' Guide.** Rockville, Md.: Woodbine House, 1988. 314 pp. $12.95 (Paper).

This "complete and compassionate guide" will help families immeasurably in learning about epilepsy, adjusting, and developing their internal resources and external supports for the road ahead. As a parent, Reisner understands clearly the need for information and support of people new to the diagnosis of epilepsy in a child; she has gathered information from doctors, therapists, educators, lawyers, and other parents. There is an important chapter on helping a child develop high self-esteem. An annotated reading and cassette list, an extensive national and state-by-state Resource Guide, delightful photographs, and a glossary round out the book's valuable and significant content.

Schneider, Joseph W.; Conrad, Peter. **Having Epilepsy: The Experience and Control of Illness.** Philadelphia: Temple University Press, 1983. 280 pp. $34.95; $12.95 (Paper).

Using interviews with eighty adults who have varying degrees and types of seizures, two sociologists examine what it is like to have epilepsy from "an insider's perspective." A chapter on family life emphasizes the role of parents as "crucial sources and mediators of experience." This interesting work can help families in their understanding and guidance of a child with a seizure disorder.

Sullivan, Margaret Walker. **Living with Epilepsy.** Walnut Creek, Calif.: Bubba Press, 1981. 123 pp. $6.95 (Paper).

The author is a counselor and teacher for people with epilepsy; she had her first seizure as an adult. Using her experience, she writes, in clear and personal style, about the history of epilepsy, types of seizures, treatments, nutrition, and practical considerations.

Where to Write for Information

Abbott Laboratories. Public Affairs, Abbott Park, IL 60064.

Send a stamped, self-addressed, long business envelope for an informative pamphlet titled **Epilepsy: Breaking Down the Walls of Misunderstanding.**

Channing L. Bete Company. 200 State Road, South Deerfield, MA 01373–0200.

The booklet, **What Everyone Should Know about Epilepsy,** is 79 cents; a minimum of 25 copies must be ordered. It covers basic information in an attractive, easy-to-read format.

Epilepsy Foundation of America (EFA). 4351 Garden City Drive, Landover, MD 20785.

EFA provides information and referral, education and advocacy, and supports medical research. Write for a listing of publications on a variety of matters concerning epilepsy. Several fine publications are **Epilepsy, You, and Your Child: A Guide for Parents; Answering Your Questions about Epilepsy;** and **Seizures, Epilepsy, and Your Child. All about Epilepsy** helps a young child understand seizures. EFA's comprehensive newsletter is called **National Spokesman.** EFA will also put you in touch with families and resources in your community.

National Institutes of Health. Office of Clinical Center Communications, Warren Grant Magnuson Clinical Center, Building 10, Room 1C-255, Bethesda, MD 20892.

　　A single copy of **Epilepsy** is free of charge.

U.S. Department of Health and Human Services. Public Health Service, National Institute of Neurological and Communicative Disorders and Stroke, Office of Scientific and Health Reports, 9000 Rockville Pike, Building 31, Bethesda, MD 20892.

　　A single copy of **Hope through Research: Epilepsy** is free.

Hearing Impairment

Basic Reading

Bess, Fred H., ed. **Childhood Deafness: Causation, Assessment, and Management.** Orlando, Fla.: Grune & Stratton, 1977. 341 pp. $64.50.

This is a scholarly work which includes contributions by leading authorities in audiology, medicine, and education of children with hearing impairments. It is useful as a source of information on specific areas of deafness.

Freeman, Roger D.; Carbin, Clinton F.; Boese, Robert J. **Can't Your Child Hear? A Guide for Those Who Care about Deaf Children.** Austin: Pro-Ed, 1981. 340 pp. $19.00.

This is a practical, realistic, and readable guide to deafness. The authors offer facts, opinions, and experiences about raising a child whose hearing loss is severe or profound and occurred before the onset of normal speech. They summarize speech, speech reading, auditory training, and sign language; their clear preference is total communication. The book has been highly praised by professionals and parents; many resource persons throughout the world aided in its development.

Groce, Nora Ellen. **Everyone Here Spoke Sign Language: Hereditary Deafness on Martha's Vineyard.** Cambridge, Mass.: Harvard University Press, 1985. 169 pp. $8.95 (Paper).

For two hundred years, two towns on Martha's Vineyard had a high incidence of hereditary deafness. Based in large part on oral history, this fascinating account discusses the origin and genetics of Vineyard deafness and describes life on the Island in earlier days when people who were deaf were totally integrated and a strong support network existed; as one Vineyarder expressed it, "Those people weren't handicapped; they were just deaf." The author argues persuasively that "disabled people can be full and useful members of a community if the community makes an effort to include them. The society must be willing to change slightly to adapt to all."

Higgins, Paul C.; Nash, Jeffrey E. **Understanding Deafness Socially.** Springfield, Ill.: Charles C Thomas, 1986. 196 pp. $32.75.

Paul Higgins acknowledges the dilemma of parents receiving advice from practitioners who perceive a child who is deaf from a particular point of view—educational, audiological, medical, psychological. This book proposes a new approach, one that looks at the life of the person who is deaf within the larger social world in which he lives. To this end, chapters discuss the demography of deafness, how deafness influences socialization and behavior, the effect of a child who is deaf on family life, education, American Sign Language, "the deaf community," and the socioeconomic status of people who are deaf. The challenge is "to understand the creation by deaf and hearing people of the social reality of deafness and to aid in its remaking."

Ling, Daniel; Ling, Agnes H. **Aural Habilitation: The Foundations of Verbal Learning in Hearing Impaired Children.** Washington, D.C.: Alexander Graham Bell, 1978. 336 pp. $18.95 (Paper).

Written in 1978 for both professionals and parents, this comprehensive book describes the knowledge then available as well as the skills relating to verbal learning and suggests ways in which those skills may be used in teaching speech to children with hearing impairments. There are chapters on communication, development of spoken language, hearing aids, audiologic assessments, use of residual hearing, language and reading, and preparation of professional personnel.

Ling, Daniel. **Speech and the Hearing Impaired Child: Theory and Practice.** Washington, D.C.: Alexander Graham Bell, 1976. 402 pp. $20.95.

    Dr. Ling, an expert in the field of aural rehabilitation, examines the problems children with hearing impairments have in learning to speak, and suggests training through which speech can be effected. The book is not easy reading, but it is a source of information for parents who want to know as much as possible about teaching speech to children with hearing impairments.

Mindel, Eugene D.; Vernon, McCay, eds. **They Grow in Silence: Understanding Deaf Children and Adults.** Rev. ed. San Diego: College-Hill, 1987. 204 pp. $24.50 (Paper).

    Several authors write on a variety of topics that should help professionals better understand families dealing with a diagnosis of deafness in their child and may help families better understand their children. Some of the topics are "the impact of deaf children on their families," primary causes of deafness, developments in pediatric audiology, recent advances in the diagnosis of hearing loss in newborns and infants, language, educational directions, and employment issues.

Ogden, Paul W.; Lipsett, Suzanne. **The Silent Garden.** New York: St. Martin's, 1982. 227 pp. $12.95. Chicago: Contemporary Books. $7.95 (Paper).

    While this reassuring and helpful book does outline the different modes of communication available to people who are hearing impaired, its greatest strength lies in its consideration of the whole child. It stresses "the importance of a healthy home environment, parents' intuition, social stimulation, nonverbal communication, playfulness, open affection, humor, honest anger, and old-fashioned fair-mindedness." The primary author has been profoundly deaf since birth.

Padden, Carol; Humphries, Tom. **Deaf in America: Voices from a Culture.** Cambridge, Mass.: Harvard University Press, 1988. 134 pp. $17.95.

    Rather than focus on the fact that people who are deaf do not hear, the authors write about "their art and performances, their everyday talk, their shared myths, and the lessons they teach one another." They offer fascinating insights into people who share American Sign Language and, therefore, a culture.

Schwartz, Sue, ed. **Choices in Deafness: A Parents' Guide.** Rockville, Md.: Woodbine House, 1987. 215 pp. $12.95 (Paper).

    Parents new to the diagnosis of deafness are thrust into early decision making for the future; this important, sensitive resource will help them make their own best choice of educational options and develop confidence in themselves and in their children. The three major methodologies—oral/aural programming, total communication, and cued speech—are discussed by professionals and twelve families who share their stories of discovery, choice, and commitment. Medical and audiological information is easy to understand. A reading list, audio and visual materials, and directories of national organizations and state programs for people with hearing impairments add to the value of this guide.

Your Child at Home

Adams, John W. **You and Your Hearing-Impaired Child: A Self-Instructional Guide for Parents.**
Washington, D.C.: Gallaudet University Press, Clerc Books, 1988. 142 pp. $9.95 (Paper).

Attractively designed to help parents of a child with a hearing impairment learn more about the disability, how to cope with feelings, behavior management, nonverbal communication, problem-solving, and other topics, this pleasant guidebook offers information and interesting written activities to reinforce the knowledge and skill building presented in the text. It includes resources and suggested readings.

Calvert, Donald R. **Parents' Guide to Speech and Deafness.** Washington, D.C.: Alexander Graham Bell, 1984. 62 pp. $9.50 (Paper).

The author contends that parents are essential in helping children with hearing impairments learn to talk. To that end, he offers, in lucid and concrete style, general observations, helpful information, and practical suggestions for dealing with school and clinic programs and for helping at home.

McArthur, Shirley Hanawalt. **Raising Your Hearing-Impaired Child: A Guideline for Parents.**
Washington, D.C.: Alexander Graham Bell, 1982. 238 pp. $12.95 (Paper).

Writing with the empathy of a parent (two of her four children are hearing impaired) and the knowledge of an educator (she is certified as a teacher of the deaf in the State of California), the author traces steps in raising a child with a hearing impairment from first learning about hearing loss, to developing communication skills, to guiding a child through the school years to adulthood. The book is filled with sound ideas based on experience.

Murphy, Judy. **Home Care of Handicapped Children: A Guide. Hearing Impairment.** Lyons, Colo.:
Carol L. Lutey Publishing, 1982. 80 pp. $6.50 (Paper).

One of a series intended for potential caregivers of a child between the ages of three and twelve, this practical and helpful guide has good information to share with families, as well. Part I offers general guidelines concerning child health, self-help activities, social behavior, communication, play, and safety and protective measures. The second part, specific to hearing impairment, discusses causes of hearing loss, understanding the child with a hearing impairment, hearing aids, and practical hints for the caregiver.

Your Child at School

Froehlinger, Vira J., ed. **Today's Hearing Impaired Child: Into the Mainstream of Education.**
Washington, D.C.: Alexander Graham Bell, 1981. 240 pp. $12.95 (Paper).

This helpful, sensible guide is written to help parents, teachers, and administrators when children with hearing impairments are being considered for, or are placed in, mainstreamed programs. The development of oral and written language is emphasized. The role of parents within both family and school settings is sensitively discussed.

Katz, Lee; Mathis, Steve L., III; Merrill, Edward C., Jr. **The Deaf Child in the Public Schools: A Handbook for Parents of Deaf Children.** Danville, Ill.: Interstate Printers and Publishers; available from T.J. Publishers, 1978. 113 pp. $4.75 (Paper).

  This is a fine handbook for the parents of the younger or school-age child who is deaf. It presents much information about educational opportunities in integrated public school settings, offers an overview of the problems caused by deafness, and advises parents on how they can best help their child.

Northcott, Winifred R., ed. **The Hearing Impaired Child in a Regular Classroom: Preschool, Elementary and Secondary Years.** Washington, D.C.: Alexander Graham Bell, 1973. 300 pp. $9.95.

  Teacher, principal, psychologist, social worker, reading specialist, speech pathologist, hearing specialist, tutor, parent, and student all share ideas in this collection of articles about the integration of children with hearing impairments into the regular classroom setting.

Quigley, Stephen P.; Kretschmer, Robert E. **The Education of Deaf Children.** Austin: Pro-Ed, 1982. 127 pp. $19.00 (Paper).

  Highly recommended by professionals, this book is a summary of the basic issues confronting parents and educators concerning the education of children who are deaf.

Streng, Alice H.; Kretschmer, Richard B.; Kretschmer, Laura W. **Language, Learning and Deafness: Theory, Application, and Classroom Management.** Orlando, Fla.: Grune & Stratton, 1978. 232 pp. $39.50.

  This overview of the education of children who are deaf is directed to teachers, but it emphasizes the importance of parents as teachers and of cooperation between parents and professionals. Specific learning techniques are discussed.

Personal Accounts—From Those Who Have Lived It

Bitter, Grant B., ed. **Parents in Action: A Handbook of Experiences with Their Hearing Impaired Children.** Washington, D.C.: Alexander Graham Bell, 1978. 99 pp. $6.95 (Paper).

  This is a collection of true stories by parents of children with hearing impairments with plenty of practical advice on raising, disciplining, teaching, and loving a child who cannot hear.

Bowe, Frank. **Changing the Rules.** Silver Spring, Md.: T.J. Publishers, 1986. 204 pp. $20.95; $17.95 (Paper).

  Frank Bowe, a bright, charming, articulate advocate for the rights of people with disabilities, tells his story. With compelling humor and passion, he writes about how he grew up deaf in a small town with parents who ensured that he lived "a normal, average, everyday childhood," the challenges and isolation of mainstreamed schooling, his college years at Western Maryland and Gallaudet, his marriage and fatherhood, and the significant part he played in the civil rights movement that led to the issuing of the regulations governing Section 504, "the Bill of Rights" for Americans with disabilities.

Ferris, Caren. **A Hug Just Isn't Enough.** Washington, D.C.: Gallaudet College Press, 1980. 94 pp. $15.95.

Illustrated with more than eighty color and black-and-white photographs, **A Hug Just Isn't Enough** presents interviews with the parents of twenty-nine young children with hearing impairments. They speak openly and directly about their goals for their children, early reactions, frustrations with professionals, concerns, family life needs, different modes of communication, and their decisions about regular and special education. They don't all agree.

Fletcher, Lorraine. **Ben's Story: A Deaf Child's Right to Sign.** Washington, D.C.: Gallaudet University Press, 1987. 267 pp. $7.95 (Paper).

An English mother writes the story of a family's early years with a child with a profound hearing loss. Encounters with professionals, the "nightmare" of adapting to a difference, a committed family, and their early decision to teach their son British Sign Language, are well-described. Ben's mother has great energy and strong conviction; she shares her thoughts and feelings persuasively.

Forecki, Marcia Calhoun. **Speak to Me.** Washington, D.C.: Gallaudet College Press, 1985. 143 pp. $9.50 (Paper).

A single parent writes with humor and candor of her first six years as Charlie's mother. She discovered that her son was deaf when he was a year and a half old. Together they learned effective ways to understand one another; Forecki makes the challenges, the frustrations, and the triumphs delightfully clear.

Glick, Ferne Pellman; Pellman, Donald R. **Breaking Silence.** Scottdale, Pa.: Herald, 1982. 187 pp. $10.95; $6.95 (Paper).

A mother writes of the growing concerns about the behavior of twin sons, the misdiagnosis of aphasia, the professionals with whom the family dealt, private schooling which involved foster home arrangements for a time, family relationships, education in public school, and religion. The twins, grown to young men, recall along with their mother the early experiences and share their view of their deafness and its consequences.

Harris, George A. **Broken Ears, Wounded Hearts.** Washington, D.C.: Gallaudet College Press, 1983. 174 pp. $12.95.

A father writes of his child, born when her parents were nineteen; she was never definitively diagnosed. He outlines with honesty and anger his frustrations with the child, the professionals who saw and worked with her, and the effect of Jennifer on his marriage. At the close of the book, twelve-year-old Jennifer is living at a state school for the deaf; her parents are divorced.

Jacobs, Leo M. **A Deaf Adult Speaks Out.** Rev. ed. Washington, D.C.: Gallaudet College Press, 1980. 192 pp. $9.95 (Paper).

The author is deaf himself, the son of parents who were deaf, was the husband of a woman who was deaf (now dead), the father of one deaf and one hearing child, and for many years a teacher of children with hearing impairments. He offers his own rational ideas about being deaf in a hearing world, educational methods, and mainstreaming in schools and community.

Luterman, David. **Deafness in the Family.** San Diego: College-Hill, 1987. 124 pp. $24.50 (Paper).

> Written for professionals, this very readable book explores how the members of three families reacted and adjusted to the hearing impairment of their children from diagnosis to adulthood. The author's interviews with family members and his commentary, both from a clinical and personal perspective, are included. **Deafness in the Family** is a significant contribution to the literature about any family in which there is a child with a disability.

Schein, Jerome; Naiman, Doris. **For Parents of Deaf Children.** Silver Spring, Md.: National Association of the Deaf, 1977. 57 pp. $3.95 (Paper).

> This is a folksy book which discusses the problems faced by parents in raising a child who is deaf. Special attention is paid to feelings of the child and other family members.

Spradley, Thomas S.; Spradley, James P. 2d ed. **Deaf Like Me.** Washington, D.C.: Gallaudet University Press, 1985. 285 pp. $7.95 (Paper).

> With great emotion, the Spradley brothers tell the story of Lynn, their daughter and niece, who was born profoundly deaf at the time of the rubella epidemic in the 1960s. They found lip reading insufficient to teach the child until supplemented by a total communication approach with signs. An epilogue by Lynn is included in this second edition of the 1978 book. This is an angry work in many ways; it does portray the sad and difficult task of finding the best means for teaching a child who is deaf.

Star, Robin Rogoff. **We Can!** 2 Vols. Washington, D.C.: Alexander Graham Bell, 1980. 88 and 98 pp. $4.95 for the set (Paper).

> The **We Can** books are designed as a Career Education series and written at a fourth-grade readability level. They present the stories of a number of people who are hearing impaired and are leading full and independent lives in a variety of occupations.

Where to Write for Information

Alexander Graham Bell Association for the Deaf. 3417 Volta Place, N.W., Washington, DC 20007.

> The Bell Association is "dedicated to improving the techniques and knowledge necessary to broaden the educational, vocational, and personal opportunities for all hearing-impaired people." Several of the many publications on its excellent publications list are specifically for parents, notably the brochure, **Listen! Hear! For Parents of Hearing-Impaired Children,** and **Parent Kit,** a collection of articles designed for parents of children from birth to five years who are newly discovered to have hearing impairments. **Family to Family** shares the feelings of several families on topics relating to deafness, deaf education, and raising a child who is hearing impaired. A.G. Bell acts as a clearinghouse for many books relating to hearing impairment. Its newsletter is **Newsounds;** its journal is called **The Volta Review; Our Kids Magazine** is designed for parents.

American Society for Deaf Children. 814 Thayer Avenue, Silver Spring, MD 20910.

> This organization provides information and support to parents and families with children who are deaf or hard of hearing. **Endeavor,** their newsletter, is published bimonthly and includes an advice column for parents. Send $6.00 for **Years of Challenge,** a guide for parents of adolescents with hearing impairments, written by two parents.

American Speech-Language-Hearing Association (ASHA). 10801 Rockville Pike, Rockville, MD 20852.

ASHA is an organization of professionals which serves people with communication disorders. Several publications will interest parents. Write for **How Does Your Child Hear and Talk?** and **Answers and Questions about Otitis Media, Hearing, and Language Development.**

Channing L. Bete Company. 200 State Road, South Deerfield, MA 01373–0200.

The booklet, **What Everyone Should Know about Deafness,** is 79 cents; a minimum of 25 copies must be ordered. It covers basic information in an attractive, easy-to-read format. Another booklet is entitled **What Everyone Should Know about Speech and Hearing Problems.**

Gallaudet University. Public Services Division, Washington, DC 20002.

Gallaudet has many programs which provide information and services to parents of children with hearing impairments. Ask for the list of publications available through the Gallaudet Bookstore; it handles books published throughout the country on subjects of interest to people with hearing impairments and their families.

The National Association of the Deaf (NAD). 814 Thayer Avenue, Silver Spring, MD 20910.

NAD is one of the world's largest publishers of books and materials related to deafness. Membership includes a subscription to both **The NAD Broadcaster** and **The Deaf American.** Send for their lengthy catalog; it's filled with titles for people of all ages.

National Easter Seal Society. 70 East Lake Street, Chicago, IL 60601.

Dos and Don'ts for Parents of Children with Hearing Problems is available for forty cents.

National Information Center on Deafness (NICD). Gallaudet University, 800 Florida Avenue, N.W., Washington, DC 20002.

NICD is a centralized source of information on all aspects of deafness and hearing loss, including services, facts, and resources. Publications include **Growing Together: Information for Parents of Hearing Impaired Children** and a **Career Information Registry of Hearing Impaired Persons in Professional, Technical, and Managerial Occupations.**

President's Committee on Employment of People with Disabilities. 1111 20th Street, N.W., Suite 636, Washington, DC 20036.

Write for their publications list; it contains a number of items of interest concerning the employment of people with disabilities, affirmative action, and accommodations.

John Tracy Clinic. West Adams Boulevard, Los Angeles, CA 90007.

Write for information concerning the Clinic's correspondence course for parents of young children who are deaf. Other publications are also available.

U.S. Department of Health and Human Services. Public Health Service, National Institute of Neurological and Communicative Disorders and Stroke, Office of Scientific and Health Reports, 9000 Rockville Pike, Building 31, Bethesda, MD 20892.

A single copy of **Hope through Research: Hearing Loss** is free.

U.S. Government Printing Office. Washington, DC 20402.

A publication of the U.S. Department of Commerce, National Bureau of Standards called **Facts about Hearing and Hearing Aids: A Consumer's Guide** is available from the GPO. Order by Stock No. SN 003–003–02024–9 ($1.30).

Learning Disabilities, Hyperactivity, and/or Attention Deficit Disorder*

Basic Reading

Brutten, Milton; Richardson, Sylvia; Mangel, Charles. **Something's Wrong with My Child.** Orlando, Fla.: Harcourt Brace Jovanovich, 1979. 284 pp. $6.95 (Paper).

> Practical information on various aspects of raising children with learning disabilities is offered in this older, well-respected book: how to recognize the disability, where to go for help, and the specific problems of adolescence.

Cruickshank, William M. **Learning Disabilities in Home, School, and Community.** Syracuse, N.Y.: Syracuse University Press, 1977. 365 pp. $12.95 (Paper).

> This overview of learning disabilities is a reissue of Cruickshank's 1967 **The Brain-Injured Child in Home, School, and Community.** What goes on in the process of diagnosis at school and at home is discussed, and practical suggestions are offered to make life and learning better for children with learning disabilities. Teaching activities are described, and ego reinforcement is emphasized. The book will be interesting to parents as well as professionals.

Friedman, Ronald J.; Doyal, Guy T. **Attention Deficit Disorder and Hyperactivity.** Danville, Ill.: Interstate Printers and Publishers, 1987. 118 pp. $6.95 (Paper).

> Originally published in 1982 under the title **The Hyperactive Child,** this detailed booklet describes for parents various medical, behavioral, and educational treatment approaches to attention deficit disorder and hyperactivity.

Gadow, Kenneth D. **Children on Medication, Volume I: Hyperactivity, Learning Disabilities, and Mental Retardation.** San Diego: College-Hill Press, 1986. 251 pp. $16.50 (Paper).

> The goal of this work is "to provide . . . pharmacological information that will help caregivers better understand medical decisions." Gadow focuses on psychotropic drugs prescribed for hyperactivity and aggressiveness. The detailed text outlines what particular medications are intended to do and what their side effects may be.

Heiting, Kenneth. **When Your Child is Hyperactive.** St. Meinard, Ind.: Abbey Press, 1978. 96 pp. $2.45 (Paper).

> Living with and raising a child who is hyperactive is the focus of this well-written book. Parents are given practical illustrations of the problems arising from hyperactivity and specific guidance on how to cope with them without sacrificing the self-esteem of their child. Parent-school relations, discipline, and medications are among its subjects.

---

* Learning disabilities, hyperactivity, and attention deficit disorder are not necessarily mutually inclusive.

Hornsby, Beve. **Overcoming Dyslexia: A Straightforward Guide for Families and Teachers.** New York: Arco, 1984. 140 pp. $7.95 (Paper).

Written by a British psychologist-teacher-speech therapist, **Overcoming Dyslexia** has much to say to families and teachers in all English-speaking countries. It explains "dyslexia" (difficulty in learning to read and write by a child of average or above average intelligence), how a child is tested, and how a child can be helped. One chapter is addressed directly to the student or adult with dyslexia. The text is clear, and photographs, graphs, and illustrations add to its appeal.

Ingersoll, Barbara. **Your Hyperactive Child: A Parent's Guide to Coping with Attention Deficit Disorder.** New York: Doubleday, 1988. 219 pp. $7.95 (Paper).

Parents and teachers will find this guidebook useful, informative, and practical. The author, a clinical psychologist, summarizes the field of Attention-Deficit Hyperactivity Disorder (ADHD) from diagnosis to treatment, both medical and psychological, at home and in school. She rejects nutritional remedies in favor of a regimen of stimulant medication and behavior management. Anecdotal material and suggestions make the book especially interesting.

Johnston, Robert B. **Learning Disabilities, Medicine, and Myth: A Guide to Understanding the Child and the Physician.** Boston: Little, Brown, 1987. 141 pp. $19.50 (Paper).

The doctor-author's intent is to demystify the role of the physician in the identification and management of "learning and attention disabilities." He writes of serious subjects with thoughtfulness, knowledge, and wit.

Jordan, Dale R. **Attention Deficit Disorder: ADD Syndrome.** Austin: Pro-Ed, 1988. 62 pp. $9.00 (Paper).

This compact booklet defines the four forms of ADD Syndrome (formerly referred to as Minimal Brain Damage), spelling out the characteristics, illustrating ADD in the classroom, and suggesting ways to help which include medication, diet control, tight structure, written lists, supervision, understanding, consistent discipline, and working with professionals.

McWhirter, J. Jeffries. **The Learning Disabled Child: A School and Family Concern.** Lanham, Md.: University Press of America, 1988. 316 pp. $12.95 (Paper).

A psychologist who is also the parent of two sons with learning disabilities has written this very practical guide. It emphasizes steps to be taken to counteract specific problems, both educational and psychological. The book is an expansion of the original work published in 1977.

Rapp, Doris, J. **The Impossible Child in School, at Home: A Guide for Caring Teachers and Parents.** Buffalo, N.Y.: Practical Allergy Research Foundation, 1988. 160 pp. $8.95 plus $1.50 postage (Paper).

A pediatric allergist writes in a nontechnical way of food allergies, pollen, and chemical sensitivities as possible causes of behavioral symptoms and poor school performance. Her practical solutions may resolve some learning problems. Numerous readings are listed in an appendix.

Renshaw, Domeena C. **The Hyperactive Child.** Chicago: Nelson-Hall, 1974. 197 pp. $19.95.

In this older work, the author describes the child who is hyperactive and suggests means of behavior management and ways of dealing with problems arising in the family and school. Distinctions are made between hyperactivity resulting from emotional disorders and hyperactive behavior resulting from disease or brain damage.

Silver, Larry B. **The Misunderstood Child: A Guide for Parents of Learning Disabled Children.** New York: McGraw-Hill, 1984. 212 pp. $14.95.

This understanding, understandable guide is intended to help a parent become "an informed consumer" and "an assertive advocate." The author, a child psychiatrist, explains the possible causes and various symptoms of learning disabilities, the psychological, emotional, and social problems that may accompany them, how they are evaluated, how they are treated, and legal issues of importance to parents. Silver shares many suggestions, techniques, and approaches for parents to use at home and in dealing with school systems; he also outlines some of the "controversial therapies" and his personal reservations concerning them.

Stewart, Mark A.; Olds, Sally Wendkos. **Raising a Hyperactive Child.** New York: Harper & Row, 1973. 209 pp. $14.45.

Parents will like the authors' obvious understanding of the problems of daily life with a child who is hyperactive. The book includes chapters describing common attributes of such a child in his early years, in adolescence, and as an adult.

Swenson, Sally Shearer; Weisberg, Phyllis Gilman. **Questions and Answers about Learning Disabilities: The Learning Disabled, Their Parents, and Professionals Speak Out.** Austin: Pro-Ed, 1988. 107 pp. $16.00 (Spiral).

Seven professionals, four parents, and two young people with learning disabilities were interviewed. They talk about the impact of learning disabilities on emotional life—how families cope, manage, survive.

Wender, Paul H. **The Hyperactive Child, Adolescent, and Adult: Attention Deficit Disorder through the Lifespan.** New York: Oxford University Press, 1987. 162 pp. $18.95; $7.50 (Paper).

Characteristics of children with attention deficit disorder, current understanding of the causes of ADD, and its treatment—including constructive guidance for parents—are cogently presented. Originally published in 1973 as **The Hyperactive Child** and in 1978 as **The Hyperactive Child and the Learning Disabled Child: A Handbook for Parents,** this continuing update extends what has been learned about symptoms, diagnosis, and treatment into adulthood.

Your Child at Home

Crook, William G.; Stevens, Laura. **Solving the Puzzle of Your Hard-to-Raise Child.** New York: Random House, 1987. 368 pp. $17.95.

The authors, a pediatrician and a mother, have long been convinced that allergies are a major cause of behavior and learning problems. They talk about the child with allergies in today's world, describe how to recognize symptoms, and—most important—tell parents what they can to help a child feel better, act better, and be successful. Appendices list many sources of help and information.

Feingold, Ben F. **Why Your Child is Hyperactive.** New York: Random House, 1985. 211 pp. $7.95.

Dr. Feingold believes that artificial flavorings and colorings are prime offenders in causing hyperactivity, which he defines as "excessive physical activity coupled with lack of concentration and learning difficulties." He discusses medication and treatment with drugs, and offers simple diets, menus, and recipes. Dr. Feingold and Helen S. Feingold, his wife, are the authors of **The Feingold Cookbook for Hyperactive Children** (Random House, 1979, $6.95) which presents a large selection of recipes and menus which are salicylate- and additive-free.

Gardner, Richard A. **MBD: The Family Book about Minimal Brain Dysfunction.** Northvale, N.J.: Jason Aronson, 1973. 185 pp. $12.50.

Part I of this work is written for parents—a straightforward discussion that concentrates on common parental reactions to children with learning disabilities and how their children adapt to those disabilities. The second half is directed to boys and girls and deals in words and illustrations with their need for information and the common worries they may have.

Lovinger, Sophie L. **Learning Disabilities and Games.** Chicago: Nelson-Hall, 1979. 143 pp. $19.95.

Play is not only "children's business" but a useful learning process. The author points out that learning disabilities can be helped by games which encourage skills and feelings of competence, self-esteem, and responsibility. Many games are described, and suggestions are made to help the adult inconspicuously arrange things to be sure that maximum pleasure and learning result from them.

Mitchell, Janey Walls. **Help for the Hyperactive Child through Diet and Love.** Crozet, Va.: Betterway Publications, 1984. 216 pp. $7.95 (Paper).

A mother who recognized the connection between diet and her son's disruptive behavior describes how to track down hidden food allergies or sensitivities and what to do with that knowledge. She also offers guidelines and techniques for "habit training." Her tone is helpful and encouraging.

Osman, Betty. **Learning Disabilities: A Family Affair.** New York: Random House, 1979. 224 pp. $15.95.

Although the information on resources and references may be out-of-date, the book is still a gold mine of practical advice on how to cope with the home and school problems of a child with learning disabilities.

Osman, Betty B.; Blinder, Henriette. **No One to Play With: The Social Side of Learning Disabilities.** Novato, Calif.: Academic Therapy Publications, 1982. 170 pp. $10.00 (Paper). New York: Warner Books, 1986. 208 pp. $3.50 (Paper).

A specialist in the field of learning disabilities writes about the social problems experienced by many children with whom she has worked. Osman suggests strategies for raising a child's "social quotient"; her anecdotal approach displays empathy for the child and genuine understanding for siblings and parents.

Schoonover, Richard J. **Handbook for Parents of Children with Learning Disabilities.** 2d ed. Danville, Ill.: Interstate Printers and Publishers; distributed by Pro-Ed, 1983. 88 pp. $6.00 (Paper).

> The author identifies the child with a learning disability by describing his characteristics and the problems which interfere with learning. He recommends methods of treating the child in learning and behavioral situations (including forty-three ways to say "good"), gives specific aids to learning which can be used in the home, and includes a chapter on behavior modification techniques. Helpful information for the college-bound student with learning disabilities is included in the appendices.

Stevens, Suzanne H. **The Learning-Disabled Child: Ways That Parents Can Help.** Winston-Salem, N.C.: John F. Blair, 1980. 196 pp. $11.95; $6.95 (Paper).

> The author, a teacher, says that the object of the book is "to help parents raise their learning-disabled children so that they . . . will be happy, well-adjusted, and normally successful adults despite their learning disabilities." Her suggestions are many; her style is clear and readable; her anecdotal illustrations add interest.

Taylor, John F. **The Hyperactive Child and the Family: The Complete What-to-Do Handbook.** New York: Dodd, Mead, 1983. 251 pp. $8.95 (Paper).

> The book is aimed at helping the family with a child who is hyperactive deal more effectively with the child and themselves. It discusses various approaches to treatment—counseling, nutrition management, and medication, the effect of the child on family relationships, and how to help the child at home, in the neighborhood, and at school. One reviewer describes owning the book as "having my own private psychologist."

Vitale, Barbara Meister. **Unicorns Are Real: A Right-Brained Approach to Learning.** Rolling Hills Estates, Calif.: Jalmar, 1982. 118 pp. $10.95 (Paper).

> In this pleasant and helpful book, the author, who grew up with a learning disability, describes the hemispheric specialization of the brain and suggests a number of learning strategies for school and home.

Your Child at School

Ayres, A. Jean. **Sensory Integration and the Child.** Los Angeles: Western Psychological Services, 1979. 191 pp. $18.50 (Paper).

> Dr. Ayres believes that occupational therapy can help some children who have sensory processing or integrative problems to achieve more in and out of school. Her detailed, yet clearly written book elucidates her theory and the therapy practiced in her private clinic. One chapter suggests ways parents can help at home.

Behrmann, Polly. **Why Me?** Available from the author (849 Seabrooke Court, Englewood, FL 34223), 1990. Approximately 100 pp. Approximately $6.00 (Paper).

> The adolescent and young adult with learning disabilities faces many problems of disorganization, clumsiness, and insecurity when dealing with everyday situations. The author has isolated some of the most common of these situations and gives suggestions for teaching social skills,

memory skills, and math skills. This updated version adds issues around acquiring and managing a job. The book is useful for helping to build poise and confidence.

Cordoni, Barbara. **Living with a Learning Disability.** Carbondale: Southern Illinois University Press, 1987. 139 pp. $18.95; $12.95 (Paper).

    This is a fine book with concrete suggestions and examples for parents and professionals who live or work with adolescents and young adults with learning disabilities. Its concentration is on social disability and how to help. The author draws on her own experiences as a mother, a resource room teacher, and the founder of a support program for college students with disabilities. Sections on reading materials, residential programs/career training, and information sources are included.

Cruickshank, William; Morse, William C.; John, Jeannie S. **Learning Disabilities: The Struggle from Adolescence toward Adulthood.** Syracuse, N.Y.: Syracuse University Press, 1980. 285 pp. $14.95 (Paper).

    The authors give a clear description of the difficulties of adolescence for the child with a learning disability. Interviews with five adults who a decade earlier had been placed in a highly structured special education program illustrate these problems and give concrete examples of some of the possible results. The authors offer descriptions, insights, and suggestions for teachers guiding adolescents with learning disabilities. Parents will find the book readable and helpful.

Griffiths, Anita N. **Teaching the Dyslexic Child.** Novato, Calif.: Academic Therapy Publications, 1978. 128 pp. $5.00 (Paper).

    A teacher shares her gift for teaching children who are "dyslexic." Her techniques are varied and provide for a great number of practical experiences for the child, who is then encouraged and taught to describe them in writing. The author emphasizes positive, active learning experiences which may be adapted by parents.

Kronick, Doreen, ed. **What about Me? The LD Adolescent.** Novato, Calif.: Academic Therapy Publications, 1975. 219 pp. $7.00 (Paper).

    Parents have collaborated to produce a collection filled with the kinds of insights that can probably only be gained from years of family living and which should be helpful and reassuring to anyone raising a teenager with learning disabilities.

McGuinness, Diane. **When Children Don't Learn: Understanding the Biology and Psychology of Learning Disabilities.** New York: Basic Books, 1985. 310 pp. $19.95.

    A psychologist examines the research underlying assumptions about children identified as learning disabled. The majority of these labeled children are male. McGuinness is particularly interested in the ways in which boys differ from girls in their development and how those differences have been ignored by schools and researchers in the past.

Rosner, Jerome. **Helping Children Overcome Learning Difficulties: A Step-by-Step Guide for Parents and Teachers.** 2d ed. New York: Walker, 1979. 379 pp. $16.95 (Paper).

    This book for parents and teachers offers programs for teaching at home and at school, with a strong admonition to work together.

Smith, Sally L. **No Easy Answers: The Learning Disabled Child at Home and at School.** New York: Bantam, 1981. 326 pp. $4.50 (Paper).

    The author, founder and director of the Lab School of the Kingsbury Center in Washington, D.C., provides a clearly written description of the child with learning disabilities, with positive suggestions for the parent and teacher on how to cope with him. This very helpful book contains useful appendices, including one on the constructive use of television, one on the use of art in education, and one listing stock phrases to encourage a learner experiencing difficulties.

Stevens, Suzanne H. **Classroom Success for the Learning Disabled.** Winston-Salem, N.C.: John F. Blair, 1984. 314 pp. $15.95; $8.95 (Paper).

    A sensitive educator writes about Al, a school dropout whose learning disabilities were not diagnosed. How to recognize the student with learning disabilities and what teachers can do to adjust school work so that the student can succeed is the focus of this interesting and sensible discussion. Numerous examples will help parents work with teachers on designing effective strategies and adjustments.

Tomlan, Patricia S. **You're Not the Only One . . . Volume I: A Survival Guide for the Learning Disabled in School.** Littleton, Colo.: PST Educational Consultants, 1986. 99 pp. $6.75 (Paper).

    Addressed to the student with learning disabilities, **You're Not the Only One** should be helpful to parents looking for easy-to-understand explanations and practical suggestions. The chapters cover auditory, visual, motor, and language disabilities. Volume II is annotated in "Your Child Grows Up," the next section of this book.

Your Child Grows Up

Mangrum, Charles T., II; Strichart, Stephen S. **College and the Learning Disabled Student: A Guide to Program Selection, Development, and Implementation.** Orlando, Fla.: Grune & Stratton, 1984. 301 pp. $34.00.

    This guide describes the emergence of college programs for students with learning disabilities, the characteristics of the students, the components of learning disabilities programs, guidelines for assisting college students with learning disabilities, and program models.

Scheiber, Barbara; Talpers, Jeanne. **Unlocking Potential: College and Other Choices for Learning Disabled People—A Step by-Step Guide.** Bethesda, Md.: Adler & Adler; distributed by Woodbine House, 1987. 195 pp. $27.95; $12.95 (Paper).

    Much information, many ideas, and good advice for students with learning disabilities who want to continue their education past high school graduation are contained in this helpful guide. **Unlocking Potential** explains learning disabilities, describes how they are diagnosed, discusses how to make decisions about postsecondary options and courses, and outlines possible accommodations, alternative ways to learn, and study skills. (It was originally published as **Campus Access for Learning Disabled Students.**)

Tomlan, Patricia S. **You're Not the Only One . . . Volume II: Reading between the Lines for the Learning Disabled.** Littleton, Colo.: PST Educational Consultants, 1986. 69 pp. $4.25 (Paper).

Volume II of **You're Not the Only One** is written for "mature students" and adults with learning disabilities. The chapters cover organization, time-management, and memory skills; college programs and writing skills; the development of learning disabilities and dealing with its signs in children; and job selection. Parents will get good insights and resource information.

Personal Accounts—From Those Who Have Lived It

Evans, James S. **An Uncommon Gift.** Philadelphia: Westminster, 1983. 180 pp. $12.95.

Dyslexic and hyperkinetic, a young man explores his struggles in school, in relationships, with teachers and counselors, and with religious faith. He defines his disability as a "force for discipline and sensitivity," "an uncommon gift." He is an articulate spokesperson.

Hampshire, Susan. **Su₂an's ₂tory: An Autobiographical Account of My Struggle with Dyslexia.** New York: St. Martin's, 1982. 171 pp. $5.95 (Paper).

Susan Hampshire is a successful English actress. This is her account of growing up feeling that a ball of string inside her head accounted for the "tangle" in her brain. The difficulties of being an actress who has "word blindness" are sometimes amusing, often embarrassing, and frequently painful. Hampshire's coping skills are impressive.

MacCracken, Mary. **Turnabout Children: Overcoming Dyslexia and Other Learning Difficulties.** Boston: Little, Brown, 1986. 258 pp. $16.95; New York: New American Library, Signet, 1986. $3.95 (Paper).

MacCracken, a gifted teacher and a talented writer, tells the stories of five of the children with whom she has most recently worked—children with "a kind of neurological dysfunction." For parents who live with children who are exhausting, bewildering, bright, vulnerable, distractible, and impulsive, MacCracken offers hope and understanding, as well as information about diagnostic tests, therapeutic techniques, and programs.

Simpson, Eileen. **Reversals: A Personal Account of Victory over Dyslexia.** Boston: Houghton Mifflin, 1979. 246 pp. $10.95. New York: Washington Square Press, 1981. 272 pp. $5.95 (Paper).

A psychotherapist describes her painful, dyslexic youth and her eventual success in overcoming her disability.

Ungerleider, Dorothy Fink. **Reading, Writing, and Rage.** Rolling Hills Estates, Calif.: Jalmar Press, 1985. 217 pp. $12.95 (Paper).

The author, an educational therapist, shares the compelling story of Tony Petri, a young man struggling with learning disabilities and lost in the educational system. Based on fact and written as fiction, this important book allows the reader to understand the frustration and the potential for violence experienced by someone not served well enough by private or public professionals. A clear picture of Tony's mother throughout his growing up years is also offered.

Where to Write for Information

Academic Therapy Publications. 20 Commercial Boulevard, Novato, CA 94947.

Write for their catalog. Topics include tips and guides for parents at home, for teachers at school, directories of facilities and services, and many useful books and pamphlets of a nontechnical nature.

Behavioral Pediatrics. 2115 Chadbourne Avenue, Madison, WI 53705.

A booklet called **Attention Deficit Disorders, Hyperactivity and Associated Disorders: A Handbook for Parents and Professionals** is available for $5.25.

Channing L. Bete Company. 200 State Road, South Deerfield, MA 01373–0200.

The booklet, **What Everyone Should Know about Learning Disabilities,** is 79 cents; a minimum of 25 copies must be ordered. It covers basic information in an attractive, easy-to-read format.

Center for Dyslexia. 1602 Gordon Avenue, Charlottesville, VA 22903.

Write for information about diagnostic and educational facilities for people with dyslexia. Inquire about publications, as well.

The Churchill Center for Learning Disabilities. 22 East 95th Street, New York, NY 10128.

Churchill Forum shares thoughtful, in-depth articles on topics that will certainly interest parents. It is published quarterly; write for ordering information.

The Council for Exceptional Children (CEC). 1920 Association Drive, Reston, VA 22091–1589.

CEC has a Division for Learning Disabilities. **Learning Disabilities Focus** and **Learning Disabilities Research** are both published twice a year. Write for subscription information.

ERIC Clearinghouse on Adult, Career, and Vocational Education, Center on Education and Training for Employment. 1900 Kenny Road, Columbus, OH 43210–1090.

Adult Learning Disabilities is available free of charge.

ERIC Clearinghouse on Handicapped and Gifted Children, Council for Exceptional Children. 1920 Association Drive, Reston, VA 22091–1589.

Learning Disabilities; Attention Deficit Disorder; Stress Management for the Learning Disabled; College Planning for Learning Disabled Students; and **What is Dyslexia?** are one dollar each. Send for the complete Product Flyer.

Father Flanagan's Boys' Home. Public Service Division, Boys Town, NE 68010.

Boys' Town circulates a helpful booklet titled **A Parent's Guide to Learning and School Problems.**

Feingold Association of the United States. 1029 Jerico Turnpike, Smithtown, NY 11787.

　　The Association gathers and disseminates information about a nutrition program which eliminates synthetic colors, flavors, and preservatives. Write for information on the "Feingold diet" as well as for a listing of local chapters; many have newsletters.

HEATH Resource Center. One Dupont Circle, N.W., Suite 800, Washington, DC 20036–1193.

　　Send for a free copy of **Young Adults with Learning Disabilities and Other Special Needs: Guide for Selecting Postsecondary Transition Programs.**

Learning Disabilities Association of America (LDAA). 4156 Library Road, Pittsburgh, PA 15234.

　　This significant national organization for parents, adults with learning disabilities, and professionals has active state and local affiliates throughout the country. Write for a listing. Also ask for the Association's inventory of books and articles. Topics include early childhood, behavior modification, nutrition, hyperactivity/attention deficit disorder, parents, physicians, and teachers. A bimonthly newsletter is called **LDAA Newsbriefs.**

Learning Disabilities Project. 7926 Jones Branch Drive, Suite 1100, McLean, VA 22102.

　　Two 1989 titles of six-page papers are **Choosing a Doctor for Your Child with Learning Disabilities or Attention Deficit Disorders** and **Recreation for Children with Learning Disabilities.** Write for ordering information.

Minerva Press. 6653 Andersonville Road, Waterford, MI 48095.

　　"The Helpful Pamphlets People" distribute several titles of interest: **A New Look at Attention Deficit Disorder: A Problem Not Outgrown But Treatable; Attention Deficit Disorder in Teenagers and Young People; Children Who Can Hear But Can't Listen: Auditory Processing Deficit—Achievement Anxiety Syndrome; Coping with Your Inattentive Child: A Practical Guide for Management; Educational Strategies for Attention Deficit Disorder;** and **Living with a Learning Disability: A Handbook for High School and College Students.** Pamphlets cost 99 cents each. They are written by professionals for distribution by pediatricians, family practitioners, and nurses.

National Center for Learning Disabilities. 99 Park Avenue, New York, NY 10016.

　　The Center's annual magazine, **Their World,** has much of interest for parents; it sells for five dollars. It also publishes a resource guide to schools, clinics, camps, and other resources for children with learning disabilities; it costs twelve dollars.

National Easter Seal Society. 70 East Lake Street, Chicago, IL 60601.

　　Yes You Can is a 29–page booklet to help young people with learning disabilities understand and help themselves. It costs $1.75.

National Information Center for Children and Youth with Handicaps (NICHCY). P.O. Box 1492, Washington, DC 20013.

　　Do get on their mailing list. NICHCY provides fact sheets, article reprints, resource information, specialized packets, bibliographies, and addresses of parent organizations and disability-related groups on a national, state, and local level, free of charge. Two titles to ask for specifically are **What Every Parent Should Know about Learning Disabilities** and **What Every Parent Should Know about Reading Disorders.**

National Institute of Mental Health (NIMH). Public Inquiries Section, 5600 Fishers Lane, Room 15C-05, Rockville, MD 20857.
>Send for **Plain Talk About—Children with Learning Disabilities.**

National Library Service for the Blind and Physically Handicapped. Library of Congress, Washington, DC 20542.
>The free library service for "Talking Books," books recorded on tape and played on cassette players that can be borrowed without charge, extends to those with learning disabilities and other impairments that impede ability to learn from the printed word.

The Orton Dyslexia Society. 724 York Road, Baltimore, MD 21204.
>The Orton Society is devoted exclusively to helping children with specific reading and language learning disabilities. Its publications list includes items for parents as well as for educators and doctors. Its periodical is called **Annals of Dyslexia.**

President's Committee on Employment of People with Disabilities. 1111 20th Street, N.W., Suite 636, Washington, DC 20036–3470.
>Write for their publications list; it contains a number of items of interest concerning the employment of people with learning disabilities, affirmative action, and accommodations.

Public Affairs Committee. 381 Park Avenue South, New York, NY 10016.
>A pamphlet of specific interest is **Learning Disabilities: Problems and Progress.** It sells for one dollar.

Right to Education Technical Assistance Group. 150 South Progress Avenue, Harrisburg, PA 17109.
>Send for the well-done free booklet called **Steps to Independence for People with Learning Disabilities** which emphasizes practical information for and about adults with learning disabilities. The author, Dale Brown, was the first chairperson of the National Network of Learning Disabled Adults.

U.S. Department of Health and Human Services, National Maternal and Child Health Clearinghouse. 38th & R Streets, N.W., Washington, DC 20057.
>NMCHC circulates a free pamphlet called **Developmental Dyslexia and Related Reading Disorders.**

U.S. Department of Health and Human Services, Public Health Service, Alcohol, Drug Abuse, and Mental Health Administration, Information Resources Inquiries Branch. 5600 Fishers Lane, Rockville, MD 20857.
>Available publications include the **Caring about Kids** series; two titles are **Dyslexia** and **Helping the Hyperactive Child.** Single copies are free. A bibliography on learning disabilities is also available.

U.S. Department of Health and Human Services, Public Health Service, National Institute of Child Health and Human Development. P.O. Box 29111, Washington, DC 20040.

Send for the free publications, **Facts about Dyslexia** and **Facts about Childhood Hyperactivity.**

U.S. Government Printing Office. Superintendent of Documents, Washington, DC 20402.

A Head Start series, called **Mainstreaming Preschoolers,** is being revised. One excellent book in the series was titled **Children with Learning Disabilities: A Guide for Teachers, Parents, and Others Who Work with Learning Disabled Preschoolers.** Inquire about its current status.

Mental Illness and Behavior Disorders

Basic Reading

Arieti, Silvano. **Understanding and Helping the Schizophrenic: A Guide for Family and Friends.** New York: Simon & Schuster, 1981. 239 pp. $9.95 (Paper).

> This look at schizophrenia, written for the general reader by a distinguished psychiatrist, discusses the causes and warning signs of schizophrenia and typical manifestations of the condition. The book gives practical suggestions for the patient's family and friends.

Axline, Virginia M. **Play Therapy.** New York: Ballantine, 1974. 374 pp. $3.95 (Paper).

> A child psychiatrist uses specific illustrations in describing how play therapy can work to aid the hostile child, the withdrawn child, the dependent child, and the child with a disability in learning to accept and respect himself and others.

Bernheim, Kayla F.; Lewine, Richard J. **The Caring Family: Living with Chronic Mental Illness.** Chicago: Contemporary Books, 1982. 226 pp. $8.75 (Paper).

> The authors interviewed many families living with relatives with mental illness in the process of writing this book. They discuss common emotions and offer both advice about how to handle problem behaviors and suggestions for minimizing stress. The mental health system is described as well as legal issues such as involuntary commitment, the right to refuse treatment, and providing for the future of a person who will be permanently dependent.

Bernheim, Kayla F.; Lewine, Richard J. **Schizophrenia: Symptoms, Causes, and Treatments.** New York: W.W. Norton, 1979. 256 pp. $9.95 (Paper).

> This fine book proposes to provide a broad understanding of schizophrenia, its symptoms, its causes, its treatment, and prognosis. An interesting section is included comparing knowledge of treatments at the time of publication with possible preventive treatments of the future.

Busick, Bonnie Sigren; Gorman, Martha. **Ill Not Insane.** Boulder, Colo.: New Idea Press, 1986. 311 pp. $12.95 (Paper).

> The authors, both of whom have family members with chronic mental illness, contend that research proves that "large numbers of patients in the mental health system have medical problems . . . that either cause or aggravate their psychiatric symptoms." They present much information about the brain, discuss research projects, and outline the need for change in the mental health and legal system—the need to go beyond "talk therapy" and drugs to a third methodology which would use what can be learned from electronics, computer technology, and biochemistry to test for abnormal brain function.

Carlisle, Wendy. **Siblings of the Mentally Ill.** Saratoga, Calif.: R & E Publishers, 1984. 190 pp. $8.95 (Paper).

> Mental illness profoundly affects an entire family. This book describes the experiences, problems, and special needs of a group of brothers and sisters of people who became mentally ill during adolescence. Relationships with parents, relationships among siblings, relationships out-

side the home, and contacts with mental health professionals were investigated. Numerous direct quotations share both common trends and individual coping skills. A significant finding points to the almost total lack of mental health services provided to those vulnerable and often needy family members, the siblings.

Chess, Stella; Hassibi, Mahin, eds. **Principles and Practice of Child Psychiatry.** 2d ed. New York: Plenum, 1986. 550 pp. $35.00.

    This clearly written examination of child psychiatry contains sections on syndromes and methods of psychiatric intervention, personality development, descriptions of strategies, and therapeutic treatment approaches. The final chapter deals with the rights of children under law. The work is comprehensive and understandable.

Committee on Psychiatry and the Community, The Group for the Advancement of Psychiatry. **A Family Affair: Helping Families Cope with Mental Illness.** New York: Brunner/Mazel, 1986. 104 pp. $9.95 (Paper).

    A committee of The Group for the Advancement of Psychiatry studied the problems of caring for a child or adult with chronic mental illness; they used as a basis for this interesting and empathic report the responses of readers of the "Dear Abby" newspaper columnist to her request for firsthand experiences. Commentary addresses the impact of mental illness on a family, coping with treatment, care systems and mental health professionals, and how families and professionals can be more effective collaborators.

Dearth, Nona; Labenski, Barbara J.; Mott, M. Elizabeth; Pellegrini, Lillian M. **Families Helping Families: Living with Schizophrenia.** New York: W.W. Norton, 1986. 163 pp. $14.95.

    Families of people with mental illness write to help other families, "to let them know what they will be facing, to ease the burden, and to educate the public." Painful, truthful, intensely personal, the book shares experiences and thoughts of parents and siblings about the family member with schizophrenia, hospitalization, therapies and treatments, keeping a life of one's own, dealing with professionals, looking ahead, and networking. Affiliates of the National Alliance for the Mentally Ill are listed.

Gadow, Kenneth D. **Children on Medication, Volume II: Epilepsy, Emotional Disturbance, and Adolescent Disorders.** San Diego: College-Hill Press, 1986. 282 pp. $19.95 (Paper).

    This work describes antiepileptic drug therapy for seizure disorders, childhood psychoses (such as infantile autism and schizophrenia), a variety of adolescent psychiatric disorders, and, additionally, enuresis, cerebral palsy, school phobia, and Tourette syndrome. Its intent is "to provide . . . pharmacological information that will help caregivers better understand medical decisions."

Hatfield, Agnes B.; Lefley, Harriet P., eds. **Families of the Mentally Ill: Coping and Adaptation.** New York: Guilford Press, 1987. 336 pp. $40.00; $19.95 (Paper).

    The focus of this significant research-oriented book is on how a family "experiences the tragedy of mental illness" in one of its members. The authors hope that professionals in the mental health field will respond with more empathy and awareness after reading specialists in the disciplines of psychology, education, nursing, psychiatry, and rehabilitation. A general theory of coping and adapting, the subjective experience of families and their perceptions of their needs, models of family practice appropriate to adaptation theory, and new issues for research are explored.

Johnson, Julie Tallard. **Hidden Victims: An Eight-Stage Healing Process for Families and Friends of the Mentally Ill.** New York: Doubleday, 1988. 191 pp. $16.95.

Johnson is a psychiatric social worker who founded the Sibling and Adult Children's Network mentioned in the "Where to Write for Information" section. She recognizes that people with serious mental illness need their families as advocates, and, more importantly, as close and connected relatives. This "workbook" suggests ways to care for each other without guilt or fear. Johnson explores the roles that people often take—caretaker or escape artist—and suggests a self-help program through which to develop a new way of life. Her stages are awareness, validation, acceptance, challenge, releasing guilt, forgiveness, self-esteem, and growth. Support groups and organizations are listed.

McElroy, Evelyn, ed. **Children and Adolescents with Mental Illness: A Parents' Guide.** Rockville, Md.: Woodbine House, 1988. 220 pp. $12.95 (Paper).

This compassionate guide by parents and professionals is well-designed to help families cope with "the difficult reality" of a child's mental illness. Readers will learn about the symptoms and treatment of common mental illnesses, what the beginning stages involve, how to select a psychiatric hospital, hospitalization and returning home, educational services and entitlements, how to prevent youth suicide, and long-term planning. Poignant and honest parent statements following each chapter give additional insight. Valuable appendices include information about medications, directories of state organizations and other resources, a glossary, and a reading list.

Park, Clara Claiborne; Shapiro, Leon N. **You Are Not Alone.** Boston: Little, Brown, 1976. 496 pp. $8.95 (Paper).

This older, far-reaching work, written for patients, families, doctors, and other professionals dealing with mental illness, contains a detailed chapter considering the special problems of children. Chapter subheadings and running summaries in the margin are especially helpful to the reader.

Rapoport, Judith. **The Boy Who Couldn't Stop Washing.** New York: E.P. Dutton, 1989. 260 pp. $18.95.

The author is a physician, child psychiatrist, and research scientist who, since 1962, has studied obsessive-compulsive disorder, "a strange and fascinating sickness of ritual and doubts run wild." She lets parents and children tell their stories of obsessions that dominate their lives; they include washing, hoarding, pulling out hair, hearing tunes, telling jokes, getting "stuck" in doorways, feeling responsible for things that have never happened. She has observed patterns in children as young as two years of age. The book is illuminating and unusual.

Torrey, E. Fuller. **Surviving Schizophrenia: A Family Manual.** Rev. ed. New York: Harper & Row, 1988. 460 pp. $22.95.

The first edition of **Surviving Schizophrenia** was considered a classic in its field. This updated and expanded version insists on the biological basis for this "cruel disease" and offers the most up-to-date information as of 1988 on its treatment and rehabilitation. From diagnosis to services, family needs to politics, history to causes, all the subjects covered in this significant work are compellingly readable. Research centers, readings, and a state-by-state information listing are included.

Tsuang, Ming T. **Schizophrenia: The Facts.** New York: Oxford University Press, 1982. 95 pp. $16.50.

    True to his intent, the author has designed a work without technical or "psychiatric jargon" that offers detailed and practical information about schizophrenia. It includes discussions of possible genetic and environmental factors, biological and psychosocial aspects, diagnosis, treatment, and ways families can be helpful. The introduction is a personal account by a young woman whose catatonic schizophrenia was diagnosed in high school and who is now recovered and counseling others.

Vine, Phyllis; Bells, G. Christian. **Families in Pain.** New York: Pantheon, 1982. 273 pp. $6.95 (Paper).

    The author has interviewed children, siblings, spouses, and parents of teenagers and adults who are mentally ill. In this informative handbook about chronic mental illness, the descriptions of treatments and programs may help families who are beginning to recognize early symptoms of serious problems.

Walsh, Maryellen. **Schizophrenia: Straight Talk for Families and Friends.** New York: William Morrow, 1985. 288 pp. $17.95. New York: Warner. $3.95 (Paper).

    The author is a parent who has written a survival handbook for other parents; she writes straightforwardly of what it is like to live with someone with chronic long-term schizophrenia, takes "a look at where and why parent hating started," and presents solid information about schizophrenia, its treatment, and its outcome. Quotes from families across the country are shared. Appendices list helpful resources. This is an important work for families, written with compassion, clarity, and humor.

Wasow, Mona. **Coping with Schizophrenia.** Palo Alto, Calif.: Science and Behavior Books, 1982. 160 pp. $9.95 (Paper).

    Beyond the pain of her own personal experience with her son, Wasow has summoned the courage to help other families survive the devastation of schizophrenia. Information, practical help, and realistic support are offered.

Your Child at Home

Herskowitz, Joel. **Is Your Child Depressed?** New York: Pharos Books, 1988. 224 pp. $14.95.

    The author, a pediatric neurologist, offers useful tools for recognizing whether a tired, irritable, or angry child or adolescent is actually depressed or suicidal. He sets forth how to get help, who the appropriate mental health professional should be, and what current forms of treatment exist. The book is readable and interesting, with case studies and helpful checklists to aid in the diagnosis of a depressive disorder.

Love, Harold D. **Behavioral Disorders in Children: A Book for Parents.** Springfield, Ill.: Charles C Thomas, 1987. 88 pp. $16.75.

> This slim, simply written book presents an overview of behavior problems, symptoms, and where to go for help. The discussion includes the commonly used tests for assessment and diagnosis, mild emotional disorders, disorders affecting physical functioning, severe emotional disorders, and classroom strategies. There is also a chapter on prevention.

Rutter, Michael. **Helping Troubled Children.** New York: Plenum, 1976. 376 pp. $29.50.

> Designed for the general reader, this book focuses on the psychiatric difficulties of the school-age child rather than on severe mental illness. The importance of the family relationship is emphasized. Chapters deal in a reassuring and common-sense manner with subjects of child development, the child in the family, community, school, and peer groups, learning difficulties, and methods of treatment and their effect.

Your Child at School

Apter, Steven J., ed. **Focus on Prevention: The Education of Children Labeled Emotionally Disturbed.** Syracuse, N.Y.: Syracuse University Press, 1978. 135 pp. $5.00 (Paper).

> The contributions of six participants in the 1976 Syracuse University Conference on Children Labeled Emotionally Disturbed address issues concerning the prevention of mental illness in children in school and other learning situations. The role of parents is defined and their participation is sought in working out solutions.

Kauffman, James M. **Characteristics of Children's Behavior Disorders.** 3d ed. Columbus, Ohio: Merrill, 1985. 432 pp. $32.95.

> Intended as a text for an introductory course in the special education of children who are emotionally disturbed, this is a good overview of the field of minor emotional and behavioral disturbances. It gives clear descriptions of behavior disorders, and, stressing a behavioral approach, assesses means of dealing with them.

Pappanikou, H.J.; Paul, James L., eds. **Mainstreaming Emotionally Disturbed Children.** Syracuse, N.Y.: Syracuse University Press, 1981. 139 pp. $9.95.

> Thoughtful arguments concerning the problems and benefits of mainstreaming a child with an emotional disability into the regular classroom are presented. The book discusses the perils of wholesale mainstreaming as well as the advantages of selective mainstreaming.

Rubin, Judith Aron. **Child Art Therapy: Understanding and Helping Children Grow through Art.** 2d ed. New York: Van Nostrand Reinhold, 1984. 304 pp. $22.95 (Paper).

> This survey of art therapy techniques used with children who are labeled emotionally disturbed and disabled includes sections on family, mother-child, and group therapy, and emphasizes the healing and self-knowledge gained through art under the guidance of a sensitive and well-trained therapist. Many case histories are included.

Swanson, H.; Reinert, Henry R. **Teaching Strategies for Children in Conflict: Curriculum Methods and Materials.** 2d ed. Columbus, Ohio: Merrill, 1984. 256 pp. $27.95.

This college text describes the major theoretical approaches to educating children with emotional disabilities. Useful appendices contain information concerning resources which may be of help to students and the teachers who work with them.

Your Child Grows Up

Sheehan, Susan. **Is There No Place on Earth for Me?** Boston: Houghton Mifflin, 1982. $14.95. New York: Vintage, 1983. $6.95 (Paper).

Journalist Susan Sheehan's book won the Pulitzer Price for Nonfiction in 1982. It is the detailed history of "Sylvia Frumkin," who was diagnosed as schizophrenic in her late teens and spent her next seventeen years in and out of psychiatric hospitals. Sheehan describes the mediocrity of hospitalization and the lack of appropriate care in the community. This extraordinary chronicle is both a sympathetic and disturbing look at one individual and an indictment of our society's mental health system, no less true today than when it was written.

Torrey, E. Fuller. **Nowhere to Go: The Tragic Odyssey of the Homeless Mentally Ill.** New York: Harper & Row, 1988. 256 pp. $18.95.

Mental institutions four decades ago were snake pits of horror, but the promise that deinstitutionalization and community mental health centers would solve the lot of people with mental illness did not materialize. **Nowhere to Go** presents the author's view of the background and history as to why this social policy failed. Many of America's homeless today are seriously mentally ill. A final chapter outlines Torrey's recommendations for solving this critical problem. This notable work is direct and fascinating reading.

Personal Accounts—From Those Who Have Lived It

Axline, Virginia M. **Dibs: In Search of Self.** Boston: Houghton-Mifflin, 1965. 221 pp. $8.95. New York: Ballantine. $3.50 (Paper).

Still considered important reading, this old but very helpful account by a psychologist tells of the effect of play therapy on the personality of a child with mental illness.

Hayden, Torey L. **Just Another Kid.** New York: G.P. Putnam's Sons, 1988. 318 pp. $17.95.

In a class for children with emotional disabilities, a gifted teacher works her magic. Her students carry labels of autism (along with diabetes), childhood schizophrenia, elective mutism. She guides the psychologically scarred volunteer aide (who is also the mother of a student) to an understanding of herself, as well. Hayden is as remarkable a writer as she must be a teacher.

Kytle, Elizabeth. **The Voices of Robby Wilde.** Cabin John, Md.: Seven Locks Press, 1987. 329 pp. $17.95.

First person accounts of events spanning fifty years are presented from the points of view of "Robby," a person with the diagnosis of paranoid schizophrenia, and others who knew him. This unusual biography offers insight into a form of mental illness from one who heard his first "voice" in elementary school.

North, Carol. **Welcome, Silence: My Triumph over Schizophrenia.** New York: Simon & Schuster, 1987. 316 pp. $17.95. New York: Avon Books, 1989. $4.50 (Paper).

Carol North writes of the overwhelming terrors she experienced as a young child: "I was six years old and afraid of everything, day and night." As she grew, she learned to conceal her fear. The torment continued through college and medical school episodes with hospitalization, medication, suicide attempts. Amazingly, North was cured through kidney dialysis. She is now a psychiatrist working with schizophrenic patients.

Rothenberg, Mira. **Children with Emerald Eyes.** New York: E.P. Dutton, 1977. 291 pp. $8.95 (Paper).

This is a tender and beautiful account of case histories involving the treatment of several children with severe mental illness. The author was the co-founder and clinical director of the Blueberry Treatment Centers.

Sechehaye, Marguerite. **Autobiography of a Schizophrenic Girl.** New York: New American Library, Signet, 1970. 192 pp. $3.95 (Paper).

Written in 1951 before drug therapy, this is the vivid, autobiographical account of a French girl who first experienced the feelings of unreality signifying her schizophrenic condition at the age of five. She describes her psychoanalysis, her hospitalization, her perceptions, and her return to reality.

Vonnegut, Mark. **The Eden Express.** New York: Dell, 1988. 214 pp. $4.95 (Paper).

The author details his life after graduating from college. He drifted into a commune, experimented with drugs, had an excruciating bout with schizophrenia, and finally recovered. A postscript chapter assesses the illness and suggests ways of dealing with it. The book was originally published in 1975.

Wilson, Louise. **This Stranger, My Son.** New York: New American Library, Signet, 1968. 223 pp. $3.95 (Paper).

Written in 1968, this poignant story by a mother attempting to understand a child who is schizophrenic remains a painfully realistic look at the impact mental illness and misguided doctors have on an entire family.

Winnicott, D.W. **The Piggle: An Account of the Psychoanalytic Treatment of a Little Girl.** Madison, Conn.: International Universities Press, 1977. 201 pp. $26.00.

The successful treatment of a two-year-old girl with mental illness is described by her English psychiatrist.

Where to Write for Information

American Academy of Child and Adolescent Psychiatry. 3615 Wisconsin Avenue, N.W., Washington, DC 20016.

Two-page **Facts for Families** cover a variety of topics, from **The Depressed Child** to **Psychiatric Medication for Children.** Another publication is a **Glossary of Mental Illnesses Affecting Teenagers.** Send for their publications list.

Channing L. Bete Company. 200 State Road, South Deerfield, MA 01373–0200.

The booklets **What Everyone Should Know about Mental Illness in the Family** and **What Everyone Should Know about Your Child's Emotional Health** are 79 cents each; a minimum of 25 copies per title must be ordered. They cover basic information in an attractive, easy-to-read format.

California Alliance for the Mentally Ill. 2306 J Street, Suite 203, Sacramento, CA 95816.

Families Know about Coping with Serious Mental Illness, a "sharing of information and ideas on how to assist a mentally ill relative and survive the experience yourself," is a sensitive, sensible booklet with good advice and pleasant illustrations. It sells for $2.00.

Centering Corporation. P.O. Box 3367, Omaha, NE 68103–0367.

Hurting Yourself is a booklet for young people who have attempted suicide or intentionally injured themselves. It costs $2.45.

Children and Adolescent Service System Programs. CASSP Technical Assistance Center, Georgetown University Child Development Center, 3800 Reservoir Road, N.W., CG-52 BLES, Washington, DC 20007.

Designed to improve service delivery for children and adolescents with severe emotional disturbance, CASSP circulates publications of interest. One title is **Profiles of Residential and Day Treatment Programs for Seriously Emotionally Disturbed Youth.**

Consumer Information Center. P.O. Box 100, Pueblo, CO 81002.

Schizophrenia: Questions and Answers, a twenty-five page booklet from the National Institute on Mental Health, is free. Specify 556W.

The Council for Exceptional Children (CEC). 1920 Association Drive, Reston, VA 22091–1589.

CEC has a Council for Children with Behavioral Disorders. Its quarterly publication is called **Behavioral Disorders.** Its yearly monograph series is titled **Severe Behavioral Disorders of Children and Youth.** Write for ordering information.

ERIC Clearinghouse on Handicapped and Gifted Children. Council for Exceptional Children, 1920 Association Drive, Reston, VA 22091–1589.

Send for their complete Product Flyer. A two-page digest, **Emotional Disturbances,** costs one dollar.

Mental Health Law Project (MHLP). 2021 L Street, N.W., Suite 800, Washington, DC 20036–4909.

MHLP is a non-profit, public interest law firm devoted to protecting and expanding the rights of children and adults with mental illness and developmental disabilities. Their newsletter, the Mental Health Law Project **Action Line,** is sent five times a year to people who contribute at least $35.00 annually.

Minerva Press. 6653 Andersonville Road, Waterford, MI 48095.

A single copy of **Helping Families Cope with Mental Illness: A Guide to Psychiatric Hospitalization** is 99 cents.

National Alliance for the Mentally Ill (NAMI). 2101 Wilson Boulevard, Suite 302, Arlington, VA 22201.

NAMI was formed in 1979 as the first nationwide network of family advocates united on behalf of people with severe and chronic mental illness. Request information on local chapters, the five-time-a-year **NAMI News,** their brochures on schizophrenia, major affective disorders, and mental illness, and their annotated reading list of books and pamphlets, some available directly from them. Two excellent publications are **Coping with Mental Illness in the Family: A Family Guide** ($3.50) and **The Experiences of Patients and Families: First Person Accounts** ($4.50).

National Institute of Mental Health (NIMH). 5600 Fishers Lane, Room 15C-05, Rockville, MD 20857.

NIMH provides information, answers inquiries, and conducts and supports research. Send for their publication list; it includes literature on schizophrenia and depression.

National Mental Health Association. 1021 Prince Street, Alexandria, VA 22314.

The Association's publication list includes the **Directory of Children and Adolescent Programs** ($5.00). The booklet, **Children in Distress,** may be useful. The pamphlet, **Stigma: A Lack of Awareness and Understanding,** offers some facts and explodes some myths about mental illness.

PACER (Parent Advocacy Coalition for Educational Rights) Center. 4876 Chicago Avenue South, Minneapolis, MN 55417–1055.

A Guidebook for Parents of Children with Emotional Disturbances ($6.00) offers much good general information; the second half of the booklet describes Minnesota resources.

Public Affairs Committee. 381 Park Avenue South, New York, NY 10016.

Help for Your Troubled Child costs one dollar. So does **Schizophrenia: Advances in Diagnosis and Treatment.**

Portland State University Research and Training Center. Regional Research Institute for Human Services, P.O. Box 751, Portland, OR 97207–0751.

This "center for research and training to improve services for seriously emotionally handicapped children and their families" publishes several annotated bibliographies and monographs of interest to parents. **Taking Charge: A Handbook for Parents Whose Children**

Have Emotional Handicaps is an excellent self-study introductory workbook. **Focal Point,** the center's quarterly newsletter, is available without charge.

Sibling and Adult Children's Network. SAC Network/NAMI, 2101 Wilson Boulevard, Suite 302, Arlington, VA 22201.

This organization for brothers, sisters, and adult sons and daughters of persons with mental illness publishes a newsletter, **The Bond** ($10.00 a year), and circulates resource materials. Request information.

U.S. Department of Health and Human Services, Public Health Service, Alcohol, Drug Abuse, and Mental Health Administration, Information Resources Inquiries Branch. 5600 Fishers Lane, Rockville, MD 20857.

Available publications include the **Plain Talk About** series; one title is **Plain Talk About—Dealing with the Angry Child.**

U.S. Government Printing Office. Superintendent of Documents, Washington, DC 20402.

A Head Start series, called **Mainstreaming Preschoolers,** is being revised. One excellent book in the series was titled **Children with Emotional Disturbance: A Guide for Teachers, Parents, and Others Who Work with Emotionally Disturbed Preschoolers.** Inquire about its current status.

Mental Retardation

Basic Reading

Blatt, Burton. **The Conquest of Mental Retardation.** Austin: Pro-Ed, 1987. 391 pp. $28.00.

    This is called a textbook but it goes well beyond the traditional definition. It is the last work of Burton Blatt, a respected leader and thinker; here he addresses mental retardation in a way that illustrates its relevance to crucial social issues and the nature of our society. It is unique and fascinating, scholarly and personal, directed by Blatt's belief and passion. "All people are valuable, . . . all people are educable. . . . It isn't that secluding retarded people is wrong, but that secluding people is wrong." To "conquer" mental retardation, each of us must look to ourself.

Cunningham, Cliff. **Down Syndrome: An Introduction.** Rev. ed. Cambridge, Mass.: Brookline Books, 1988. 248 pp. $15.95 (Paper).

    From his supportive letter to parents recognizing the problems inherent in information overload to his concluding observation that "members of our society who are severely disabled . . . cause us to question our values, they test our compassion, they remind us that 'ability' is not all," the author illustrates his warmth, his sensitivity, his knowledge, and his understanding. Cliff Cunningham has long been involved in research about how to help the development of young children with Down syndrome in the United Kingdom. The topics he addresses include feelings and reactions, effects on the family, causes and characteristics, personality and temperament, and mental, motor, and social development. This new edition includes information relating to older children and adults.

Dybwad, Rosemary. **Perspectives on a Parent Movement: The Revolt of Parents of Children with Intellectual Deficit.** Cambridge, Mass.: Brookline Books, 1990. Write or call for ordering information.

    Gunnar Dybwad, internationally known for his contributions to the field of developmental disabilities, has collected essays written by his wife, Rosemary, over a lifetime of advocacy and reflection. Her subjects include the role of parent organizations, prevention and intervention, education, adult living, employment, human rights, public acceptance, and religious concerns.

Edgerton, Robert B. **Mental Retardation.** Cambridge, Mass.: Harvard University Press, 1979. 125 pp. $12.00; $3.95 (Paper).

    Written in an easy style, free of jargon, this book presents a brief but solid discussion of mental retardation, its genetic, environmental, and social causes, prevention, how families cope, what schools are doing, and what society's responsibilities are.

Feuerstein, Reuven; Rand, Yaacov; Rynders, John E. **Don't Accept Me as I Am: Helping "Retarded" People to Excel.** New York: Plenum, 1988. 322 pp. $24.95.

    The psychologist-authors argue that educators, be they parents or teachers, can be "active modifiers" of the intelligence and competence of persons with mental retardation. Starting from the belief that the individual *can* go beyond his present observable level of functioning, they set forth the steps of "instrumental enrichment/mediated learning." Significant progress can be made with the necessary time, effort, skill, patience, commitment, and love. A chapter on reconstructive plastic surgery for people with Down syndrome is included.

Gadow, Kenneth D. **Children on Medication, Volume I: Hyperactivity, Learning Disabilities, and Mental Retardation.** San Diego: College-Hill Press, 1986. 251 pp. $16.50 (Paper).

 The goal of this work is "to provide . . . pharmacological information that will help caregivers better understand medical decisions." Gadow focuses on psychotropic drugs prescribed for hyperactivity and aggressiveness. The detailed text outlines what particular medications are intended to do and what their side effects may be.

Pueschel, Siegfried M.; Tingey, Carol; Rynders, John E.; Crocker, Allen C.; and Crutcher, Diane M. **New Perspectives on Down Syndrome.** Baltimore: Paul H. Brookes, 1987. 393 pp. $32.95.

 Leading professionals from the fields of biomedicine, education, psychosocial studies, and community living gathered in Boston in April 1985, to participate in the Down Syndrome State-of-the-Art Conference. Each book chapter is an update of one of the major conference presentations; it is followed by comments from peer reviewers. Although the papers are research-oriented, the serious parent-reader will find much of interest.

Scheerenberger, R.C. **A History of Mental Retardation.** Baltimore: Paul H. Brookes, 1983. 311 pp. $27.95.

 As its title states, this is an historical text. Part I discusses what is known of the "understanding, social care, and treatment" of people with mental retardation in Western Europe from earliest times until the twentieth century. Part II covers the history of mental retardation in the United States from the colonial years through 1959. A final, very brief chapter highlights happenings from 1960 through 1979. Supplemental readings are suggested.

Scheerenberger, R.C. **A History of Mental Retardation: A Quarter Century of Promise.** Baltimore: Paul H. Brookes, 1987. 318 pp. $26.95.

 In an ambitious sequel to the previous entry, Scheerenberger covers the history of mental retardation from 1960 through 1984, almost exclusively in the United States. Its purpose is "to set forth . . . some of the major decisions, events, and personages of the times." While he concludes that often "promise far outweighed progress," the twenty-five years of which he writes were ones of remarkable forward change.

Seltzer, Marsha Mailick; Krauss, Marty Wyngaarden. **Aging and Mental Retardation: Extending the Continuum.** Washington, D.C.: American Association on Mental Retardation, 1987. 187 pp. $20.00 (Paper).

 This monograph, reflecting the results of a national survey, examines programs and services, both in the community and institutionally based, that are set up for people with mental retardation over the age of 55. The literature on aging and mental retardation is reviewed and issues are discussed. The authors suggest implications for research, services, and policy development.

Stray-Gundersen, Karen, ed. **Babies with Down Syndrome: A New Parents' Guide.** Rockville, Md.: Woodbine House, 1986. 244 pp. $12.95 (Paper).

A complete introduction to Down syndrome for new families, this work covers it all: what Down syndrome is, adjusting, medical concerns, daily care, family life, development, early intervention, legal rights, and advocacy. Parent statements at the end of each chapter share real experiences, thoughts, and advice. An annotated reading list, an extensive national and state-by-state Resource Guide, charming photographs, and a glossary help to make this truly "the first book that parents and family should read" and one to which they will refer again and again.

Tingey, Carol, ed. **Down Syndrome: A Resource Handbook.** San Diego: College-Hill, 1988. 209 pp. $19.50 (Paper).

A compilation of articles by professionals and family members covers basic medical issues, family concerns, early development, and education and community activities. Tingey is a mother as well as a professional in the field of mental retardation; she has collected here what she refers to as "the best answers from the most experienced people."

Treffert, Darold A. **Extraordinary People: Understanding "Idiot Savants."** New York: Harper & Row, 1989. 291 pp. $17.95.

For more than twenty-five years, psychiatrist Treffert has been intrigued by Savant syndrome—"an exceedingly rare condition in which persons with serious mental handicaps . . . or major mental illness . . . have spectacular islands of ability or brilliance which stand in stark, markedly incongruous contrast to the handicaps." His fascinating book tells some remarkable stories of savants of yesterday and today, their caring families, teachers, and caregivers, and the new theories and research advanced to explain an intriguing paradox. Dr. Treffert gently guides the reader to a greater "appreciation, admiration and awe for these special people and their equally special families."

Your Child at Home

Cunningham, Cliff; Sloper, Patricia. **Helping Your Exceptional Baby: A Practical and Honest Approach to Raising a Mentally Handicapped Child.** New York: Pantheon, 1980. 336 pp. $12.95; $6.95 (Paper).

This practical and helpful book for parents of babies with developmental disabilities (especially those with Down syndrome) contains good advice on coming to terms with the disability, guidelines for measuring development, and suggestions for learning activities according to developmental level.

Dmitriev, Valentine. **Time to Begin.** Milton, Wash.: Caring, 1982. 248 pp. $30.00; $20.00 (Paper).

Drawn from a model program at the University of Washington which was developed and coordinated by the author, this easy-to-follow text presents early intervention exercises and activities to use with infants and young children with Down syndrome. The importance of the human element—warmth, gentleness, and "a deep and tender caring for each child's uniqueness and human potential"—is stressed as vital. Helpful basic information and many charming pictures are included.

Frank, Roger A.; Edwards, Jean P. **Building Self-Esteem in Persons with Developmental Disabilities.**
Austin: Pro-Ed, 1988. 106 pp. $15.00 (Paper).

"Healthy self-esteem is an essential human need and crucial to our psychological well-being."
A discussion of the importance of self-esteem is followed by common-sense strategies for promoting self-confidence and enhancing self-respect in people with developmental disabilities. This
small handbook will encourage better parenting techniques.

Gordon, Michael Lewis; Ryan, David H.; Shilo, Tamar. **Helping the Trainable Mentally Retarded
Child Develop Speech and Language: A Guidebook for Parents, Teachers, and Paraprofessionals.**
Springfield, Ill.: Charles C Thomas, 1979. 68 pp. $14.95.

Prespeech exercises and a simple program for developing listening skills and language are outlined for the use of parents and professionals.

Hanson, Marci J. **Teaching the Infant with Down Syndrome: A Guide for Parents and Professionals.** 2d ed. Austin: Pro-Ed, 1987. 268 pp. $21.00.

This expanded and updated second edition of a popular guide for parents of babies with Down
syndrome presents encouraging information on the progress of infants taught by their parents.
The author describes how to observe and analyze behavior and how to break it down into steps;
she then presents suitable activities for each developmental milestone. Directions are clear and
easy to follow. With or without professional assistance, this guide offers a program which parents
can do at home in the course of caring for or playing with their child. Photographs, references,
suggested readings, a Baby Record for monitoring progress, and other useful information add to
the book's value.

Johnson, Vicki M.; Werner, Roberta A. **A Step-by-Step Learning Guide for Retarded Infants and
Children.** Syracuse, N.Y.: Syracuse University Press, 1975. 195 pp. $12.95 (Paper).

A sequenced checklist for determining a child's current skills and a curriculum of activities to
permit and reinforce learning each step of the way are provided in this very helpful manual. The
format is simple and clear and the approach through observable behaviors makes this a good
resource for parents.

Murphy, Judy. **Home Care of Handicapped Children: A Guide. Mental Retardation.** Lyons, Colo.:
Carol L. Lutey Publishing, 1982. 87 pp. $6.50 (Paper).

One of a series intended for potential caregivers of a child between the ages of three and
twelve, this practical and helpful guide has good information to share with families, as well. Part I
offers general guidelines concerning child health, self-help activities, social behavior, communication, play, and safety and protective measures. The second part, specific to mental retardation, includes causes, understanding the child, and recreation.

Ohio State University Research Foundation Staff. **Toilet Training: Help for the Delayed Learner.**
New York: McGraw-Hill, 1978. 106 pp. $17.60 (Paper).

Considered one of the best manuals of its kind, this book presents illustrated instructions on
how to go about toilet training children with developmental delay at various ages and stages.
Steps for teaching handwashing are also included. Sample schedules are provided.

Pader, Olga F. **A Guide and Handbook for Parents of Mentally Retarded Children.** Springfield, Ill.: Charles C Thomas, 1981. 254 pp. $27.00.

> Information about the development and capabilities of children who are mentally retarded, techniques and programs for teaching appropriate behaviors, and a discussion of family relationships and parenting skills are offered. The book grew out of a course outline for parent groups.

Your Child at School

Gorski, Berni. **Beyond Limitations: The Creative Art of the Mentally Retarded.** Springfield, Ill.: Charles C Thomas, 1979. 135 pp. $19.75.

> This is a collection of pictures and art objects made by people with mental retardation in schools, institutions, and community programs, with a brief section of commentary by teachers who have worked successfully with artists who have developmental disabilities.

Hirst, Cynthia; Michaelis, Elaine. **Retarded Kids Need to Play.** Champaign, Ill.: Leisure Press, 1983. 288 pp. $12.95 (Paper).

> This book presents a program of physical education activities and sport skills ranging from simple to advanced. The purpose of each exercise and directions for doing it are outlined. Suggestions and photographs help to clarify the curriculum.

Johnson, Vicki M.; Werner, Roberta A. **A Step-by-Step Learning Guide for Older Retarded Children.** Syracuse, N.Y.: Syracuse University Press, 1977. 214 pp. $10.95 (Paper).

> How to break large tasks down into smaller ones so that step-by-step learning becomes possible is clearly demonstrated in this very useful book. It presents two hundred and sixty-five activities, organized into various areas—self-care, fine and gross motor development, language, and perception. Other chapters address behavior management and give general advice to parents.

Sussman, Ellen J. **Art Projects for the Mentally Retarded Child.** Springfield, Ill.: Charles C Thomas, 1976. 98 pp. $16.25.

> The author describes and illustrates thirty-nine classroom art projects, some of which can be done in the home. The text gives step-by-step instructions, lists of materials, and estimates of time needed to complete the projects.

Wilcox, Barbara; Bellamy, G. Thomas. **The Activities Catalog: An Alternative Curriculum for Youth and Adults with Severe Disabilities.** 84 pp. **A Comprehensive Guide to the Activities Catalog.** 195 pp. Baltimore: Paul H. Brookes, 1987. $29.95.

> The unusual **Catalog** displays hundreds of ways for promoting leisure time activities, personal management, and work skills for persons with moderate and severe disabilities. Parents are advised to decide which of the many activities would increase the quality of life for their son or daughter, fill out a (provided) order form, and turn it in at the next IEP or IHP (individualized habilitation plan) meeting. The **Guide** describes the application of the **Catalog** in high schools, supported employment, and residential services. These companion volumes offer an innovative and impressive approach to designing a meaningful curriculum that will ensure appropriate adult interests and abilities.

Your Child Grows Up

Bellamy, G. Thomas; Rhodes, Larry E.; Mank, David M.; Albin, Joyce M. **Supported Employment: A Community Implementation Guide.** Baltimore: Paul H. Brookes, 1988. 287 pp. $19.95 (Paper).

> This book offers "practical advice on how to develop, organize, operate, manage, and evaluate supported employment efforts." It will be of value to all who should operate as a team in making supported employment work: the parents and advocates who seek to make the lives of people with severe disabilities meaningful, service providers, state and local agencies, and employers.

Evans, Daryl Paul. **The Lives of Mentally Retarded People.** Boulder, Colo.: Westview Press, 1983. 306 pp. $42.00; $15.95 (Paper).

> This interesting, helpful, and sympathetic account of how integration into community life is experienced by those so long excluded is written from the perspective of a sociologist who has spent significant time in classrooms, workplaces, residential homes, and institutions. For his discussion of education, social psychology of mental retardation, the family, rights, the occupational world, residential lives, the judicial and penal systems, sexuality, marriage, geriatrics, and prevention, he uses literature, his own observations, and learnings from the people he has interviewed.

Gold, Marc W. **Try Another Way (Training Manual).** Champaign, Ill.: Research Press, 1980. 112 pp. $10.95 (Paper).

Gold Marc W. **Marc Gold: "Did I Say That?"** Champaign, Ill.: Research Press, 1980. 349 pp. $19.95 (Paper).

> Marc Gold was one of the best known and most imaginative developers of materials for teaching daily living skills and vocational tasks to people with severe and profound retardation. **Try Another Way** materials are all based on Gold's conviction that the limit of a person's functioning is determined by the availability of training technology and by the amount of resources society is willing to allocate, not by significant limitations in one's biological potential. **Marc Gold: "Did I Say That?"** is a collection of twenty-seven articles and commentaries about the **Try Another Way** system.

Gollay, Elinor; Freedman, Ruth; Wyngaarden, Marty; Kurtz, Norman R. **Coming Back: The Community Experiences of Deinstitutionalized Mentally Retarded People.** Cambridge, Mass.: Abt Books, 1978. 227 pp. $30.00.

> **Coming Back** presents the results of a study of over four hundred people with mental retardation who, in the early years of the deinstitutionalization movement, left institutions to live in various settings in the community. Through their own words and through the author's analysis of data, the reader learns about where they live, what they do, and how they feel about their new lives. The results of the study should reassure those who may still be apprehensive about the risks of community living. The study also illuminates the main reasons for failures, as true today as they were a dozen years ago; insufficient support services and lack of job opportunities are high on the list.

Halpern, Andrew S.; Close, Daniel W.; Nelson, Debra J. **On My Own: The Impact of Semi-Independent Living Programs for Adults with Mental Retardation.** Baltimore: Paul H. Brookes, 1986. 189 pp. $15.95 (Paper).

    On My Own is a very readable, in-depth study of the lives of three hundred adults with mild mental retardation who live in apartments and receive drop-in staff services. Detailed interviews were held with the residents, staff, and administrators around the issues of homes and neighborhoods, employment and finances, social relationships and leisure activities, and programs and services. While basically encouraging, the study does outline the problems of semi-independent living programs. It also suggests a model for better programs and services.

Hauerwas, Stanley. **Responsibility for Devalued Persons: Ethical Interactions between Society, the Family, and the Retarded.** Springfield, Ill.: Charles C Thomas, 1982. 112 pp. $16.25.

    This transcript of a symposium dealing with moral and ethical issues concerning responsibility for persons with mental retardation makes fascinating reading. Questions raised by professionals and parents include who should speak for persons who are retarded, the role of the family, the status of citizens who are retarded, and society's responsibility.

Huff, Gary; Tyler, Virginia. **Free Time Fun: Low-Cost, Leisure Time Activities for Special Populations.** For People First International; distributed by Pro-Ed, n.d. 59 pp. $12.00 (Spiral).

    Written for adults with developmental disabilities or their "support workers," the manual talks about leisure and recreational activities available in the community or at home, alone or with others, that don't cost too much money. The suggestions are practical and possible.

McLoughlin, Caven S.; Garner, J. Bradley; Callahan, Michael. **Getting Employed, Staying Employed: Job Development and Training for Persons with Severe Handicaps.** Baltimore: Paul H. Brookes, 1987. 239 pp. $22.95 (Paper).

    This step-by-step guide to planning, negotiating, placement, and training of persons with severe disabilities in integrated settings, written for job developers, should prove valuable to families and advocates who want to understand the nuts and bolts of creating employment options. Underlying the concepts in this book is Marc Gold's pioneering "Try Another Way" approach. Eighteen appendices offer sample forms, letters, and guidelines.

Pueschel, Siegfried M., ed. **The Young Person with Down Syndrome: Transition from Adolescence to Adulthood.** Baltimore: Paul H. Brookes, 1988. 237 pp. $21.00 (Paper).

    A number of professionals, advocates, and family members discuss innovative programs, practical strategies, and underlying philosophies relating to issues of transition for young adults with Down syndrome. Chapters cover parenting, biology, psychology, communication, social integration, community participation, leisure, vocational training programs, continuing education, school to work issues, independent living, self-esteem, sexuality, policy issues, human rights, and advocacy.

Vanier, Jean, et al. **The Challenge of L'Arche**. New York: Harper & Row, 1982. 286 pp. $9.95 (Paper).

>Jean Vanier, one of the founders of the first l'Arche home, and eighteen other authors who live or have lived in l'Arche communities sharing life with people with disabilities, speak of thoughts and experiences with gratitude and humility, and sometimes with gentle humor.

Wehman, Paul; Moon, M. Sherril; Everson, Jane M.; Wood, Wendy; Barcus, J. Michael. **Transition from School to Work: New Challenges for Youth with Severe Disabilities.** Baltimore: Paul H. Brookes, 1988. 315 pp. $23.95 (Paper).

>Young adults with severe disabilities who are leaving school are all too often graduating only to waiting lists for adult services. Although written for educators, rehabilitators, and community service personnel, this significant work from leaders in the field of transitional services should aid parents in understanding what it takes to make an effective transition program and how to team with school and adult service providers to make the necessary coordination between service systems possible. Helpful appendices include an annotated bibliography on supported employment and transition.

Williams, Paul; Shoultz, Bonnie. **We Can Speak for Ourselves: Self-Advocacy by Mentally Handicapped People.** London: Souvenir Press; distributed in the U.S. by Brookline Books, 1982. 245 pp. $17.95 (Paper).

>Expectations for people with mental retardation have for too long ignored possibilities; the self-advocacy movement is proving that people with mental retardation *can* speak for themselves. Readers will learn about People First of Oregon, Project 2 of Nebraska, and their English counterparts. Chapters describe principles of self-advocacy and the group process from its inception through its development; nonlabeled people are only minimally involved as advisers. Particularly impressive are the words of the self-advocates themselves, as they describe their past history, claim their rights, and work to help free their peers from institutions. Parents will find much food for thought in these provocative pages.

Personal Accounts—From Those Who Have Lived It

Bakely, Donald C. **Bethy and the Mouse: God's Gifts in Special Packages.** Newton, Kans.: Faith and Life Press, 1985. 164 pp. $10.95 (Paper).

>In poems, in pictures, and in preschool evaluation reports, **Bethy and the Mouse** chronicles the feelings of a father as he writes of two of his children. The "Mouse" who had microcephaly, died in his fifth year. Bethy, who has Down syndrome, is, at the close of the book, about to enter a typical kindergarten class. "God, the ultimate artist, has a better sense of beauty than we have." "Together, child, we have helped to make each other whole." The author writes with humor, with tenderness; he offers much for reflection.

Bogdan, Robert; Taylor, Steven J. **Inside Out: The Social Meaning of Mental Retardation**. Toronto, Ontario: University of Toronto Press, 1982. 231 pp. $15.95.

>The autobiographical accounts of two people who carry the label "mentally retarded" and spent years in institutions before becoming independent, contributing members of society should help readers to understand what life has been like for them and how they view the world and

themselves. Their perceptive insights, expressed in their own words, challenge societal preconceptions of mental retardation; their interviewers draw important conclusions for new societal directions.

Bolnick, Jamie Pastor. **Winnie: "My Life in the Institution."** New York: St. Martin's, 1985. 248 pp. $14.95.

Winnie lived in state institutions for most of her life. In reaction to being called "mentally retarded" by a relative, she wrote a twenty-page "book" to prove she "got something upstairs, instead of nothing." Based on that work and on hundreds of hours of interviews with the author, **Winnie** tells of the sad times and the good times, the frustrations and the triumphs, with humor and poignancy. Her voice is one that should be heard.

Bondo, Ulla. **Ida: Life with My Handicapped Child.** Winchester, Mass.: Faber and Faber, 1980. 128 pp. $9.95 (Paper).

A Danish mother details her daughter's progress in diary format from her birth in 1966 through the next twelve years. Ida has Down syndrome. Helpful developmental charts are included.

Cook, Ellen, ed. **Sharing the Journey: Active Reflections on the Church's Presence with Mentally Retarded Persons.** Dubuque, Iowa: William C. Brown, 1986. 132 pp. $6.95 (Paper).

An interesting set of articles, written by members of the National Apostolate with Mentally Retarded Persons, offers reflections on the personal experiences of the authors in relating to people with mental retardation. Each has learned that people with mental retardation can bring gifts to families, as well as difficulties. Faith plays a large role in the authors' lives but many topics are discussed, such as managing the medical profession, financial planning, educational and residential alternatives, sexuality, and parent advocacy.

Dickerson, Martha Ufford. **Our Four Boys: Foster Parenting Retarded Teenagers.** Syracuse, N.Y.: Syracuse University Press, 1978. 222 pp. $9.95 (Paper).

Martha Dickerson, a professional in the field of mental retardation, tells how she and her husband became the foster parents of four boys with mental retardation after raising their own two children. She openly describes feelings of resentment and futility as well as the more frequent times of joy and fulfillment. The preface is a call to everyone working with young people with mental retardation to aim toward providing the same commitment and quality of care in residential services so evident in the Dickersons' foster-parenting.

Dougan, Terrell; Isbell, Lyn; Vyas, Patricia, comps. **We Have Been There**. Nashville: Abingdon, 1983. 206 pp. $10.95 (Paper).

Written with honesty and humor, **We Have Been There** is a compilation of personal vignettes offering insights on a variety of subjects: how to survive the initial diagnosis, raising a child who is mentally retarded, the laws affecting education, concerns of brothers and sisters, joining organizations, the service system, anger. In the final section, people with mental retardation speak for themselves.

Edwards, Jean; Dawson, David. **My Friend David: A Source Book about Down Syndrome and a Personal Story about Friendship.** Austin: Pro-Ed, 1983. 125 pp. $12.00.

David Dawson writes his own forty-six-year story, using taped interviews with his mother to help him. Jean Edwards writes about her "ever understanding, ever accepting, touching, wise friend." As a "salute" to their friendship, the third part of this very special book describes Down syndrome and offers emotional support, strategies for sponsoring appropriate behavior, and information about education, residential and vocational options, and resources. The book is filled with wonderful photographs.

Gauchat, Dorothy; Lyons, Arthur. **All God's Children.** New York: Ballantine, 1985. 224 pp. $2.50 (Paper).

This is the story of a remarkable couple who, many years ago, started out taking one foster child with a disability into their home, then another, and ended up building a house for thirty-five children with disabilities.

Hebden, Joan. **A Very Special Child.** New York: Demos, 1985. 159 pp. $10.95 (Paper).

For over a year after Cathy Hebden was born in England in 1961, her family did not know that she had Down syndrome. Undaunted by the cynicism, pessimism, and fears of others, a determined mother (who remembered her early experiences with polio) designed training programs for her child. Reinforced in school, Cathy learned to read, sew, cook, iron, shop, and travel independently. At the age of twenty-three, she received the Duke of Edinburgh Gold Award, having completed numerous requirements; she is the first person with Down syndrome to be so honored. This is important reading for parents of young children.

Jablow, Martha Moraghan. **Cara: Growing with a Retarded Child.** Philadelphia: Temple University Press, 1982. 205 pp. $24.95; $12.95 (Paper).

Cara, born with Down syndrome, was enrolled at one month of age in an intensive early intervention program. Before she was five, she was reading. Much useful information accompanies her story, told by her journalist-mother, which will hearten parents and enlighten professionals.

Kanat, Jolie. **Bittersweet Baby.** Irving, Calif.: CompCare Publishers, 1987. 156 pp. $8.95 (Paper).

A "book about discovery" by the mother of a daughter with Down syndrome, **Bittersweet Baby** shares journal entries recorded during her child's first year of life. In their determination and love, the family explored all possible avenues—infant stimulation, cross-patterning, vitamin therapy, cell therapy, a university research project, sign and speech classes. As the title suggests, the record is one of pain and delight, sorrow and recovery, sadness and fun.

Kaufman, Sandra Z. **Retarded Isn't Stupid, Mom!** Baltimore: Paul H. Brookes, 1988. 230 pp. $15.00.

The author has used her interest and training in anthropology and ethnography to write about her daughter's world. Nicole is mildly mentally retarded. Kaufman gives a fascinating account of Nicole as she grows to adulthood and struggles to live independently. Nicole's family stays involved—they "underwrite her independence"—but allows risk-taking. Kaufman paints a very real picture, complete with problems and frustrations and economic difficulties of people integrated into the community and yet often penalized by society for their normalization. The account is a provocative one.

MacDonald, C. Scott; Oden, Chester W., Jr. **Moose.** Cambridge, Mass.: Brookline Books, 1978. 200 pp. $10.95 (Paper).

   Moose is the focus of a spirited account of life with a child with Down syndrome in the midst of a large, active, devoted family. Parents, brothers, and sisters see to it that Moose assumes every bit of possible independence.

Mantle, Margaret. **Some Just Clap Their Hands: Raising a Handicapped Child.** New York: Adama Books, 1985. 263 pp. $16.95.

   In exploring the realities and the feelings involved in raising a child with mental retardation, the author uses her own story and quotations from a number of others. She refers to herself as "an ordinary person doing her best to cope with an extraordinary situation" as she describes the times of "finding out," "holding on," and "letting go."

Moise, Lotte E. **As Up We Grew with Barbara.** Minneapolis: Dillon, 1980. 232 pp. $8.95.

   Lotte Moise, a leader in the movement to make services available and to help communities understand mental retardation, writes of experiences in her family and her professional life. Her daughter Barbara was born in the early 1950s when parent advocates were first organizing to work for their children with mental retardation.

Rimland, Ingrid. **The Furies and the Flame.** Novato, Calif.: Arena, 1984. 218 pp. $15.00.

   The author writes with anger and passion of her journey from the jungles of Paraguay to Canada and eventually to the United States, where she learned English, became a clinical psychologist and writer, and raised her two children to adulthood. Her first child was apparently brain-damaged during primitive surgery at the age of six weeks.

Where to Write for Information

American Association on Mental Retardation (AAMR). 1719 Kalorama Road, N.W., Washington, DC 20009–2684.

   AAMR publishes a newsletter called **News and Notes,** monographs, and two bimonthly publications—**American Journal on Mental Retardation** and **Mental Retardation.** Its publications are primarily for professionals; its focus is to inform, educate, and provide its members with leadership opportunities.

ARC (Association for Retarded Citizens) Resources Center. 246 South River, Holland, MI 49423.

   Request their **Independent Living Materials** catalog which features practical aids for the non-reader. **101 Picture Recipes** was developed by a special education teacher and is in notebook format; it costs $25.00 plus $6.00 for shipping and handling.

Association for Children with Down Syndrome (ACDS). 2616 Martin Ave., Bellmore, NY 11710.

   ACDS offers several useful publications for families with young children, including a guide to help children accept eyeglasses, a self-help curriculum, a movement and dance curriculum, and bibliographies.

Association for Persons in Supported Employment (APSE). P.O. Box 27523, Richmond, VA 23261–7523.

APSE was formed to promote the concept of paid integrated employment and full community participation for all individuals. Parent membership is welcomed. A newsletter, **The Advance,** is published quarterly. Regular membership is $35.00; $20.00 for a person with a disability.

Association for Retarded Citizens/Montgomery County (Maryland). Family and Community Resources, 11600 Nebel Street, Rockville, MD 20852.

A packet, called the **Down Syndrome Kit** ($2.00), is addressed to new parents of a baby with Down syndrome. It is filled with parent-to-parent guidance, information, exercise and stimulation suggestions, basic reading ideas, and photographs. Ask for a list of their **Someday I May Want to Know . . .** fact sheets; while all are specific to local resources, some have helpful generic text.

Association for Retarded Citizens of the United States (ARC/US). National Headquarters, 2501 Avenue J, Arlington, TX 76005.

The ARC/US is a national grassroots organization involved in training, research, developing model programs, and information and referral. The Association circulates a number of titles of interest to families. Send for their order form that lists helpful booklets for nominal cost, such as **Make the Most of Your Baby** about meaningful play experiences, **Toilet Training for Children with Mental Retardation,** and **An Overview of Down Syndrome. ARCFacts** are two-page fact sheets about topics of current interest; one of them addresses **Mental Illness in Persons with Mental Retardation. The ARC** is a newspaper sent to all members of local chapters six times a year; **Government Report** is published semi-monthly and is available by subscription.

Channing L. Bete Company, Inc. 200 State Road, South Deerfield, MA 01373–0200.

The booklet, **What Everyone Should Know about Mental Retardation,** is 79 cents; a minimum of 25 copies must be ordered. It covers basic information in an attractive, easy-to-read format.

Brown County Association for Retarded Citizens, Citizen Advocacy Program. 1673 Dousman Street, P.O. Box 12770, Green Bay, WI 54307.

On Your Own in the Kitchen, a cookbook for non-readers, is available for $16.95, which includes postage and handling.

Council for Exceptional Children (CEC). 1920 Association Drive, Reston, VA 22091–1589.

CEC has a Division on Mental Retardation that publishes a quarterly journal called **Education and Training in Mental Retardation.** Write for ordering information.

Down's Syndrome Association of Ontario. 157 Hazelwood Drive, Whitby, Ontario, Canada L1N 3L9.

Two good booklets, **The Development of Language and Reading Skills in Children with Down's Syndrome** and **Reading and Language Development in Children with Down's Syndrome: A Guide for Parents and Teachers,** are based on a research project and accompany video tapes. This organization also circulates a book, **The Adolescent with Down's Syndrome,** which presents findings of a survey of ninety families who live in the county of Hampshire, England.

ERIC Clearinghouse on Handicapped and Gifted Children. Council for Exceptional Children, 1920 Association Drive, Reston, VA 22091–1589.

Mental Retardation and **Down Syndrome** each cost one dollar. Request their complete Product Flyer.

International League of Societies for Persons with Mental Handicaps. Avenue Louise, 248–bte 17, B-1050, Brussels, Belgium.

The League shares ideas and experiences from countries around the world in an attempt to promote a better quality of life for people with mental retardation everywhere. It publishes the results of symposia, conferences, and world congresses, pamphlets, and an international newsletter translated into four languages. Past subjects have included aging, advocacy, education, and rights.

March of Dimes. Public Health Education and Community Services Department, 1275 Mamaroneck Avenue, White Plains, NY 10605.

Down Syndrome, an easy-to-read information sheet, is available free of charge.

Mississippi University Affiliated Program for Persons with Developmental Disabilities. University of Southern Mississippi, Southern Station Box 5163, Hattiesburg, MS 39406–5163.

A series of single-concept flyers designed for both parents and school personnel is called **Providing Services for Students with Moderate and Severe Handicaps.** Individual titles include **How Can Students Be Integrated?; What Are the Roles of Related Service Personnel?; How Can Parents Participate in School Programs?;** and **What Are the Key Elements of Transition Plans?**

National Down Syndrome Congress. 1800 Dempster Street, Park Ridge, IL 60068–1146.

This national organization of parents and professionals is concerned with promoting the welfare of people with Down syndrome. Its ten-issues-a-year newsletter is called **Down Syndrome News.** Publications include a booklet called **Down Syndrome,** and a bibliography especially for new parents that lists books, pamphlets, journal articles, and films.

National Down Syndrome Society. 141 Fifth Avenue, New York, NY 10010.

The Society publishes fact sheets and a booklet called **This Baby Needs You Even More,** specifically for parents of newborn children with Down syndrome.

National Information Center for Children and Youth with Handicaps (NICHCY). P.O. Box 1492, Washington, DC 20013.

NICHCY provides fact sheets, article reprints, resource information, specialized packets, bibliographies, and addresses of parent organizations and disability-related groups on a national, state, and local level, free of charge. Get on their mailing list.

The Ohio State University Nisonger Center. 1581 Dodd Drive, Columbus, OH 43216.

Parents: A Guide for Teaching Persons with Moderate, Severe, and Profound Mental Retardation in Home and Community Settings sells for ten dollars.

Pilot Parents. Omaha Association for Retarded Citizens, 3610 Dodge, Omaha, NE 68131.

Write for information on starting a parent group; their handbook is detailed and helpful.

President's Committee on Employment of People with Disabilities. 1111 20th Street, N.W., Suite 636, Washington, DC 20036–3490.

Write for their publications list; it contains a number of items of interest concerning the employment of people with disabilities, affirmative action, and accommodations.

President's Committee on Mental Retardation (PCMR). North Building, 330 Independence Avenue, S.W., Room 4723, Washington, DC 20201.

The Problem of Mental Retardation was written in 1979 and is still available. PCMR's annual reports to the President include the title **The Mentally Retarded Worker: An Economic Di$covery.**

Public Affairs Committee. 381 Park Avenue South, New York, NY 10016.

Two pamphlets of interest to parents of children with mental retardation are **The Retarded Child Gets Ready for School** and **Mental Retardation—a Changing World** (written in 1979). Each pamphlet costs one dollar.

Rehabilitation Research and Training Center, Virginia Commonwealth University (RRTC-VCU). 1314 West Main Street, Box 2011, Richmond, VA 23284–2011.

The RRTC-VCU conducts research and training on supported employment for citizens with developmental and other severe disabilities. Their interesting newsletters share articles of interest about supported employment. Ask to get on their mailing list.

The G. Allan Roeher Institute. York University, Kinsmen Building, 4700 Keele Street, Downsview, Ontario M3J 1P3, Canada.

The G. Allan Roeher Institute is Canada's National Institute for the Study of Public Policy Affecting Persons with an Intellectual Impairment. It publishes material in a wide range of areas, with a major focus on public policy and funding, on studies of innovative social programs, and on the development of policy alternatives. The Institute sells for $6.00 a small, wise, and helpful first guide called **The Family Book: A Resource for Parents Who Have Learned Their Child Has a Mental Handicap.** A five part series is **Making a Difference: What Communities Can Do to Prevent Mental Handicap and Promote Lives of Quality.** Its quarterly magazine, **entourage,** promotes community living for people with mental handicaps and is written in both French and English. Write for the publication list; it includes some hard-to-get books from other publishers.

Special Additions. 23 Boulder Brook Road, Greenwich, CT 06830.

Special Additions offers an illustrated guide to twelve complete dinners, called **Picture This.** An eight-piece stainless steel measuring set with handles color-coded to the illustrations is also available. Write for ordering information.

The Association for Persons with Severe Handicaps (TASH). 7010 Roosevelt Way, N.E., Seattle, WA 98115.

      TASH materials have long been recognized as state-of-the-art in promoting integrated, community-based services for people who have traditionally been labeled "severely intellectually disabled." TASH publishes a journal known as the **Journal of the Association for Persons with Severe Handicaps (JASH),** a newsletter filled with information, and the **DC Update** which shares news about governmental affairs. Parents are encouraged to write for information and referral.

U.S. Department of Health and Human Services, National Maternal and Child Health Clearinghouse. 38th & R Streets, N.W., Washington, DC 20057.

      Send for **Facts about Down Syndrome;** a single copy is free. So is **Clinical Programs for Mentally Retarded Children.**

U.S. Government Printing Office. Superintendent of Documents, Washington, DC 20402.

      A Head Start series called **Mainstreaming Preschoolers** is being revised. One excellent book in the series was titled **Children with Mental Retardation: A Guide for Teachers, Parents, and Others Who Work with Mentally Retarded Preschoolers.** Inquire about its current status.

Multiple Disabilities

Your Child at Home

Perske, Robert; Clifton, Andrew; McLean, Barbara M.; Stein, Jean Ishler, eds. **Mealtimes for Persons with Severe Handicaps.** Baltimore: Paul H. Brookes, 1986. 136 pp. $17.50 (Paper).

Parents and professionals from all over contributed their ideas for making mealtimes a more successful experience for persons with severe disabilities, as well as for the people who care for them. The collection, a re-release of a 1977 publication, is a testimony to people's ingenuity and sensitivity. Martha Perske's illustrations are a great asset.

Rogow, Sally M. **Helping the Visually Impaired Child with Developmental Problems: Effective Practice in Home, School, and Community.** New York: Teachers College Press, 1988. 200 pp. $28.95; $16.95 (Paper).

The author has worked with children with multiple disabilities and their families; she is also a teacher trainer. She clearly believes that all children can learn and grow and that interaction with people and the environment is essential to the process. Her book describes visual impairments and associated neurological problems; the needs of children as they learn to cope; how teachers sponsor language communication, play, and social interaction; mobility training; the promise of technology; and how to encourage "social and personal competence." Parents will like her humanistic approach.

Scott, Eileen P.; Jan, James E.; Freeman, Roger D. **Can't Your Child See? A Guide for Parents of Visually Impaired Children.** 2d ed. Austin: Pro-Ed, 1985. 238 pp. $19.00 (Paper).

The authors drew on many years of experience in writing this excellent book designed to help parents raise a child with visual impairment. A chapter on the child with multiple disabilities is included.

Stainback, Susan B.; Healy, Harriet A. **Teaching Eating Skills: A Handbook for Teachers.** Springfield, Ill.: Charles C Thomas, 1982. 99 pp. $17.50 (Paper).

A special educator and an occupational therapist have prepared practical, easy-to-understand information on techniques to foster basic eating skills and independent eating skills for children with severe motor development problems. They contrast normal and abnormal development, talk about positioning, appropriate sucking, swallowing, and chewing, the use of utensils, new foods, and socially acceptable ways of eating. The book is meant for teachers. Since parents are the teachers of their children, this concise and helpful book should serve them well.

Your Child at School

DeVore, M. Susan. **Individualized Learning Program for the Profoundly Retarded.** Springfield, Ill.: Charles C Thomas, 1977. 250 pp. $29.25.

Designed for the use of parents or instructors, this manual offers over sixty lesson plans for teaching self-care, socialization, communication, cognitive, gross motor, and fine motor skills to children or adults with severe or profound mental retardation.

Eddy, Junius. **The Music Came from Deep Inside.** Updated ed. Cambridge, Mass.: Brookline Books, 1989. 178 pp. $17.95 (Paper).

    This is a chronicle in words and photographs of what happened in three school settings when the National Committee, Arts for the Handicapped, sponsored a project to improve the quality of life of children with severe and profound retardation and, through the use of arts strategies, their functional skills as well. An update spanning the ten years following the experiment is included in this 1989 edition. It offers some interesting and significant messages.

McInnis, J.M.; Treffry, J.A. **Deaf-Blind Infants and Children.** Toronto, Ontario: University of Toronto Press, 1982. 284 pp. $27.50.

    Much information from professionals and centers working with children who are deaf and blind is assembled in this guide. It includes methods and activities to encourage development in the areas of social and emotional skills, communication, gross and fine motor ability, perceptual and cognitive-conceptual understandings, orientation and mobility, and life skills.

Orelove, Fred P.; Sobsey, Dick. **Educating Children with Multiple Disabilities: A Transdisciplinary Approach.** Baltimore: Paul H. Brookes, 1987. 367 pp. $28.00 (Paper).

    For parents of children with severe to profound mental retardation who also have one or more significant motor or sensory impairments, this textbook may prove useful. It describes a model for providing services that emphasizes cooperation between teachers, therapists, nurses, and parents. Specific techniques for teaching communication, mealtime, toileting, and dressing skills are described.

Sherrill, Claudine, ed. **Creative Arts for the Severely Handicapped.** 2d ed. Springfield, Ill.: Charles C Thomas, 1979. 286 pp. $32.75.

    Dance, music, film, drama, movement—all of the arts are shown to be adaptable and very effective in working with the child with severe disabilities.

Sontag, Ed; Smith, Judy; Certo, Nick, eds. **Educational Programming for the Severely and Profoundly Handicapped.** Reston, Va.: Council for Exceptional Children, 1977. 472 pp. $9.95 (Paper).

    Written for educators back in 1977, some articles are either too technical or too theoretical to be of much interest to most parents. However, for those who want to gain a thorough understanding of all the issues, achievements, and problems involved in the earliest days of providing educational services to students with severe to profound disabilities from birth to age twenty-one, this is a very useful and interesting collection.

Your Child Grows Up

Covert, Angela M.; Fredericks, Bud, eds. **Transition for Persons with Deaf-Blindness and Other Profound Handicaps: State of the Art.** Monmouth, Oreg.: Teaching Research Publications, 1987. 163 pp. $10.00 (Paper).

    Papers from the 1986 National Conference on the Transition of Profoundly/Multiply Handicapped Deaf-Blind Youth have been collected in this volume. The four major areas discussed were residential, vocational, leisure and recreational, and health services. All participants agreed that all services for people with deaf-blindness and other profound disabilities need to be community-based. A number of recommendations were offered.

Personal Accounts—From Those Who Have Lived It

de Vinck, Christopher. **The Power of the Powerless.** New York: Doubleday, 1988. 153 pp. $14.95.

    This is a remarkable book, well-written, gentle, and forceful, about the profoundly positive effect people with severe disabilities can have. Oliver, blind, mute, "in a permanent state of helplessness" for all of his thirty-two years, sharpened his brother's vision. Through his writing, Christopher de Vinck sharpens ours.

Kupfer, Fern. **Before and after Zachariah.** Chicago: Academy Chicago Publishers, 1988. 241 pp. $7.95 (Paper).

    This breathtakingly personal account of a family makes clear the plight, the hurt, the depth of the sadness when parents decide that they cannot continue to live with a child with multiple, severe disabilities. "Lives are smashed and rearranged without any preparation on our part." Kupfer helps us to understand the totality of her experience, the "different kinds of courage" it takes to find a positive alternative.

Rose, Harriet Wallace. **Something's Wrong with My Child!** Springfield, Ill.: Charles C Thomas, 1987. 196 pp. $26.75.

    The mother of a young adult with severe multiple handicaps writes about a number of myths concerning families in which there is a child with a disability. Each myth is debunked with humor, common sense, and descriptions of the life experiences of her family. This optimistic, realistic, appealing book abounds with good advice for the parent new to the experience of disability; parents and professionals will learn from it.

Tuttle, David R. **To Brian . . . With Love.** West Chester, Pa.: Brian's House, 1981. 173 pp. $12.95.

    The father of a son who is profoundly retarded chronicles the history of Brian's House, a remodeled Civil War mansion converted into a licensed home for twelve children with retardation.

Where to Write for Information

American Foundation for the Blind. 15 West 16th Street, NY 10011.

    Reach Out and Teach is a two-volume set intended to give parents the information they need to raise a child with visual or multiple disabilities. Write for ordering information.

Association for Retarded Citizens of the United States (ARC/US). National Headquarters, 2501 Avenue J, Arlington, TX 76005.

    Opportunities after High School for Persons Who Are Severely Handicapped costs one dollar. **Augmentative Communication** is a set of five booklets providing information on assessment, device/technique selection, training, and other topics ($5.00).

Canadian Deaf-Blind and Rubella Association. P.O. Box 1625, Meaford, Ontario N0H 1Y0, Canada.
A $25.00 yearly subscription in Canadian money brings three publications: **Intervention,** a newsletter/bulletin, **Talking Sense,** an English quarterly, and **Deaf-Blind Education,** the Journal of the International Association for the Education of the Deaf-Blind.

ERIC Clearinghouse on Handicapped and Gifted Children. Council for Exceptional Children, 1920 Association Drive, Reston, VA 22091–1589.
Send one dollar each for **Severe Disabilities** and **Orientation and Mobility for Blind, Multiply Handicapped Infants**. Ask for the Product Flyer for a complete listing.

National Information Center for Children and Youth with Handicaps (NICHCY). P.O. Box 1492, Washington, DC 20013.
NICHCY provides fact sheets, article reprints, resource information, specialized packets, bibliographies, and addresses of parent organizations and disability-related groups on a national, state, and local level, free of charge. Get on their mailing list.

The Ohio State University Nisonger Center. 1581 Dodd Drive, Columbus, OH 43216.
Parents: A Guide for Teaching Persons with Moderate, Severe, and Profound Mental Retardation in Home and Community Settings sells for ten dollars.

The Association for Persons with Severe Handicaps (TASH). 7010 Roosevelt Way, N.E., Seattle, WA 98115.
TASH materials have long been recognized as state-of-the-art in promoting integrated, community-based services for people who have traditionally been labeled "severely intellectually disabled." TASH publishes a journal known as **JASH,** a newsletter filled with information, and the **DC Update** which shares news about national policies and trends affecting the lives of people with severely handicapping conditions. Parents are encouraged to write for information and referral.

Physical Disabilities

Basic Reading

Bloom, Beth-Ann; Seljeskog, Edward. **A Parent's Guide to Spina Bifida.** Minneapolis: University of Minnesota Press, 1988. 92 pp. $14.95.

Compact and clear, informal yet informative, practical and honest, this guide will answer the questions parents most often ask when a baby is diagnosed as having spina bifida. Its subjects include signs and symptoms, causes, associated medical and health problems, care, and treatment. How a family can best help a child to cope from infancy to adulthood, including issues of self-image, independence, and sexuality, is sensitively presented. Photographs and an appendix of technical terms, resources, and reading materials contribute to the book's usefulness.

Fraser, Beverly A.; Hensinger, Robert N. **Managing Physical Handicaps: A Practical Guide for Parents, Care Providers, and Educators.** Baltimore: Paul H. Brookes, 1983. 256 pp. $17.95.

Based on a program of physical therapy in Wayne County, Michigan schools, this is an illustrated guide to help in the day-to-day care of students with severe physical disabilities. Techniques for communicating with and handling people and a chapter on wheelchairs and transportation offer some practical guidance. Manufacturers and distributors of prescriptive equipment are listed.

Myers, Gary J.; Cerone, Sharon Bidwell; Olson, Ardis L., eds. **A Guide for Helping the Child with Spina Bifida.** Springfield, Ill.: Charles C Thomas, 1981. 307 pp. $36.25.

This reference book for parents provides general information on the family and on social aspects of raising a child with spina bifida, a consideration of medical problems, and personal accounts of involved individuals and families.

Powers, Paul W.; Orto, Arthur E. Dell, eds. **Role of the Family in the Rehabilitation of the Physically Disabled.** Austin: Pro-Ed, 1980. 554 pp. $22.00 (Paper).

Written primarily for health professionals and rehabilitation counselors, this book addresses several issues of interest to parents—the psychological and emotional effects of disability and chronic illness in children, the reaction of all family members to disability and chronic illness, and strategies for professionals to use in helping families adjust to trauma and crisis by developing effective coping styles. A number of personal statements by people with disabilities and parents of children with disabilities are included.

Russell, Philippa. **The Wheelchair Child: How Handicapped Children Can Enjoy Life to Its Fullest.** New York: Prentice Hall, 1985. 262 pp. $9.95 (Paper).

Children who use wheelchairs "can achieve emotional, educational, social and vocational successes *if* they have the opportunity." To this end, a British parent-professional has written a book jam-packed with a wealth of practical suggestions, descriptions of aids, modifications, and products, and solid advice for every parent of a child who uses a wheelchair.

Schleichkorn, Jay. **Coping with Cerebral Palsy: Answers to Questions Parents Often Ask.** Austin: Pro-Ed, 1983. 196 pp. $18.00 (Paper).

Based on material gathered from parent questionnaires and interviews, this book provides answers to questions concerning what cerebral palsy is; its causes; the growth and development of the child with cerebral palsy; medical and surgical problems; dealing with medical, dental, podiatric, nutritional, and therapeutic services; psychological, social, and educational concerns; "life experiences"; and research.

Simmons, Richard. **Reach for Fitness: A Special Book of Exercises for the Physically Challenged.** New York: Warner Books, 1986. 316 pp. $17.95.

Two programs of exercise, nutrition, and information designed for children and adults with physical disabilities are presented in easy-to-follow words and photographs. The appendix contains specific exercise tips for forty medical and handicapping conditions.

Thompson, Charlotte E. **Raising a Handicapped Child: A Helpful Guide for Parents of the Physically Disabled.** New York: William Morrow, 1986. 276 pp. $17.95.

This powerful and significant book could well serve initially as a primer for survival for parents new to the arena of disabilities or chronic illness, and as a problem-solving helper as time goes on. With a kind, compassionate, and realistic approach, Dr. Thompson explores the "roller coaster of emotions" following a devastating diagnosis, and offers strategies and practical advice for searching out the best care and services, coping with costs, and keeping up on medical research. Comprehensive appendices include listings of health professionals, definitions of physical handicaps, a resource directory of national organizations, private and governmental agencies listed by state, toll-free information numbers, selected accessible recreational facilities, and a bibliography.

Wright, Beatrice A. **Physical Disability—A Psychosocial Approach.** 2d ed. New York: Harper & Row, 1983. 520 pp. $32.50.

Long recognized as an authority on the psychology of adjustment to physical illness and disability, Dr. Wright describes and analyzes the psychosocial sources of positive and negative beliefs by and about people with disabilities. Using numerous examples of life experiences of people with a variety of physical disabilities, and guided by "value-laden beliefs and principles," she indicates the ways in which behavior may be affected by attitudes, reactions of others, and the environment. Written for the practitioner in the field of rehabilitation, this important work will be valuable to families, people with disabilities, and policy-makers, as well.

Your Child at Home

Finnie, Nancie R. **Handling the Young Cerebral Palsied Child at Home.** New York: E.P. Dutton, 1975. 337 pp. $8.95 (Paper).

Considered a classic, this informative and very useful manual includes drawings and explanations of methods for handling the everyday problems of management and development of the young child with cerebral palsy. Parents will appreciate its tone and its content.

Hanson, Marci J.; Harris, Susan R. **Teaching the Young Child with Motor Delays: A Guide for Parents and Professionals.** Austin: Pro-Ed, 1986. 218 pp. $29.00 (Paper).

 This attractive and helpful reference book for parents of young children with movement difficulties provides basic information, suggests resources, and offers teaching and handling strategies to stimulate motor, social, cognitive, and communication skills. Personal accounts and photographs are included. There are, in addition, charts of developmental milestones, a glossary of terms parents will hear from professionals, commercial sources of adaptive equipment, reading lists, resource organizations, and a section to record the baby's progress.

Murphy, Judy. **Home Care of Handicapped Children: A Guide. Orthopedic Handicaps.** Lyons, Colo.: Carol L. Lutey Publishing, 1982. 153 pp. $6.50 (Paper).

 One of a series intended for potential caregivers of a child between the ages of three and twelve, this practical and helpful guide has good information to share with families, as well. Part I offers general guidelines concerning child health, self-help activities, social behavior, communication, play, and safety and protective measures. The second part, specific to orthopedic disability, includes types of handicaps (cerebral palsy, spinal cord injury, spina bifida, and the muscular dystrophies), guidelines for lifting, lowering, carrying, transfers, and positioning, caring for a child who is bed-ridden, specific self-help activities, understanding the child who is orthopedically disabled, accessibility issues, and special equipment.

Pensis, Nancy T.; Maloney, Mary Ann. **Mealtimes for People with Handicaps: A Guide for Parents, Paraprofessionals, and Allied Health Professionals.** Springfield, Ill.: Charles C Thomas, 1983. 143 pp. $15.25 (Spiral).

 Designed to use in training families and other caregivers who assist someone with a physical disability at mealtimes, this manual offers techniques for the positioning of the helper, the person being fed, and the food.

Your Child at School

Adams, Ronald C.; Daniel, Alfred N.; Rullman, Lee. **Games, Sports, and Exercises for the Physically Handicapped.** 3d ed. Philadelphia: Lea & Febiger, 1982. 400 pp. $28.50.

 Designed as a resource guide for the teacher of students who are physically disabled, this all-encompassing work emphasizes the need for physical activity in the daily life of people with disabilities and describes specific activities, necessary adaptations of equipment, and appropriate activities for specific disabilities.

Stainback, Susan B.; Healy, Harriet A. **Teaching Eating Skills: A Handbook for Teachers.** Springfield, Ill.: Charles C Thomas, 1982. 99 pp. $17.50 (Paper).

 A special educator and an occupational therapist have prepared practical, easy-to-understand information on techniques to foster basic eating skills and independent eating skills for children with severe motor development problems. They contrast normal and abnormal development, talk about positioning, appropriate sucking, swallowing, and chewing, the use of utensils, new foods, and socially acceptable ways of eating. The book is meant for teachers. Since parents are the teachers of their children, this concise and helpful book should serve them well.

Williamson, G. Gordon, ed. **Children with Spina Bifida: Early Intervention and Preschool Programming.** Baltimore: Paul H. Brookes, 1987. 231 pp. $25.00.

Contributors in the fields of nursing, occupational therapy, physical therapy, psychology, orthopedic surgery, rehabilitation medicine, social work, special education, and speech-language pathology write of current research. Both extensive and practical, the book is written for professionals but should prove useful to parents in understanding the educational and therapeutic programs offered the young child with spina bifida.

Your Child Grows Up

Lifchez, Raymond; Winslow, Barbara. **Design for Independent Living: The Environment and Physically Disabled People.** Berkeley: University of California Press, 1981. 208 pp. $14.95.

These very personal profiles of seven men and women from the community of people with physical disabilities in Berkeley, California, where the Independent Living movement began, assess their needs in terms of specific activities such as housing, sleeping, sexuality, grooming, feeding, excreting, gaining accessibility to work and recreation, and eliminating barriers. The book discusses the support network necessary for these adults to participate in life as normally and as self-sufficiently as possible. Thoughtful design and personal adaptation make all the difference.

Maddox, Sam. **Spinal Network: The Total Resource for the Wheelchair Community.** Boulder, Colo.: Spinal Network, 1987. 372 pp. $42.95; $27.95 (Spiral).

While many of its articles discuss spinal cord injury, **Spinal Network** is an encyclopedic resource book for most people who participate in "the wheelchair lifestyle." It covers medical questions, sports and recreation, travel, media and images, computers, sex and romance, disability and rights, legal and financial issues, resource connections, and a potpourri of other topics. Illustrations, photographs, and cartoons add to its lively layout. Its tone is upbeat, yet realistic; its focus is on possibility and choice.

Personal Accounts—From Those Who Have Lived It

Browne, Susan E.; Connors, Debra; Stern, Nanci. **With the Power of Each Breath: A Disabled Women's Anthology.** Pittsburgh: Cleis Press, 1985. 354 pp. $9.95 (Paper).

The fifty-four women who contributed to this anthology span the years from teenagers to women in their eighties; their disabilities are both visible and invisible, recent and lifelong. They write about "surviving the system," anger, growing up in families, self-image, motherhood, and friendship. The writings range from informational to clever to poetic. They are powerful in their messages of strength and reward, of needs and challenges.

Grandle, Julia Nelle. **Pot of Gold.** New York: Vantage Press, 1985. 115 pp. $8.95.

In simple prose, a mother writes of her son Chris, born with spina bifida and given little chance to live. A determined and loving family with faith in God sees him become an engineer and marry.

Jewell, Geri; Weiner, Stewart. **Geri.** New York: Ballantine, 1984. 224 pp. $3.50 (Paper).

Geri Jewell's autobiography of a person with cerebral palsy who becomes a celebrated comedienne tells also of a supportive family.

Nolan, Christopher. **Dam-Burst of Dreams.** Athens: Ohio University Press, 1981. 96 pp. $9.95 (Paper).

This is a collection of the remarkable writings of a most remarkable person. Christy Nolan was brain-damaged at birth and as a result has never been able to speak or control his body. A muscle-relaxant drug, first administered when he was eleven, allowed him, with the aid of a head device and in partnership with his mother, sufficient control to type his unique, incredible verse, short stories, plays, and autobiography. "Mankind meditates on lovely tear-making manners in other people. . . ."

Nolan, Christopher. **Under the Eye of the Clock.** New York: St. Martin's, 1987. 162 pp. $16.95. New York: Delta, 1989. $7.95 (Paper).

Christopher Nolan, the incredible, young, award-winning poet-writer, whose cerebral palsy keeps him unable to move or talk, "zoo-caged," "able only to think," has created a most extraordinary autobiography. His language is energetic, original, and often puzzling, but for the reader who perseveres, glimpses of Nolan's thoughts and feelings are movingly revealed, his family is described, his life-experience is chronicled.

Pieper, Elizabeth. **Sticks and Stones: The Story of Loving a Child.** Syracuse, N.Y.: Human Policy Press, 1977. 88 pp. $4.50 (Paper).

In this well-done account of the birth and development of a baby with spina bifida, Pieper describes her painful progress toward knowledge of her child's problems and the challenges of dealing with doctors, authorities, educators, counselors, and government agencies. Betty Pieper is a fighter, and she presents a good case for more sensitivity on the part of professionals who care for people who are disabled and more assertiveness on the part of parents of a child with a disability.

Rush, William L. **Journey out of Silence.** Lincoln, Nebr.: Media Productions & Marketing, 1986. 217 pp. $14.95.

While athetoid cerebral palsy has disallowed the author the use of his arms, legs, and voice, it has not robbed him of intelligence and the ability to communicate. Rush tells his life history and explores, with humor, insight, and a journalist's skill, significant issues of living with a physical disability.

Sienkiewicz-Mercer, Ruth; Kaplan, Steven B. **I Raise My Eyes to Say Yes: A Memoir.** Boston: Houghton Mifflin, 1989. 225 pp. $17.95.

Encephalitis at the age of five weeks left Ruth Sienkiewicz with no control of her body and unable to develop speech. She lived sixteen of her years at Belchertown State School in Massachusetts; her story supports her case for the closure of institutions. Now an advocate for all people with disabilities and married to another former resident of Belchertown, Sienkiewicz-Mercer has written of her experiences with the help of an "interlocutor" and communication boards.

Zola, Irving Kenneth. **Missing Pieces: A Chronicle of Living with a Disability.** Philadelphia: Temple University Press, 1982. 246 pp. $29.95; $9.95 (Paper).

The author defines his book as a "socio-autobiography, a personal and social odyssey that chronicles not only my beginning acknowledgment of the impact of my physical differences on my life but also my growing awareness of the ways in which society invalidates people with a chronic disability." The framework is a visit to Het Dorp, a sixty-five-acre village specifically designed to house four hundred adult Netherlanders with severe disabilities.

Travel Guides

Hecker, Helen. **Travel for the Disabled: A Handbook of Travel Resources and 500 Worldwide Access Guides.** Vancouver, Wash.: Twin Peaks Press, 1985. 185 pp. $11.95 (includes postage) (Paper).

There has been in recent years an explosion of travel guides to help the adult traveler with a physical disability find accessible accommodations and resources. Travelling families will find this comprehensive guide quite useful in deciding what information is available to order and where to call. Listings include travel agencies, clubs, books, magazines, hotel and motel information, parks and playgrounds, summer camps, access guides to places here and abroad, and much more.

Weiss, Louise. **Access to the World: A Travel Guide for the Handicapped.** Rev. ed. New York: Henry Holt, 1986. 240 pp. $12.95 (Paper).

Chock-full of facts and tips that will make travelling with a disability as easy as possible, **Access to the World** spells out airline policies, bus, train, and ship information, access guides, tour operators, travel agents and travel organizations, hotel and motel accommodations, and vacation ideas here and abroad. Parents travelling with a child with a physical disability will appreciate its practicality and specificity.

Where to Write for Information

Accent on Information. P.O. Box 700, Bloomington, IL 61701.

The **Accent on Living** magazine prints articles about people with physical disabilities and advertises aids and resources. There is an annual **Buyer's Guide** and several Accent Special Publications. A particularly helpful booklet, called **Ideas for Making Your Home Accessible,** contains both ideas and product listings. **Ideas for Kids on the Go** is an encouraging booklet for children and teenagers with physical limitations; it describes and illustrates products for recreation, day-to-day living, and computer adaptations. Ask for the **Books for Better Living** brochure.

Channing L. Bete Company. 200 State Road, South Deerfield, MA 01373–0200.

The booklet, **What Everyone Should Know about Cerebral Palsy,** is 79 cents; a minimum of 25 copies must be ordered. It covers basic information in an attractive, easy-to-read format.

ERIC Clearinghouse on Handicapped and Gifted Children. Council for Exceptional Children, 1920 Association Drive, Reston, VA 22091–1589.

> **Students with Physical Disabilities and Health Impairments** costs $1.00. Request the Product Flyer for a complete listing of publications.

March of Dimes. Public Health Education and Community Services Department, 1275 Mamaroneck Avenue, White Plains, NY 10605.

> A single copy of an easy-to-read Public Health Education Information Sheet called **Spina Bifida** is free.

National Clearing House of Rehabilitation Training Materials. 115 Old USDA Building, Oklahoma State University, Stillwater, OK 74078.

> Send for **The Helping Hand: A Manual Describing Methods for Handling the Young Child with Cerebral Palsy** ($2.00 plus $1.00 postage). This helpful guide, developed at the Children's Rehabilitation Center in Charlottesville, Virginia, answers many of the questions parents ask about cerebral palsy, their children, and their own feelings. It also sets out in words and pictures the basic principles of Neurodevelopmental Treatment, a therapy also referred to as "the Bobath method."

National Easter Seal Society. 70 East Lake Street, Chicago, IL 60601.

> The National Easter Seal Society offers a broad array of quality print materials in leaflet, pamphlet, booklet, reference, and guidebook format. Topics range from accessibility and attitudes to dental care, independent living, and speech. Titles include **Feeding the Cerebral Palsied Child, Self-Help Clothing for Children Who Have Physical Disabilities,** and **Camps for Children with Disabilities: Make the Right Choice for Your Child.** Write for ordering information.

National Information Center for Children and Youth with Handicaps (NICHCY). P.O. Box 1492, Washington, DC 20013.

> NICHCY provides fact sheets, article reprints, resource information, specialized packets, bibliographies, and addresses of parent organizations and disability-related groups on a national, state, and local level, free of charge. Get on their mailing list.

National Library Service for the Blind and Physically Handicapped. Library of Congress, Washington, DC 20542.

> The free library service for "Talking Books," books recorded on tape and played on a free loaned cassette player, can be a most valuable resource for learning and for leisure time. Write for information.

National Rehabilitation Information Center (NARIC). 8455 Colesville Road, Suite 935, Silver Spring, MD 20910.

> NARIC can supply research reports, bibliographies, and computer searches on any question relating to the rehabilitation needs or concerns of people with disabilities. Request a description of their services.

President's Committee on Employment of People with Disabilities. 1111 20th Street, N.W., Suite 636, Washington, DC 20036.

Send for their publication list; it contains a number of items of interest concerning the employment of people with disabilities, affirmative action, and accommodations.

Spina Bifida Association of America (SBAA). 1700 Rockville Pike, Suite 540, Rockville, MD 20852.

SBAA has a network which provides support and information through local chapters. Their current publications list has many fine, low-priced materials for parents. Titles include **Introduction to Spina Bifida, Giant Steps for Steven** (the sharing of a six year old), **Sociological Aspects of Spina Bifida,** and **SBAA Spotlights,** which address issues of physical, sociological, and legal concern. Free pamphlets include **What the Teacher Needs to Know** and **Taking Charge of Your Life: A Guide to Independence for Teens with Physical Disabilities.** The association's bimonthly newsletter is called **Insights.**

United Cerebral Palsy Associations (UCP). 7 Penn Plaza, Suite 804, New York, NY 10001.

UCP can put you in touch with a local chapter and supply a publication list with general information on cerebral palsy. Their newsletter on legislation, called **Word from Washington,** is available from UCP Governmental Activities Office, 425 Eye Street, N.W., Washington, DC 20001.

U.S. Architectural and Transportation Barriers Compliance Board. 1111 18th Street, N.W., Suite 501, Washington, DC 20202.

Write for information on accessibility standards, enforcement regulations, the complaint process, and a **Selected Bibliography on School Design for Students with Disabilities.**

U.S. Department of Housing and Urban Development. 451 7th Street, S.W., Washington, DC 20410.

The Office of Independent Living for the Disabled, Room 9106, can supply information and publications. Two useful pamphlets are **Changing Environments for People with Disabilities** and **Pathways to Independent Living.**

U.S. Department of Health and Human Services. Public Health Service, National Institute of Neurological and Communicative Disorders and Stroke, National Institutes of Health, 9000 Rockville Pike, Building 31, Room 8A06, Bethesda, MD 20892.

Single copies of the **Hope through Research** series are free. Specific titles include **Cerebral Palsy** and **Spina Bifida.**

Speech and Language Disabilities

Barach, Carol. **Help Me Say It: A Parent's Guide to Speech Problems.** New York: New American Library, 1983. 272 pp. $8.95 (Paper).

Easy to read and packed with information for parents looking for guidance, **Help Me Say It** answers questions about communication and community resources and suggests ways parents can help their child. Normal speech and language development is outlined, followed by chapters on various types of communication disorders and how they can be identified and remedied by parents and professionals. The author uses fictional children as examples.

Brooks, Mary; Engmann, Deedra; Johnson, Merrily. **Your Child's Speech and Language.** Austin: Pro-Ed, 1978. 55 pp. $5.95 (Paper).

This breezily written guide is intended to help parents to encourage normal speech development and to aid in the early detection of communication disorders. The guide covers infancy through preschool years, giving indications of normal development and suggesting parent activities to stimulate and respond to language development.

de Villiers, Peter; de Villiers, Jill G. **Early Language.** Cambridge, Mass.: Harvard University Press, 1979. 160 pp. $4.95 (Paper).

A brief and very readable description explains how language is first learned by the developmentally "normal" child. The book also covers obstacles to language development such as deafness, aphasia, and autism.

Jeffree, Dorothy M.; McConkey, Roy. **Let Me Speak.** New York: Taplinger, 1977. 176 pp. $7.95 (Paper).

This is a delightful collection of many games and activities designed to help parents aid children who are slow in acquiring language skills. Language development charts pinpoint developmental needs and relate them to the specific learning activities spelled out in the text. In an easy style, with good, clear instructions, **Let Me Speak** encourages parents to teach and motivate their children through play.

Karnes, Merle B. **Learning Language at Home: Level I and Level II.** Reston, Va.: Council for Exceptional Children, 1977. $19.95 (Paper).

The Level I kit contains two hundred activity cards to stimulate language for preschoolers or for somewhat older children with disabilities. They are designed for use by parents to teach language skills at home. Level II has two hundred cards designed for children ages six to nine or for an older child with a delay. The activities are sequenced in order of difficulty. Manuals that accompany the kits give instructions for keeping track of progress.

Schwartz, Sue; Miller, Joan E. Heller. **The Language of Toys: Teaching Communication Skills to Special-Needs Children.** Rockville, Md.: Woodbine House, 1988. 280 pp. $12.95 (Paper).

This charming book will provide delightful and stimulating playtime for a parent and child; the time spent will increase the child's language skills, as well. Contents include background information on language development and delays and detailed suggestions for how to use toys, along with sample language dialogues arranged sequentially by language developmental age from birth to sixty months. The sensitive writing, attractive photographs, developmental checklists, and lists of resources, toy manufacturers, children's books, and suggestions for homemade toys help to make this parents' guide particularly useful.

Where to Write for Information

American Speech-Language-Hearing Association (ASHA). 10801 Rockville Pike, Rockville, MD 20852.

>Several publications will interest parents. Write for **Answers and Questions about Stuttering; Answers and Questions about Articulation Problems; Answers and Questions about Otitis Media, Hearing, and Language Development;** and **How Does Your Child Hear and Talk? Recognizing Hearing Disorders.**

Channing L. Bete Company. 200 State Road, South Deerfield, MA 01373–0200.

>The booklet, **What Everyone Should Know about Speech and Language Disorders,** is 79 cents; a minimum of 25 copies must be ordered. It covers basic information in an attractive, easy-to-read format.

The Council for Exceptional Children (CEC). 1920 Association Drive, Reston, VA 22091–1589.

>CEC has a Division for Children with Communication Disorders. It publishes the **Journal of Childhood Communication Disorders** twice a year. Write for subscription information.

National Easter Seal Society. 70 East Lake Street, Chicago, IL 60601.

>**Understanding Stuttering: Information for Parents** is available for $1.20.

National Institute of Neurological and Communicative Disorders and Stroke. Office of Scientific and Health Reports, Building 31, Room 8A-06, Bethesda, MD 20892.

>Send for **Stuttering: Hope through Research.**

National Stuttering Project. 1269 Seventh Avenue, San Francisco, CA 94122.

>Monthly newsletters for parents and students called **Letting Go** and **Letting Go, Jr.** and **A Brochure for Parents of Children Who Stutter** are available.

The Ohio State University Nisonger Center. 1581 Dodd Drive, Columbus, OH 43216.

>**Conversations with Children: A Model for Early Communication Development** costs $7.00.

Speech Foundation of America. P.O. Box 11749, Memphis, TN 38111.

>For a $1.00 donation, you can receive a booklet called **If Your Child Stutters: A Guide for Parents.** It distinguishes between normal disfluencies and stuttering, and outlines warning signs, possible causes, and how parents can help their child. The Foundation also offers a booklet called **Do You Stutter: A Guide for Teens.**

U.S. Government Printing Office. Superintendent of Documents, Washington, DC 20402.

A Head Start series, called **Mainstreaming Preschoolers,** is being revised. One excellent book in the series was titled **Children with Speech and Language Impairments: A Guide for Teachers, Parents, and Others Who Work with Speech and Language Impaired Preschoolers.** Inquire about its current status.

Visual Disabilities

Basic Reading

Fraiberg, Selma; Fraiberg, Louis. **Insights from the Blind: Comparative Studies of Blind and Sighted Infants.** New York: New American Library, 1977. 297 pp. $4.95 (Paper).

An important report of a ten-year study of infants who were blind outlines findings on how the baby who cannot see differs from the sighted child in learning, ego development, and relations with other people, and what adaptations are helpful in overcoming developmental delays resulting from blindness.

Lowenfeld, Berthold. **The Changing Status of the Blind—From Separation to Integration.** Springfield, Ill.: Charles C Thomas, 1975. 336 pp. $39.25.

This is an old but still interesting overview by a noted professional which offers an historical perspective on the social status of people who are blind.

Warren, David H. **Blindness and Early Childhood Development.** Rev. ed. New York: American Foundation for the Blind, 1984. 377 pp. $12.00 (Paper).

This scholarly work by an associate professor of psychology at the University of California reviews the available knowledge of the effects of visual impairment on child development, including motor, perceptual, language and cognition, social, emotional, and personality development. Measures to counter developmental lag are discussed.

Your Child at Home and School

Kastein, Shulamith; Spaulding, Isabelle; Scharf, Battia. **Raising the Young Blind Child.** New York: Human Sciences Press, 1980. 208 pp. $29.95; $14.95 (Paper).

Three specialists in the education of children with visual disabilities discuss how children with visual impairments grow and how parents can help their child cope with each developmental milestone. Insights into the emotional reactions of children and families are also presented.

Lowenfeld, Berthold. **Our Blind Children: Growing and Learning with Them.** 3d ed. Springfield, Ill.: Charles C Thomas, 1971. 244 pp. $19.75.

Written for parents, this older, well-respected book presents both facts on blindness and practical advice on teaching the skills of daily living to infants and children who are blind, through the adolescent years. Parent concerns are addressed in this helpful book.

Maloney, Patricia L. **Practical Guidance for Parents of the Visually Handicapped Preschooler.** Springfield, Ill.: Charles C Thomas, 1981. 78 pp. $14.95 (Paper).

This compact, common-sensical guide offers both help in coping with the emotions of having a child who is blind and instruction in care, training, and education. Written by a mother who obviously weathered the early years successfully, the book provides valuable and practical advice to parents just beginning.

Murphy, Judy. **Home Care of Handicapped Children: A Guide. Visual Impairments.** Lyons, Colo.: Carol L. Lutey Publishing, 1982. 76 pp. $6.50 (Paper).

One of a series intended for potential caregivers of a child between the ages of three and twelve, this practical and helpful guide has good information to share with families, as well. Part I offers general guidelines concerning child health, self-help activities, social behavior, communication, play, and safety and protective measures. A short second section discusses causes and understanding the child with a visual impairment, and offers a few practical hints concerning orientation, safety, mobility, eating, and recreational activities.

Rogow, Sally M. **Helping the Visually Impaired Child with Developmental Problems: Effective Practice in Home, School, and Community.** New York: Teachers College Press, 1988. 200 pp. $28.95; $16.95 (Paper).

The author has worked with children with multiple disabilities and their families; she is also a teacher trainer. She clearly believes that all children can learn and grow and that interaction with people and the environment is essential to the process. Her book describes visual impairments and associated neurological problems; the needs of children as they learn to cope; how teachers sponsor language communication, play, and social interaction; mobility training; the promise of technology; and how to encourage "social and personal competence." Parents will like her humanistic approach.

Scott, Eileen P.; Jan, James E.; Freeman, Roger D. **Can't Your Child See? A Guide for Parents of Visually Impaired Children.** 2d ed. Austin: Pro-Ed, 1985. 238 pp. $19.00 (Paper).

The authors drew on many years of experience in writing this excellent book designed to help parents raise a child with visual impairment. The effect of blindness on the developing child is discussed from infancy through the school years to adulthood; the guide is filled with practical suggestions to help all family members through the different stages of growth. A chapter on the child with multiple disabilities is included. Parents will find this a most valuable resource.

Swallow, Rose-Marie; Huebner, Kathleen Mary, eds. **How to Thrive, Not Just Survive: A Guide to Developing Independent Life Skills for Blind and Visually Impaired Children and Youths.** New York: American Foundation for the Blind, 1987. 93 pp. $9.00 (Paper).

This small but comprehensive manual is packed full of guidelines and strategies that parents can use to help youngsters who are blind or visually impaired to develop necessary skills. The areas discussed are daily living—eating, toileting, dressing, hygiene, grooming, behavior, and self-esteem; orientation—including awareness of body and environment; and leisure time and recreational activities. Photographs and a listing of resources round out the helpful contents.

Personal Account—From One Who Has Lived It

Ulrich, Sharon; Wolf, Anna W.M. **Elizabeth.** Ann Arbor: University of Michigan Press, 1972. 122 pp. $5.95.

Elizabeth's mother describes the first five years in the life of "a normal child who is blind"; many practical and useful ideas for home training are part of her heartening, helpful family story.

Framing her detailed account is an introduction by Selma Fraiberg, then Director of the University of Michigan Child Development Project for the Department of Psychiatry, who describes the project for children who were blind and their families, and a lengthy commentary by Edna Adelson, research psychologist with the project, who discusses the psychology of the infant and the early education of the child who is blind.

Where to Write for Information

American Alliance for Health, Physical Education, Recreation, and Dance (AAHPERD). P.O. Box 10375, Alexandria, VA 22310.

Get a Wiggle On and its sequel, **Move It!** provide suggestions for helping infants and children who are blind or visually impaired grow and learn like other children. Both books are helpful and delightful in format. **Physical Education and Recreation for the Visually Impaired** is also available. Write for ordering information.

American Foundation for the Blind (AFB). 15 West 16th Street, New York, NY 10011.

AFB provides information and consultation for persons who are blind or visually impaired. AFB's publications catalog has a number of books and pamphlets that will be of interest to parents. **Show Me How** is a manual for parents of preschool children; **Reach Out and Teach** is a two-volume set intended to give parents the information they need to raise a child who is visually or multiply disabled. Another useful booklet is **Parenting Preschoolers: Suggestions for Raising Young Blind and Visually Impaired Children. A Different Way of Seeing** is written as a letter to children. A free catalog describes **Products for People with Vision Problems.**

American Printing House for the Blind. P.O. Box 6085, Louisville, KY 40206.

The Printing House publishes and distributes materials for people with visual impairment. Send for a list of publications; some titles are of interest to parents for use with their children.

Blind Children's Center. 4120 Marathon Street, P.O. Box 29159, Los Angeles, CA 90029–0159.

The Center offers an Educational Correspondence Program and publications that include **Talk to Me; Move with Me; Learning to Play;** and **Heart to Heart: Parents of Blind and Partially Sighted Children Talk about Their Feelings** ($1.00 each). A good booklet to share with school systems is **When You Have a Visually Handicapped Child in Your Classroom: Suggestions for Teachers.**

Blind Children's Fund. 230 Central Street, Auburndale, MA 02116–2399.

This organization collects, develops, and disseminates information, materials, and services for infants and young children with visual impairments. Publications include **Parent Packet; Watch Me Grow;** and a pamphlet on the Children's Braille Book Club.

Comprehensive Eye Center. Children's Hospital, 700 Children's Drive, Columbus, OH 43205.

Written for parents, a thirty-four-page manual called **Moving and Doing: How to Help Visually Impaired Children Know Their World** is available for $3.00.

Council for Exceptional Children (CEC). 1920 Association Drive, Reston, VA 22091–1589.

> CEC has a Division for the Visually Handicapped. Write for information about publications.

ERIC Clearinghouse on Handicapped and Gifted Children. Council for Exceptional Children. 1920 Association Drive, Reston, VA 22091–1589.

> Send for their complete Product Flyer. A two-page digest, **Visual Impairments,** costs $1.00.

National Association for Parents of the Visually Impaired (NAPVI). P.O. Box 562, Camden, NY 13316.

> NAPVI provides support and service to the parents of children of all ages with visual impairment. It distributes **Mainstreaming the Visually Impaired Child** (Orlansky, 1977) for $13.00, and **Preschool Learning Activities for the Visually Impaired Child: A Guide for Parents** ($7.00). The ninety-one-page **Guide** was prepared by the Illinois Department of Education and is well-organized and practical with suggestions for selected skill-teaching games and activities for parents to use with young children who have visual impairments.

National Association for the Visually Handicapped. 22 West 21st Street, New York, NY 10010.

> The Association is devoted solely to providing information and resources for and about people with partial vision. Ask for its publication called **Family Guide: Growth and Development of the Partially Seeing Child.**

National Braille Press, Inc. 88 St. Stephen Street, Boston, MA 02115.

> A self-paced workbook that will help a parent learn to identify the braille alphabet, numbers, and contractions is called **Just Enough to Know Better** and sells for $12.50.

National Federation of the Blind. 1800 Johnson Street, Baltimore, MD 21230.

> This consumer group answers questions, makes referrals, and offers written information. Publications include **Future Reflections,** published quarterly and designed specifically for parents of children who are blind ($8.00 for a Family Membership), **A Resource Guide for Parents and Educators of Blind Children** ($5.95), and many free articles on a variety of topics.

National Library Service for the Blind and Physically Handicapped. Library of Congress, Washington, DC 20542.

> The free library service for "Talking Books," books recorded on tape and played on a free loaned cassette player, can be a most valuable resource for learning and for leisure time. Write for information.

President's Committee on Employment of People with Disabilities, 1111 20th Street, N.W., Suite 636, Washington, DC 20036.

> Write for their publications list; it contains a number of items of interest concerning the employment of people with disabilities, affirmative action, and accommodations.

Public Affairs Committee. 381 Park Avenue South, New York, NY 10016.

> **Creating Careers for Blind People: Rehabilitation and Technology** is $1.00.

U.S. Government Printing Office. Superintendent of Documents, Washington, DC 20402.

A Head Start series called **Mainstreaming Preschoolers** is being revised. One excellent book in the series was titled **Children with Visual Handicaps: A Guide for Teachers, Parents, and Others Who Work with Visually Handicapped Preschoolers.** Inquire about its current status.

SPECIFIC TOPICS
OF INTEREST

PART III

Advocacy

Anderson, Winifred; Chitwood, Stephen; Hayden, Deidre. **Negotiating the Special Education Maze: A Guide for Parents and Teachers.** 2d ed. Rockville, Md.: Woodbine House, 1990. 269 pp. $12.95 (Paper).

Based on a training program to teach parents to be educational advocates and using case studies for illustrations, this practical, readable, step-by-step guide explains how to plan, secure, and oversee a child's special education. A new and important chapter on transition appears in this second edition as well as information on Public Law 99–457, which mandates services for infants and toddlers with disabilities. Appendices offer addresses of federal and state offices and national organizations. Parents of children new to special education and parents who are veterans in working through the maze of special rules, policies, procedures, and professionals will find much of value in the pages of this book.

Biklen, Douglas. **Let Our Children Go: A Classic Organizing Manual for Parents and Advocates.** Syracuse, N.Y.: Human Policy Press, 1974. 144 pp. $4.50 (Paper).

Let Our Children Go is an effectively presented handbook for parents and others advocating to change the system for children who are not getting what they need from it. It was written before the Education for All Handicapped Children Act; it is still useful.

Budoff, Milton; Orenstein, Alan. **Due Process in Special Education: On Going to a Hearing.** Cambridge, Mass.: Brookline Books, 1982. 352 pp. $17.95 (Paper).

Prior to the passage of Public Law 94–142, Massachusetts had enacted Chapter 766, which reformed special education. Budoff and Orenstein use the Massachusetts experience to study the special education appeals system. Experiences of parents, school administrators, and hearing officers are documented. The authors conclude that a hearing is all too often traumatic and adversarial and frequently does not resolve disagreements between parents and schools over appropriate programming for a child with special needs. Two chapters present tips for schools to minimize hearings and tips for parents who go to hearings.

Des Jardins, Charlotte. **How to Get Services by Being Assertive.** Chicago: Coordinating Council for Handicapped Children, 1980. 114 pp. $6.00 (includes postage) (Paper).

This delightful, ten-year-old booklet is still as relevant, readable, and helpful as when it was first written. Parents will develop self-confidence and learn strategies for getting necessary services for their children by practicing the assertive communication techniques described.

Des Jardins, Charlotte. **How to Organize an Effective Parent/Advocacy Group and Move Bureaucracies.** Chicago: Coordinating Council for Handicapped Children, 1980. 126 pp. $4.50 (Paper).

Living with a child with a disability has turned many a parent into an effective advocate for his or her own child. By joining with other parents "and their helpers," significant global happenings can occur. This easy-to-read guide answers all possible questions about organizing an effective advocacy group that can deal with current problems and prevent future crises.

Hazel, Robin; Barber, Patricia A.; Roberts, Sally; Behr, Shirley K.; Helmstetter, Edwin; Guess, Doug. **A Community Approach to an Integrated Service System for Children with Special Needs.** Baltimore: Paul H. Brookes, 1988. 264 pp. $24.00 (Paper).

> For advocates and activists who want to help their community develop a plan to meet the special needs of families with infants and toddlers who have disabilities or chronic illness, this basic guidebook of strategies and activities will supply the step-by-step practical skills and action plans necessary. The authors suggest forming a CAISS (Community Approach to an Integrated Service System) committee and describe how to go about doing just that. One group exercise, "The Shoes Test," invites participants to walk in the shoes of a family that includes a child with a disability and get a feel for their needs.

Markel, Geraldine Ponte; Greenbaum, Judith. **Parents Are to Be Seen and Heard: Assertiveness in Educational Planning for Handicapped Children.** Ann Arbor, Mich.: Greenbaum & Markel, 1985. 145 pp. $6.95 (Paper).

> The goal of the handbook is to create knowledgeable parents who can communicate what they know and want for their children with disabilities—parents who can assert themselves as authoritatively as school personnel so often do. Skills in verbal and nonverbal communication, listening, and note taking are taught in this instructional program.

Paul, James L.; Neufeld, G.R.; Pelozi, John. **Child Advocacy within the System.** Syracuse, N.Y.: Syracuse University Press, 1977. 165 pp. $9.95.

> Awareness of the failure of any of our major institutions which are there to give services to children—health, education, recreation, welfare—begins with parents who are engaged in the daily management of their children's well-being. That premise lends urgency to the authors' definition of advocacy, their discussion of individual and systems advocacy, of ways to bring about change, and of the personal effects such work has on the individual, whether parent, professional, or paraprofessional.

Rousso, Harilyn; O'Malley, Susan Gushee; Severance, Mary. **Disabled, Female, and Proud!** Boston: Exceptional Parent Press, 1988. 136 pp. $9.95 (Paper).

> Ten women with a variety of disabilities who are leading interesting and satisfying lives share their stories. This book is designed to help counter societal stereotypes and encourage young women with disabilities to make their own choices. Parents will find much to think about.

School, Beverly A.; Cooper, Arlene. **The IEP Primer and the Individualized Program.** Rev. ed. Novato, Calif.: Academic Therapy Publications, 1981. 129 pp. $7.00 (Paper).

> Intended to help teachers design individual programming that conforms to the requirements of the law, this handbook includes a brief but good chapter giving tips for parents.

Shields, Craig V. **Strategies: A Practical Guide for Dealing with Professionals and Human Service Systems.** Richmond Hill, Ontario: Human Services Press; distributed by Paul H. Brookes, 1987. 144 pp. $16.00 (Paper).

> Effective parent advocates for children with special needs rarely spring forth full-blown; they learn through experience. **Strategies** may be a shortcut to the process of becoming an advocate since it offers strategies for dealing with the most common questions, situations, and problems

parents will meet when working with professionals and agencies. The appendices set out the master list of strategies and list support groups for parents in Canada and the United States.

Shore, Kenneth. **The Special Education Handbook: A Comprehensive Guide for Parents and Educators.** New York: Teachers College Press, 1986. 224 pp. $14.95 (Paper).

Kenneth Shore's valuable book guides parents, with clarity and respect, from the time of their child's initial referral to special education through the diagnostic evaluation to the implementation of programs and services, including the resolution of any conflict along the way. And it does far more; it will help parents to be confident participants, effective communicators, and well-prepared advocates as they team with school personnel to design the best educational program for their child.

Sutherland, Allan T. **Disabled We Stand.** Cambridge, Mass.: Brookline Books, 1984. 159 pp. $17.95 (Paper).

In this thought-provoking work, Sutherland, who has epilepsy, effectively challenges the stereotypes, stigma, and humiliations inflicted by society on people with disabilities. He and others he interviewed articulate convincingly their conviction that people with disabilities should be in charge of decisions affecting their lives. They express their pain and anger at the denial of fundamental human rights to access, employment, and education. (Issues relating to mental disability are not included.)

Taylor, Steven J.; Biklen, Douglas. **Understanding the Law.** Syracuse, N.Y.: Human Policy Press, 1980. 67 pp. $4.25 (Paper).

This advocate's guide to the law and developmental disabilities provides necessary background for the nonlawyer on how the legal system is set up, how it works, how to research the law, and how to build a case.

Williams, Paul; Shoultz, Bonnie. **We Can Speak for Ourselves: Self-Advocacy by Mentally Handicapped People.** London: Souvenir Press; distributed in the U.S. by Brookline, 1982. 245 pp. $17.95 (Paper).

Expectations for people with mental retardation have for too long ignored real possibilities; the self-advocacy movement is proving that people traditionally thought to need the voices of others can speak for themselves. Readers will learn about People First of Oregon, Project 2 of Nebraska, and their English counterparts. Chapters describe the principles of self-advocacy and the group process from its inception through its development; people who are not disabled are only minimally involved as advisers. Particularly impressive are the words of the self-advocates themselves as they describe past history, claim their rights, and work to free their peers from institutions. Parents and professionals will find much food for thought in these fascinating pages.

Where to Write for Information

Children's Defense Fund. 122 C Street, N.W., Washington, DC 20001.

The Children's Defense Fund has long specialized in advocacy for children's rights, exposing federal and state policies and programs which fail children or put them at risk. Send for **94–142 and 504: Numbers That Add Up to Educational Rights for Children with Disabilities** ($6.25),

It's Time to Stand Up for Your Children: A Parent's Guide to Child Advocacy ($1.00), and **Your Child's School Records** ($2.75). Add $1.50 postage and handling for orders under $25.00. The organization's newsletter is called **CDF Reports.**

Federation for Children with Special Needs. 312 Stuart Street, Boston, MA 02116.
    Roots and Wings . . . A Manual about Self-Advocacy costs $5.00.

Mental Health Law Project (MHLP). 2021 L Street, N.W., Suite 800, Washington, DC 20036–4909.
    MHLP is a non-profit, public interest law firm devoted to protecting and expanding the rights of children and adults with mental illness and developmental disabilities. Their newsletter, the Mental Health Law Project **Action Line,** is sent five times a year to people who contribute at least $35.00 annually.

National Association of Protection and Advocacy Systems (NAPAS). 220 Eye Street, N.E., Washington, DC 20202.
    NAPAS can tell you the address of the federally mandated protection and advocacy (P & A) office serving people with disabilities in your state. It responds to individual inquiries and may provide legal assistance. Many state P & A offices circulate newsletters and publications that will be of interest to parents.

National Committee for Citizens in Education (NCCE). 10840 Little Patuxent Parkway, Suite 301, Columbia, MD 21044.
    NCCE is an education-advocacy organization which has organized a Parents' Network open to any individuals or groups interested in improving education for all children. The newsletter is called **Network.** Send for the helpful **Special Education Checkup** to learn what Federal law requires in educating your child.

Office of Civil Rights (OCR). U.S. Department of Education, Room 5000, Switzer Building, 330 C Street, S.W., Washington, DC 20202–1328.
    Free Appropriate Public Education for Students with Handicaps outlines requirements under Section 504 of the Rehabilitation Act of 1973; **The Rights of Individuals under Federal Law** is another OCR publication.

PACER (Parent Advocacy Coalition for Educational Rights) Center, 4876 Chicago Avenue South, Minneapolis, MN 55417–1055.
    This parent organization provides a variety of resources, including a long list of excellent publications. Among their many fine titles are **Parents Can Be the Key . . . To an Appropriate Education for Their Handicapped Child** ($1.00), **Unlocking Doors: A Guide to Effective Communications** ($2.50), and **Thoughts for Those Helping Parents to Become Effective Advocates for Their Children with Handicaps** ($1.00).

Parent Resources on Disabilities (PROD). P.O. Box 14391, Portland, OR 97214.
    PROD is a parent-run organization devoted primarily to advocacy on medical issues for parents of children with disabilities. Its quarterly publication is called **The Bridge** and covers subjects of interest in depth. A year's subscription costs $10.00.

Attitudes

Baum, Dale D., ed. **The Human Side of Exceptionality.** Austin: Pro-Ed, 1982. 283 pp. $21.00 (Paper).

This book is a collection of articles from popular magazines exploring the "humanistic dimensions of handicapping conditions." The book is designed to be used as a supplement in professional training programs and includes commentaries and discussion questions on a variety of disabilities. The selections make interesting reading; many are by parents.

Borba, Michele; Borba, Craig. **Self-Esteem: A Classroom Affair.** New York: Harper & Row, 1978, 1982. 2 vols. Vol. 1: 148 pp. $8.95 (Paper). Vol. 2: 144 pp. $9.95 (Paper).

These charming, helpful books were written to show teachers how to build a child's sense of achievement in the classroom.

Brightman, Alan J., ed. **Ordinary Moments: The Disabled Experience.** Syracuse, N.Y.: Human Policy Press, 1985. 160 pp. $10.95.

This extraordinary book is about people who share what it means to be "a magnet for whispers." Read it slowly and step for a moment into the shoes of another. **Ordinary Moments** uses words and photographs to make the experiences and feelings of eight individuals with physical disabilities intensely real. "First impressions aside," says one, "I'm a lot more like you than you probably imagine." Brightman also includes brief samplings from his favorite books about disability.

Campling, Jo, ed. **Images of Ourselves: Women with Disabilities Talking.** New York: Routledge & Kegan Paul, 1981. 140 pp. $9.95 (Paper).

This is a collection of thoughts and personal insights from twenty-five English women, ranging in age from seventeen to seventy-five, from a variety of backgrounds, with many different disabilities. They talk about their experiences, relationships, sexuality, motherhood, education, employment, and, most significantly, their own attitudes and the attitudes of others toward disability.

DeLoach, Charlene; Greer, Bobby G. **Adjustment to Severe Physical Disability: A Metamorphosis.** New York: McGraw-Hill, 1981. 310 pp. $32.95.

The authors are professors of special education and rehabilitation at Memphis State University and have physical disabilities themselves. They have written this text on "the issues, the attitudes, the barriers, and the debates" of the psycho-social aspects of disability for students, professionals, and families of people with disabilities. Vignettes add to the readability of this interesting book that discusses the societal misconceptions that impede the physical, psychological, and social adjustment of people who have physical disabilities.

Derman-Sparks, Louise; The A.B.C. Task Force. **Anti-Bias Curriculum: Tools for Empowering Young Children.** Washington, D.C.: National Association for the Education of Young Children, 1989. 148 pp. $10.95 (Paper).

A task force of early childhood educators fashioned this fine curriculum to help the youngest children learn about diversity: racial and cultural differences and similarities, gender identity, and disabilities. This is more than a suggested series of activities. Principles and methodology, information about children, anecdotes, photographs, and resources make this a particularly important approach. Teachers will find much help in making their classrooms inclusive environments; parents will learn how to examine their own biases and ensure that their children will be part of a welcoming world.

Dudley, James R. **Living with Stigma: The Plight of the People Who We Label Mentally Retarded.** Springfield, Ill.: Charles C Thomas, 1983. 125 pp. $14.75.

Based on a study of the lives of twenty-seven adults with mental retardation, this important work portrays clearly and movingly the pervasive problems of stigmatization by a world where a wall of misconceptions and prejudice still exist. The community-based service delivery system has brought physical integration but social segregation remains a barrier to full participation by people with mental retardation. The author suggests ways in which people who are assigned "the label" can be empowered.

Eisenberg, Myron G.; Griggins, Cynthia; Duval, Richard J., eds. **Disabled People as Second-Class Citizens.** New York: Springer, 1982. 300 pp. $26.95.

This interesting compilation of articles focusing on the discrimination experienced by people who are physically disabled suggests some remedies.

Fine, Michelle; Asch, Adrienne, eds. **Women with Disabilities: Essays in Psychology, Culture, and Politics.** Philadelphia: Temple University Press, 1988. 347 pp. $34.95.

The work of many fine writers and thinkers is collected to explore how disability and gender interact. The book makes provocative and challenging reading. It raises issues beyond the investigation of disability and sexism; it is a searing look at the way our society treats "difference."

Fox, C. Lynn. **Communicating to Make Friends: A Program for the Classroom Teacher.** Rolling Hills Estates, Calif.: B.L. Winch & Associates, 1980. 125 pp. $9.95 (Paper).

This is a program designed to change the social climate of a classroom. Each student learns to discover and talk about common interests and feelings with a partner through tested classroom activities.

Fox, C. Lynn; Weaver, Francine Lavin. **Unlocking Doors to Friendship.** Rolling Hills Estates, Calif.: B.L. Winch & Associates, 1983. 210 pp. $14.95 (Paper).

These creative activities are designed to help adolescents in grades 7 through 12 explore their attitudes, feelings, and actions toward others, and, in the process, learn to accept and value themselves and their peers. The methods and lesson plans are clear and concise and easily implemented into the regular secondary school curriculum.

Froschl, Merle; Colon, Linda; Rubin, Ellen; Sprung, Barbara. **Including All of Us: An Early Childhood Curriculum about Disability.** New York: Education Equity Concepts; distributed by Gryphon House, 1984. 144 pp. $10.95 (Paper).

Teachers and parents will be heartened by this nonsexist, multicultural guide to three popular preschool through first grade subjects: Same and Different, Body Parts, and Transportation. Hearing impairment, visual disability, and physical disability are incorporated in activities for teaching the traditional units. The guide celebrates individual differences and encourages the development of a positive self-image for all children. Materials are listed and photographs from the classrooms used for the pilot project are included.

Gartner, Alan; Joe, Tom, eds. **Images of the Disabled, Disabling Images.** New York: Praeger, 1987. 218 pp. $35.95.

The editors point out that throughout recorded history people with disabilities have been portrayed as either less or more than human. The collection of essays by a number of scholars and activists examines the ways in which this has happened and how those portrayals affect, and are affected by, public policy. Disability in western literature and television, the newspaper treatment of Baby Doe and Elizabeth Bouvia, education, employment, everyday living, and treatment of the high risk newborn are its subjects. The work calls for a new approach to assure equal rights through coalition-building around issues of broad significance.

Groce, Nora Ellen. **Everyone Here Spoke Sign Language: Hereditary Deafness on Martha's Vineyard.** Cambridge, Mass.: Harvard University Press, 1985. 169 pp. $8.95 (Paper).

For two hundred years, two towns on Martha's Vineyard had a high incidence of hereditary deafness. Based in large part on oral history, this fascinating account discusses the origin and genetics of Vineyard deafness and describes life on the Island in earlier days when people who were deaf were totally integrated and a strong support network existed; as one Vineyarder expressed it, "Those people weren't handicapped; they were just deaf." The author argues persuasively that "disabled people can be full and useful members of a community if the community makes an effort to include them. The society must be willing to change slightly to adapt to all."

Jones, Reginald L., ed. **Reflections on Growing Up Disabled.** Reston, Va.: Council for Exceptional Children, 1983. 103 pp. $10.50 (Paper).

These firsthand perspectives by people with disabilities, as well as the views of parents, are meant to "fill a real void in the attitudinal literature" about children with special needs. Several contributors make compelling arguments against the differential treatment and lowered expectations of sheltered experiences. The final chapter, tracing "the distance traveled" in attitude change by parents over two decades, was authored by the late Peg Morton, to whom this **Reader's Guide** is dedicated.

Stehle, Bernard F. **Incurably Romantic.** Philadelphia: Temple University Press, 1985. 241 pp. $ 29.95.

Photographs and words of couples at a private, total-care institution, once known as "The Philadelphia Home for Incurables," makes it clear that people with physical disabilities can and do have romantic relationships. Viewing the "profound affirmation of . . . [people's] essential normality" challenges stereotypical thought.

Stilma, Lize. **Portraits.** New York: Mosaic Press, 1985. 94 pp. $15.95; $8.95 (Paper).

An amazing Dutch poet paints pictures of real people—people with mental retardation, people with physical handicaps, people with emotional disabilities, people who live in institutions. Through her words of compassion, sensitivity, and insight, she allows us to see who they really are. "How tenderly two people can be in tune . . . When one wants to meet the depth of the other."

Sutherland, Allan T. **Disabled We Stand.** Cambridge, Mass.: Brookline Books, 1984. 159 pp. $17.95 (Paper).

In this thought-provoking work, Sutherland, who has epilepsy, effectively challenges the stereotypes, stigma, and humiliations inflicted by society on people with disabilities. He and others he interviewed articulate convincingly their conviction that people with disabilities should be in charge of decisions affecting their lives. They express their pain and anger at the denial of fundamental human rights to access, employment, and education. (Issues relating to mental disability are not included.)

Ward, Michael J.; Arkell, Robert N.; Dahl, Harry G.; Wise, James H. **Everybody Counts!** Reston, Va.: Council for Exceptional Children, 1979. 73 pp. $14.95 (Paper).

Directions and materials for planning, organizing, and conducting a workshop for adults to increase sensitivity to, and awareness of, the frustrations experienced by people with disabilities are presented. Twenty-five simulation activities are outlined; a tape cassette, "An Unfair Hearing Test," is included.

Wolfensberger, Wolf. **The Origin and Nature of Our Institutional Models.** Syracuse, N.Y.: Human Policy Press, 1975. 88 pp. $5.25 (Paper).

Originally written in 1968, this history of institutions continues to raise issues of importance today. Wolfensberger's examination of the perceptions of people with mental retardation which led to the justification for their segregation quotes from documents of the past and calls for new attitudes. The author has, of course, long been a distinguished and articulate leader in the march toward "normalization," and, more recently, "social role valorization."

Wolfensberger, Wolf. **The Principle of Normalization in Human Services.** Downsview, Ontario: G. Allen Roeher Institute, 1972. 258 pp. $12.50 (Paper).

With four distinguished colleagues—Bengt Nirje, the Swedish originator of the principle of "normalization," Simon Olshansky, Robert Perske, and Phillip Roos—Wolfensberger put together a collection of thoughtful essays on how the concept of normalization can reshape the world in which people with mental retardation live.

Wright, Beatrice A. **Physical Disability—A Psychosocial Approach.** 2d ed. New York: Harper & Row, 1983. 520 pp. $32.50.

Long recognized as an authority on the psychology of adjustment to physical illness and disability, Dr. Wright describes and analyzes the psychosocial sources of positive and negative beliefs by and about people with disabilities. Using numerous examples of life experiences of people with a variety of physical disabilities, and guided by "value-laden beliefs and principles," she indicates the ways in which behavior may be affected by attitudes, reactions of others, and the environment. Written for the practitioner in the field of rehabilitation, this important work will be valuable to families, people with disabilities, and policy-makers, as well.

Zola, Irving Kenneth. **Missing Pieces: A Chronicle of Living with a Disability.** Philadelphia: Temple University Press, 1982. 246 pp. $29.95; $9.95 (Paper).

A "socio-autobiography, a personal and social odyssey that chronicles not only my beginning acknowledgment of the impact of my physical differences on my life but also my growing awareness of the ways in which society invalidates people with a chronic disability" is the way the author describes his book. The framework is a visit to Het Dorp, a sixty-five-acre village specifically designed to house four hundred adult Netherlanders with severe disabilities.

Attitudes—For the Younger Reader

Brown, Tricia; Ortiz, Frank. **Someone Special, Just Like You.** New York: Henry Holt, 1984. 64 pp. $14.95. (Ages 3–6)

Intended to help preschoolers become comfortable with the children with disabilities with whom they will more and more often share classrooms, **Someone Special, Just Like You** offers wonderful black-and-white photographs of children with a variety of disabilities doing all the ordinary things all children enjoy doing. The charming text is a delightful guide to understanding what is really important about all people.

Cohen, Miriam. **See You Tomorrow, Charles.** New York: Greenwillow Books, 1983. Unpaginated. $2.95 (Paper). (Ages 4–7)

One of Miriam Cohen's delightful stories of a first grade class, **See You Tomorrow, Charles** introduces a new student. Charles is blind. The plot is simple and the unstated message will help develop a young child's appreciation of all people.

Exley, Helen, ed. **What It's Like to Be Me.** 2d ed. New York: Friendship Press, 1984. 127 pp. $10.95. (Ages 9–12)

In words and drawings, children and teenagers with disabilities share their thoughts and feelings. Through their work, compiled during the International Year of Disabled People, the contributors make the point in many ways that they do not want to be judged on the basis of disability but rather to be accepted for who they are. "Some think I'm different. I'm not." "I am not my disability, I'm me."

Quinsey, Mary Beth. **Why Does That Man Have Such a Big Nose?** Seattle, Wash.: Parenting Press, 1986. 26 pp. $4.95. (Ages 4–7)

Written "to help parents and teachers foster positive attitudes in children towards all kinds of people," the text and photographs do deal in several instances with disabilities. A helpful note to adults is included.

Schwier, Karin Melberg. **Keith Edward's Different Day.** Downsview, Ontario: G. Allan Roeher Institute, 1988. 28 pp. $4.95 (Paper). (Ages 4–7)

In the course of a day, five-year-old Keith Edward discovers that different isn't bad, "just different!" A parent/teacher discussion guide will help adults who are helping young children develop positive acceptance of people with differences.

Shalom, Debra Buchbinder. **Special Kids Make Special Friends.** Bellmore, N.Y.: Association for Children with Down Syndrome, 1984. 43 pp. $5.00 (Paper). (Ages 3–6)

Written to educate the very young about Down syndrome, this pleasant booklet illustrates, in photographs and text, students learning and playing in their special preschool class. Its emphasis is on their similarities with typical children.

Stein, Sara Bonnett. **About Handicaps: An Open Family Book for Parents and Children Together.** New York: Walker, 1974. 47 pp. $10.95; $6.95 (Paper). (Ages 4–8)

This unique book has separate texts for adults and children. Vivid photographs and a reassuring, honest story explore the relationship between two young boys, one of whom has cerebral palsy. The text for parents provides specific detail and is designed to help adults prepare their children for the realities of the world about them.

Wolf, Bernard. **Don't Feel Sorry for Paul.** New York: Harper & Row, Harper Junior, 1974. 96 pp. $18.50. (Ages 5–8)

Good photographs illustrate the true story of two weeks in the life of seven-year-old Paul, born with his hands and feet incompletely formed. Paul and his family have adapted well to his physical differences; his experiences indicate the need for changes in the attitudes of outsiders.

Yashima, Taro. **Crow Boy.** New York: Viking Penguin, Puffin Books, 1955. Unpaginated. $3.95 (Paper). (Ages 6–10)

In this small book with a big message, a strange, shy boy isolated by his differences from the other children in his Japanese village school, is helped to find his special talents by an understanding teacher.

Where to Write for Information

Channing L. Bete Company. 200 State Road, South Deerfield, MA 01373–0200.

The booklet, **What Everyone Should Know about People with Disabilities,** is 79 cents; a minimum of 25 copies must be ordered. It speaks of the need for changing attitudes in an attractive, easy-to-read format.

Center on Human Policy. Syracuse University, 200 Huntington Hall, Second Floor, Syracuse, NY 13244.

The Center's excellent materials include publications, films, posters, and slide shows designed to help eradicate discriminatory attitudes. Send for a resource catalog.

Educational Equity Concepts. 114 East 32nd Street, New York, NY 10016.

Write for their brochure. It lists interesting materials, such as **Building Community: A Manual Exploring Issues of Women and Disability.**

ERIC Clearinghouse on Handicapped and Gifted Children. Council for Exceptional Children, 1920 Association Drive, Reston, VA 22091–1589.

Being at Ease with Handicapped Children is $1.00.

Governor's Planning Council on Developmental Disabilities. Harrison Building, 143 West Market Street, Suite 404, Indianapolis, IN 46204.

A good booklet to help elementary age students understand developmental disabilities is titled **Awareness Activities.** Write for ordering information.

The Lighthouse. The New York Association for the Blind, 111 East 59th Street, New York, NY 10022–1202.

My Friend Jodi is Blind is a short booklet designed to help young children feel more comfortable with someone who is blind. Send $1.00.

National Easter Seal Society. 70 East Lake Street, Chicago, IL 60601.

The following titles are among those available in the Attitudes/Awareness listing: **Disabling Myths about Disabilities; Myths and Facts about People Who Have Disabilities;** and **Myths and Facts about People without Disabilities.**

National Mental Health Association. 1021 Prince Street, Alexandria, VA 22314.

Send for the pamphlet, **Stigma: A Lack of Awareness and Understanding.** It offers some facts and explodes some myths about mental illness.

PACER (Parent Advocacy Coalition for Educational Rights) Center. 4876 Chicago Avenue South, Minneapolis, MN 55417–1055.

PACER's "COUNT ME IN" Project uses puppets for school disability awareness programs. The written materials for the Project include a **Resource Manual on Disabilities** ($15.00), a **Coordinator's Handbook** ($8.00), a **Secondary Supplement** ($3.00) that includes answers to questions asked by older students about disabilities, and a booklet with stories about seven teenagers with handicapping conditions called **Disabled? Yes. Able? Also, Yes** ($1.50). PACER's materials are consistently good.

Pediatric Projects, Inc. P.O. Box 1880, Santa Monica, CA 90406–9920.

Pediatric Projects, Inc. is an organization helping children to understand health care, illness, disability, and hospitalization. **A Buyer's Guide to Medical Toys and Books** is a quarterly guide to medical toys, books, videos, films, and audiotapes; a one-year subscription is $12.00.

President's Committee on Employment of Persons with Disabilities. 1111 20th Street, N.W., Suite 636, Washington, DC 20036–3470.

People Just Like You—An Activity Guide has activities for every age group aimed at increasing understanding of children and adults with disabilities. The goal is to promote positive self-images for those who have disabilities as well as for those who don't. A single copy is free.

Rochester Institute of Technology. National Technical Institute for the Deaf, Public Information Office, One Lomb Memorial Drive, P.O. Box 9887, Rochester, NY 14623–0887.

A nice booklet is called **TIPS You Can Use When Communicating with Deaf People.**

The Woman's Action Alliance. 370 Lexington Avenue, Suite 603, New York, NY 10017.

Equal Play, a national journal on nonsexist education, features major issues in educational equity for children. An early issue of the journal was called **Mainstreaming Disabled Children.** It is still available for $4.50.

Behavior Modification

There is no shortage of books on behavior modification. Most of them are written for the use of parents and teachers encountering "normal" but nonetheless difficult to manage behavior problems with children in the home or in the classroom. In general, these books outline the principles of behavior change, tell how to collect baseline data, how to choose and use reinforcers, and how to carry out the strategies for changing the troublesome behaviors.

There are books for trainers of parents. Others are written expressly for parents. Some are designed specifically for parents of children with special needs. And a few describe techniques that are non-punishing to use with people with the most challenging behaviors.

Of the titles listed, any would be a good resource for parents interested in learning about behavior modification. Those with a more specific, less general, focus are annotated.

Baldwin, Victor L.; Fredericks, H.D. Bud; Brodsky, Gerry. **Isn't It Time He Outgrew This? A Training Program for Parents of Retarded Children.** Springfield, Ill.: Charles C Thomas, 1973. 230 pp. $15.00.

Becker, Wesley C. **Parents Are Teachers: A Child Management Program.** Champaign, Ill.: Research Press, 1971. 194 pp. $10.95 (Paper).

Lovett, Herbert. **Cognitive Counseling and Persons with Special Needs: Adapting Behavioral Approaches to the Social Context.** New York: Praeger, 1985. 160 pp. $29.95; $16.95 (Paper).

This is a significant and articulate work that promotes respect for the dignity of human beings and argues for techniques for helping individuals achieve appropriate behavior control without punitive intervention. Lovett works from the premise that the person best suited to set behavioral limits is the individual with the "inappropriate" behavior and that only by forming a working relationship with that person can one hope to be helpful. He shares a number of anecdotal examples of people with severe disabilities who respond to being taught "ordinary, dignified social responsibility."

McGee, John J.; Menolascino, Frank J.; Hobbs, Daniel C.; Menousek, Paul E. **Gentle Teaching: A Nonaversive Approach for Helping with Mental Retardation.** Richmond Hill, Ontario: Human Services Press, 1987. 204 pp. $24.95.

The authors suggest an alternative to the "mechanistic and authoritarian approach" of some caregivers to persons with aggressive or self-injurious behaviors. Ignoring those behaviors, redirecting, and rewarding positive change results instead in bonding between the caregiver and the individual. A number of examples are offered and answers to frequently asked questions are given. Parents will find the book useful in helping people who work with their sons and daughters with challenging behaviors to find an approach that precludes punishment.

Patterson, Gerald R. **Families: Applications of Social Learning to Family Life.** Champaign, Ill.: Research Press, 1975. 171 pp. $10.95 (Paper).

Patterson, Gerald R. **Living with Children: New Methods for Parents and Teachers.** Champaign, Ill.: Research Press, 1976. 114 pp. $9.95 (Paper).

Rioux, Marcia H.; Yarmol-Franko, Karen, eds. **The Language of Pain.** Downsview, Ontario: G. Allan Roeher Institute, 1988. 180 pp. $14.95 (Paper).

> This collection of essays explores the consequences of the use of aversive conditioning techniques—punishment—as a form of "therapy" to control and modify the behavior of people with mental retardation. Canada's National Institute for the Study of Public Policy examines the issue from the viewpoint of doctors, lawyers, psychologists, and the people and their families who have experienced aversive procedures—the language of pain. The authors articulate the social, ethical, legal, scientific, and personal reasons for finding other ways to change behavior.

Turecki, Stanley. **The Different Child: A New Step by Step Approach for Understanding and Managing Your Hard-to-Raise Child.** New York: Bantam, 1987. 240 pp. $6.95 (Paper).

> The "difficult" child is not necessarily a child with a disability. A child with a disability can, however, be temperamentally difficult. Child psychiatrist Stanley Turecki defines the factors that make for difficulty and details the management strategies that can make a difference. Clear advice and numerous examples abound.

Computer Technology and Technical Aids

Levin, Jackie; Scherfenberg, Lynn. **Breaking Barriers: How Children and Adults with Severe Handicaps Can Access the World through Simple Technology.** Minneapolis: Ablenet, 1986. 66 pp. $13.95 (Paper).

Simple technology can increase access to new experiences, activities, and environments for people of all ages with severe physical or mental disabilities. This helpful booklet shares creative ways that automated learning devices can be used in home, school, work, and community settings. It also lists "device manufacturers" and "adaptable toys."

Levin, Jackie; Scherfenberg, Lynn. **Selection and Use of Simple Technology in Home, School, Work, and Community Settings.** Minneapolis, MN: Ablenet, 1987. 88 pp. $17.95 (Spiral-bound).

This booklet is designed to help parents and teachers make decisions about the most appropriate technology to use for the learning and functional independence of people with severe physical disabilities. It describes automated learning devices and discusses how to analyze objectives, abilities, and barriers, and decide on solutions. A number of case studies and resources are included.

LINC Associates. **The Specialware Directory, 2nd Edition: A Guide to Software for Special Education.** Columbus, Ohio: LINC Associates, 1986. 160 pp. $22.50 (Paper).

Computer technology is proving to be a significant educational boon for students with disabilities. This comprehensive directory identifies more than three hundred software programs for special education. Indexes will help the user to locate programs to match specific skill needs and exceptionality; a directory of publishers and distributors also appears.

The Nordic Committee on Disability. **The More We Do Together: Adapting the Environment for Children with Disabilities.** New York: World Rehabilitation Fund, 1985. 84 pp. $5.00 (Paper).

Charming illustrations are plentiful in this delightful monograph that presents technical aids to assist children with physical, visual, and hearing impairments in their homes, schools, and communities. Translated from Swedish, this booklet includes a lengthy listing of suppliers and resources in the United States.

Pressman, Harvey, ed. **Making an Exceptional Difference: Enhancing the Impact of Microcomputer Technology on Children with Disabilities.** Boston: The Exceptional Parent Press, 1987. 300 pp. $24.95 (Paper).

This collection of articles, illustrating the new possibilities that computer technology is offering people with disabilities, provides much practical information. Readers can learn from stories of individuals and research and demonstration projects how computers have been used successfully with very young children with disabilities, children with communication impairments, older children with mental, physical, and emotional disabilities, and adults looking for employment opportunities. Helpful chapters on choosing "the right stuff" and contact information on resources, publications, and commercial vendors adds to the book's usefulness.

Where to Write for Information

Ablenet. 1081 Tenth Avenue, S.E., Minneapolis, MN 55414.

Send for their catalog; it offers products and identifies toys and games to promote integration for people with disabilities. **ALDetails** is a quarterly publication that focuses on applications of automated learning devices for play/leisure, domestic, vocational, and learning environments for persons with severe disabilities.

Canadian Rehabilitation Council for the Disabled. International Secretariat, One Yonge Street, Suite 2110, Toronto, Ontario M5E 1E5, Canada.

Write for ordering information for a booklet titled **Activities Using Headsticks and Optical Pointers: A Description of Methods**.

National Library Service for the Blind and Physically Handicapped. Library of Congress, Washington, DC 20542.

The free library service for "Talking Books," books recorded on tape and played on a free loaned cassette player, can be a most valuable resource for learning and for leisure time. Write for information.

Death, Dying, and Grieving

Burton, Lindy, ed. **Care of the Child Facing Death.** New York: Routledge & Kegan Paul, 1974. 225 pp. $19.95.

    This book illuminates the problems of parents and others involved in the care of a dying child. Personal accounts illustrate the devastation inflicted on a family by the loss of a child, but the authors also concentrate attention on the positive contributions that can be made by loving parents towards helping the dying child experience the most in the life that remains to him. The book is divided into sections dealing with fatal diseases of childhood, specific problems of such illnesses, helping the child, and, finally, helping the parent.

Deford, Frank. **Alex: The Life of a Child.** New York: New American Library, 1984. 208 pp. $3.50 (Paper).

    A father starts and ends his book with the death of his daughter at age eight of cystic fibrosis. He writes of the charm and the joy of a most extraordinary child. He writes of loving, of missing, of anger. This is not grim writing; Deford is wonderfully gifted and there are moments of humor along with the anguish. **Alex** is deeply touching and profoundly moving.

Farnsworth, Elizabeth Brooks. **Journey through Grief.** Atlanta: Susan Hunter Publishing, 1988. 84 pp. $7.95 (Paper).

    This small book shares—in narrative and poetry—the story of a family that survived the birth and death of a son with Down syndrome and heart disease. How this mother worked through her early grieving feelings may prove helpful to others.

Friedman, Rochelle; Gradstein, Bonnie. **Surviving Pregnancy Loss.** Boston: Little, Brown, 1982. 244 pp. $16.45; $10.95 (Paper).

    This is an empathetic and helpful book for those who live through the overwhelming experience of losing a pregnancy.

Grollman, Earl A. **Talking about Death: A Dialogue between Parent and Child.** Boston: Beacon, 1976. 98 pp. $6.95 (Paper).

    Written to help parents explain death to a child, the main text is meant to be read to or with the child. The parents' portion of the book covers various topics such as a child's loss of a sibling, suicide, and how adults can face bereavement.

Grollman, Sharon. **Shira: A Legacy of Courage.** New York: Doubleday, 1988. 84 pp. $12.95. (Ages 10 and up)

    Shira Putter died at the age of nine from a very rare form of diabetes. This book shares the child's poems and thoughts and uses personal accounts from her family and friends to create a journal about her short life in and out of hospitals. Shira was "smart, spunky, funny . . . gifted and unique." **Shira** is a real and moving portrait.

Klaus, Marshall H.; Kennell, John H. **Parent-Infant Bonding: The Impact of Early Separation or Loss on Family Development.** 2d ed. St. Louis: C.V. Mosby, 1982. 314 pp. $18.95 (Paper).

    The potential for closeness, richness, and beauty of the bond formed between a mother or father and her or his newborn baby and the impact of separation or loss are topics of this study. Chapters on caring for parents of infants with congenital malformations, premature or sick infants, or infants who die, describe the range of reactions and how sensitive and understanding physicians and other medical professionals can ease the impact and help families deal with their distress.

Kushner, Harold S. **When Bad Things Happen to Good People.** New York: Avon Books, 1981. 149 pp. $6.95 (Paper).

    Rabbi Kushner's son died of a rare and dreadful disease, progeria (premature aging). Struggling to make sense of this tragedy, the author has written his book for people who "want to believe in God's goodness and fairness but find it hard." The book has proved of comfort to many.

Levy, Erin Linn. **Children Are Not Paper Dolls: A Visit with Bereaved Siblings.** Incline Village, Nev.: Publishers Mark, 1982. 121 pp. $8.95 (Paper).

    Children, too, go through a grieving process when a brother or sister dies. Pictures and quotes in this book are shared by six bereaved siblings. They address the subjects of funerals, family, friends, school, feelings, and holidays. The book offers significant and important understanding.

Martinson, Ida Marie, ed. **Home Care for the Dying Child: Professional Approaches.** Brooklyn: Center for Thanatology Research, 1976. 332 pp. $9.95 (Paper).

    This is a collection of chapters on various aspects of home care of a dying child, including descriptions of specific cases and model programs for care. One section deals with the family's reaction to death. The essays are sensitively written, comprehensive, and practical.

Miller, Robyn. **Robyn's Book: A True Diary.** New York: Scholastic, 1986. 179 pp. $2.75 (Paper).

    Robyn Miller was born with cystic fibrosis and, surprisingly, experienced good health for her first sixteen years. For the five years that remained to her, things were very different. Her remarkable journal shares her pain, the loss of friends, her feeling of being lucky "to have the day," her understanding of the magic that is life. **Robyn's Book** is powerful and extraordinary writing; it has much to say.

Schiff, Harriet Sarnoff. **The Bereaved Parent: A Book of Counsel for Those Who Suffer This Heartbreaking Experience.** New York: Crown, 1987. 160 pp. $14.95. New York: Penguin, 1978. $6.95 (Paper).

    From her own experience of losing a ten-year-old son to death, Sarnoff has created a survival guide for others. It is practical, compassionate, powerful.

Schwiebert, Pat; Kirk, Paul. **Still to be Born: A Guide for Bereaved Parents Who Are Making Decisions about Their Future.** 2d ed. Portland, Oreg.: Perinatal Loss, 1985. 112 pp. $3.25 (Paper).

    For those who have experienced the tragedy of losing a baby, a nurse and doctor have prepared an understanding, compassionate guide. Parents write of their feelings and their fears. The authors give coping suggestions, and offer hope. **When Hello Means Goodbye,** from the same writing team, is a guide for parents whose child dies before birth, at birth, or shortly after birth.

Stinson, Robert and Peggy. **The Long Dying of Baby Andrew.** Boston: Little, Brown, 1983. 375 pp. $17.95.

Andrew Stinson was born sixteen weeks prematurely, and, through a succession of medical calamities, was kept alive for nearly six months. His parents chronicle the long days and their individual reactions. Brutal, painful, and honest, their book raises important ethical questions about doctor decisions, parent rights, and the routine use of sophisticated neonatal technology.

Where to Write for Information

Centering Corporation. P.O. Box 3367, Omaha, NE 68103–0367.

Write for their catalog. It carries a large number of low-priced and well-written booklets dealing with grief, miscarriage, stillbirth, and infant death. Their quarterly newsletter is called **Caring Concepts.**

Compassion Book Service. 216 Via Monte, Walnut Creek, CA 94598.

If you cannot find the book you're looking for, send for their catalog; they are a comprehensive distributor of books on all aspects of death and dying.

Medic Publishing Company. P.O. Box 89, Redmond, WA 98073–0090.

A short and very fine booklet called **Sibling Grief: How Parents Can Help the Child Whose Brother or Sister Has Died** is filled with excellent and helpful suggestions. Write for ordering information.

Integration*

Berres, Michael S.; Knoblock, Peter, eds. **Program Models for Mainstreaming: Integrating Students with Moderate to Severe Disabilities.** Austin: Pro-Ed, 1987. 311 pp. $31.00.

The chapter contributors believe that both social and instructional integration is possible for all students; they are, for the most part, educators working to prove that segregated, exclusionary practices are unnecessary. They postulate that integration largely depends upon the attitudes and problem-solving skills of educators and that these attitudes are at least as important as the skills of students. Beyond the philosophy and the program descriptions, this fine book also offers a planning process and examples of how change might occur. Students in the programs described include those with visual, hearing, and orthopedic disabilities, as well as autism, serious behavioral disturbance, and developmental disability. Two chapters deal with preschool integration.

Biklen, Douglas; Bogdan, Robert; Ferguson, Dianne L.; Searl, Sanford J., Jr.; Taylor, Steven J. **Achieving the Complete School: Strategies for Effective Mainstreaming.** New York: Teachers College Press, 1985. 206 pp. $15.95 (Paper).

Biklen and his co-authors have marshalled the arguments, suggested the ways, and written a practical, readable guide for parents, district administrators, principals, and teachers who want to make integration of students with special needs into typical schools a reality. They acknowledge the barriers to mainstreaming and share specific principles, strategies, organizational methods, and vignettes that illustrate that those barriers can be toppled. The comprehensive set of recommendations are based on data from successful programs in real schools and classrooms across the country.

Biklen, Douglas; Ferguson, Philip; Ford, Alison. **Schooling and Disability.** Chicago: NSSE; distributed by Paul H. Brookes, 1988. 281 pp. $27.00.

This Eighty-Eighth Yearbook of the National Society for the Study of Education offers a comprehensive view of the issues in special education today. It explores the potential relationship between special and "regular" education, defines the goals of education for students with disabilities, examines current effective educational practice, and raises "broad issues of ideology and policy." Parent perspectives are included. Written for educators, **Schooling and Disability** should prove of interest to any reader concerned about the state of education today.

Crossley, Rosemary; McDonald, Anne. **Annie's Coming Out.** New York: Penguin, 1980. 256 pp. $6.95 (Paper).

Born with cerebral palsy, Anne McDonald lived in an Australian institution for people with profound retardation from the ages of three to eighteen. Rosemary Crossley, a ward assistant, helped Annie to establish communication, to assert her independence, and, in a case that went to the country's Supreme Court, to move into the community. This is their story; it speaks to important medical and societal issues. Both women are articulate and passionate spokespeople.

---

* For books relating to the integration of students with hearing impairments, refer to the section "Your Child at School" in the category on *Hearing Impairments*.

Evans, Daryl Paul. **The Lives of Mentally Retarded People.** Boulder, Colo.: Westview Press, 1983. 306 pp. $42.00; $15.95 (Paper).

This interesting, helpful, and sympathetic account of how integration into community life is experienced by those so long excluded is written from the perspective of a sociologist who has spent significant time in classrooms, workplaces, residential homes, and institutions. For his discussion of education, social psychology of mental retardation, the family, rights, the occupational world, residential lives, the judicial and penal systems, sexuality, marriage, geriatrics, and prevention, he uses literature, his own observations, and learnings from the people he has interviewed.

Forest, Marsha. **Education/Integration: A Collection of Readings on the Integration of Children with Mental Handicaps into Regular School Systems.** Downsview, Ontario: G. Allan Roeher Institute, 1984. 87 pp. $12.00 (Paper).

This delightful collection of articles and ideas about integration stems from the author's deep conviction that children with disabilities belong in typical classrooms in regular schools in their home communities. **Education/Integration** describes model programs, shares rationale for integration, discusses strategies, and answers the arguments of skeptics. There is much to learn here from different points of view.

Forest, Marsha, ed. **More Education/Integration: A Further Collection of Readings on the Integration of Children with Mental Handicaps into Regular School Systems.** Downsview, Ontario: G. Allan Roeher Institute, 1987. 176 pp. $15.00 (Paper).

A second collection of articles offers further arguments for the integration of students labeled disabled into typical schools. One particularly helpful chapter called "The Kaleidoscope: Challenge to the Cascade" describes MAPS—an approach to help team members plan for the integration of students with challenging needs into typical, age-appropriate classrooms. There are many quotable entries.

Gold, Deborah; McGill, Judith, eds. **The Pursuit of Leisure: Enriching Lives with People Who Have a Disability.** Downsview, Ontario: G. Allan Roeher Institute, 1988. 111 pp. $12.50.

This is a provocative and exciting look at the advantages integrated leisure opportunities provide, shared by parents, people who have lived with labels, friends, and advocates. They are all clear in their commitment to participation and inclusion in the life of one's community. Beyond the many strategies for sponsoring activities, parents will find a wealth of ideas to support or shape their individual thinking about what real integration means.

Gollay, Elinor; Freedman, Ruth; Wyngaarden, Marty; Kurtz, Norman R. **Coming Back: The Community Experiences of Deinstitutionalized Mentally Retarded People.** Cambridge, Mass.: Abt Books, 1978. 227 pp. $30.00.

Coming Back presents the results of a study of over four hundred people with mental retardation who, in the early years of the deinstitutionalization movement, left institutions to live in various settings in the community. Through their own words and through the author's analysis of data, the reader learns about where they live, what they do, and how they feel about their new lives. The results of the study should reassure those who may still be apprehensive about the risks of community living. The study also illuminates the main reasons for failures, as true today as they were a dozen years ago; insufficient support services and lack of job opportunities are high on the list.

Groce, Nora Ellen. **Everyone Here Spoke Sign Language: Hereditary Deafness on Martha's Vineyard.** Cambridge, Mass.: Harvard University Press, 1985. 169 pp. $8.95 (Paper).

For two hundred years, two towns on Martha's Vineyard Island had a high incidence of hereditary deafness. Based in large part on oral history, this fascinating account discusses the origin and genetics of Vineyard deafness and describes life on the Island in earlier days when people who were deaf were totally integrated and a strong support network existed; as one Vineyarder expressed it, "Those people weren't handicapped; they were just deaf." The author argues persuasively that "disabled people can be full and useful members of a community if the community makes an effort to include them. The society must be willing to change slightly to adapt to all."

Hutchison, Peggy; Lord, John. **Recreation Integration: Issues and Alternatives in Leisure Services and Community Involvement.** Leisurability Publications; distributed by G. Allan Roeher Institute, 1979. 152 pp. $14.00 (Paper).

Two Canadian authors make convincing arguments that people of all ages with disabilities belong in the mainstream of community activities, that physical integration can help to facilitate social integration, and that with proper planning, development, and action, communities can make a significant difference in the lives of all their members. Parents can help in the process by being involved advocates, community educators, and team members with service systems; this book describes how. Published in 1979, it is still right on target.

Kunc, Norman. **Ready, Willing, and Disabled.** Toronto, Ontario: Personal Library; distributed by G. Allan Roeher Institute, 1981. 111 pp. $12.00 (Paper).

The author, who was born with cerebral palsy, writes of the process of integrating a student with a physical handicap into a regular classroom. He proposes viewing this situation as one in which a teacher has a class of students to educate and that one of them has special needs and requirements. The problem, then, is not the student with the disability but rather an environment not set up for inclusion. His book is filled with insights, practical advice, and stories drawn from his own experience.

Lipsky, Dorothy Kerzner; Gartner, Alan, eds. **Beyond Separate Education: Quality Education for All.** Baltimore: Paul H. Brookes, 1989. 302 pp. $32.00.

The editors believe that schools can be organized so that students of varying skills can work and learn together successfully and profit from the integration. They see school reform and the use of good educational practices as a societal imperative. Chapters by a number of articulate authors cover the background and current situation, discuss a variety of possible educational practices, speak to the role of teachers, parents, and students, and outline next steps. This is a fascinating look at what schools are and could be doing.

Long, Kate. **Johnny's Such a Bright Boy, What a Shame He's Retarded: In Support of Mainstreaming in Public Schools.** Boston: Houghton Mifflin, 1977. 361 pp. $4.95 (Paper).

    The author uses a fictional story of a warm, sensible special education supervisor to dramatize the painful effects on children of labeling and placement in segregated schools and classes. The book is interspersed with chapters giving information about the issues involved in mainstreaming. Altogether, the result is a very engrossing work in support of integrating children as much as possible with their typical peers.

Lord, John. **Participation: Expanding Community and Leisure Experiences for People with Severe Handicaps.** Downsview, Ontario: G. Allan Roeher Institute, 1981. 75 pp. $12.50 (Paper).

    This Canadian resource was "designed to assist communities in the initiation, planning, and implementation of a *process* for expanding community and leisure experiences to include people with severe handicaps." It outlines clearly and helpfully the "whys" and "how to's" in sponsoring a supportive and cooperative community.

Murray-Seegert, Carola. **Nasty Girls, Thugs, and Humans Like Us: Social Relations between Severely Disabled and Nondisabled Students in High School.** Baltimore: Paul H. Brookes, 1989. 198 pp. $22.00.

    The author, a special education teacher who has studied anthropology, spent one year as a classroom volunteer in an inner-city high school in San Francisco where she got to know teenagers involved in a special education program designed to encourage interactions between students with severe intellectual disabilities and their typical peers. While "dump and hope" programs that merely place students with and without disabilities in the same settings are unlikely to promote positive social relations, this doctoral study confirms that with systematic intervention students without disabilities can experience positive academic and social outcomes. Planned integration works for everyone. This is engaging reading with important implications.

Pancsofar, Ernest; Blackwell, Robert. **A User's Guide to Community Entry for the Severely Handicapped.** Albany: State University of New York Press, 1986. 182 pp. $18.95 (Paper).

    This text for planners of residential services, administrators, and direct care staff will be quite helpful to families exploring or evaluating community residential options. The authors write of quality-of-life issues; they also offer practical guidance about financial, procedural, and programmatic concerns.

Pappanikou, H.J.; Paul, James L., eds. **Mainstreaming Emotionally Disturbed Children.** Syracuse, N.Y.: Syracuse University Press, 1981. 139 pp. $9.95.

    Thoughtful arguments concerning the problems and benefits of mainstreaming a child with an emotional disability into the regular classroom are presented. The book discusses the perils of wholesale mainstreaming as well as the advantages of selective mainstreaming.

Perske, Robert. **Circles of Friends.** Nashville: Abingdon, 1988. 94 pp. $9.95 (Paper).

    Written by Robert Perske, illustrated by Martha Perske, **Circle of Friends** is a loving look at how "people with disabilities and their friends enrich the lives of one another." As with all the Perske books, profound messages are delivered in its easy-to-read, delightful-to-look-at pages.

Perske, Robert. **New Life in the Neighborhood.** Nashville: Abingdon, 1980. 78 pp. $9.95 (Paper).

This book offers compelling discussion to demonstrate "how persons with retardation and other disabilities can help make a good community better." Martha Perske's sensitive and charming illustrations complement the descriptions of "normalized environments."

Reynolds, Maynard C.; Birch, Jack W. **Adaptive Mainstreaming: A Primer for Teachers and Principals.** 3d ed. New York: Longman, 1988. 396 pp. $22.95.

Intended for educators, this revision of a significant textbook challenges typical schools to become more effective and adaptive. The authors give cogent argument and strategies for accommodating students with learning disabilities, educable mental retardation, and behavior problems, as well as those with speech and language, hearing, visual, physical, and health impairments in the mainstream. Adaptive instruction in regular classes and activities in neighborhood schools, they contend, is "feasible, desirable, and economical now for most exceptional children."

Sailor, Wayne; Anderson, Jacki L.; Halvorsen, Ann T.; Doering, Kathy; Filler, John; Goetz, Lori. **The Comprehensive Local School: Regular Education for All Students with Disabilities.** Baltimore: Paul H. Brookes, 1989. 274 pp. $33.00.

Studies were conducted from 1982 to 1987 by the California Research Institute on Integration of Students with Severe Handicaps. Analysis was also made by CRI of the literature regarding the education of students with mild disabilities. The authors of this detailed work believe the least restrictive environment the field of education has to offer is the comprehensive local school—the public school a student would attend if he or she did not need special education services. They propose a five-phase model: mainstreaming the youngest children, integrated educational services, community intensive instruction, transition from school to work and community service, and integrated supported work and community living.

Schleien, Stuart J.; Ray, M. Tipton. **Community Recreation and Persons with Disabilities: Strategies for Integration.** Baltimore: Paul H. Brookes, 1988. 277 pp. $25.95 (Paper).

The authors provide a practical and philosophical basis for including children and adults with disabilities in already-existing community recreational activities. They describe the planning process, the implementation, and the evaluation of integrated leisure services. Tools for problem solving and strategizing are included. Six exemplary programs in Minnesota are presented. For professionals and for families wishing to influence professionals in ensuring full participation in the leisure life of a community for *all* its citizens, this textbook should prove most helpful.

Stainback, Susan; Stainback, William; Forest, Marsha. **Educating All Students in the Mainstream of Regular Education.** Baltimore: Paul H. Brookes, 1989. 286 pp. $34.00.

The editors and chapter contributors look at the merger of special and regular education as necessary and possible. They refuse to settle for anything less than true "integration, oneness, belonging, and an egalitarian, quality system of education for all students and teachers." This would mean modifying the way resources are allocated as well as reassigning students. An historical overview and rationale for merger are presented. Case histories and working examples are shared. Organizational strategies, educational practices, and friendship support systems (MAPS) are spelled out. The book also discusses family and community support. In short, this provocative textbook offers reasons why merger should happen and strategies for how it can happen. It is practical and readable.

Stainback, Susan; Stainback, William. **Integration of Students with Severe Handicaps into Regular Schools.** Reston, Va.: Council for Exceptional Children, 1985. 145 pp. $17.00 (Paper).

  The authors have written elsewhere of their "personal belief that the special/regular education dichotomy that now exists will one day be dissolved." Until that happens, special efforts to integrate students with severe handicaps into typical neighborhood schools will have to be made. This persuasive, coherent work discusses why integration should happen, what teachers need to know to make it happen, practical ways to promote positive interaction, why and how to educate nonhandicapped students about individual differences, training students with severe handicaps in social skills, the use of peers, integration in community settings, and model program strategies.

Stainback, William; Stainback, Susan, eds. **Support Networks for Inclusive Schooling: Interdependent Integrated Education.** Baltimore: Paul H. Brookes, 1990. 259 pp. $24.00 (Paper).

  How to support all students in the mainstream of school and community life is the focus of this practical, readable book, designed to help teachers and administrators turn their schools into welcoming environments. What inclusive schooling is, how a number of support options (including peer friendships, peer tutoring, cooperative learning, team teaching, and collaborative consultation) can be used, and the development of caring and supportive schools and communities are the subjects of sixteen chapters written by a number of contributors who are involved in making integrated education happen.

Taylor, Steven J.; Biklen, Douglas; Knoll, James, eds. **Community Integration for People with Severe Disabilities.** New York: Teachers College Press, 1987. 231 pp. $31.95; $21.00 (Paper).

  State of the art in community integration of people with severe disabilities has taken our society beyond debating issues of whether people should live in institutions to an examination of how people with the most challenging needs can *best* be served in the community. Chapter contributors share exciting examples, describe new possibilities, promote real relationships. Based on "deeply held beliefs and values," this provocative work speaks with conviction and passion.

Taylor, Steven J.; Racino, Julie A.; Knoll, James A.; Lutfiyya, Zana. **The Nonrestrictive Environment: On Community Integration for People with the Most Severe Disabilities.** Syracuse, N.Y.: Human Policy Press, 1987. 112 pp. $8.95 (Paper).

  This manual, developed at The Center on Human Policy at Syracuse University, makes compelling arguments for abandoning the continuum concept, which assumes a progression from the most to the least restrictive environments as people learn the appropriate skills. It outlines basic principles for community integration, describes model programs, and offers ideas, strategies, and resources for serving people with the most severe disabilities in integrated community environments. Parents and professionals will find this discussion thoughtful, reasoned, articulate, and well-organized.

Zigler, Richard. **Principals and Principles of Integration: A Practical Guide for School Level Administrators to Develop Integration Practices for Children with Severe and Multiple Handicaps.** Peace River, Alberta: Zigler Keyes Associates, 1989. 172 pp. $32.90 (Paper).

As the subtitle implies, **Principals and Principles of Integration** goes beyond a presentation of philosophy. Following an overview of the history of the integration movement, it settles into a discussion of the concerns and the role of a principal and how that principal can develop strategies and influence staff in a smooth transition to an integrated educational system. Many suggestions are included. School board members, superintendents, central and local administrators, and teachers will learn much from this comprehensive handbook.

Where to Write for Information

Association for Persons in Supported Employment (APSE). P.O. Box 27523, Richmond, VA 23261–7523.

APSE was formed to promote the concept of paid integrated employment and full community participation for all individuals. Parent membership is welcomed. A newsletter, **The Advance,** is published quarterly. Regular membership is $35.00; $20.00 for a person with a disability.

Association for Retarded Citizens Minnesota. 3225 Lyndale Avenue South, Minneapolis, MN 55408.

For one dollar, you can receive a most helpful parent handbook called **Integration in Action: Achieving an Integrated School Program.**

California Research Institute on the Integration of Students with Severe Disabilities. San Francisco State University, 612 Font Boulevard, San Francisco, CA 94132.

Send for a listing of the **Written Products from Activities of the California Research Institute on the Integration of Students with Severe Disabilities. Strategies** is a quarterly bulletin that documents and promotes the process of statewide systems change.

Center for Urban Affairs and Policy Research. Publications Department, Northwestern University, 2040 Sheridan Road, Evanston, IL 60208.

Mary O'Connell's **The Gift of Hospitality: Opening the Doors of Community Life to People with Disabilities** tells the stories of people with disabilities who have gotten connected with others in their communities and in the process have found their way out of isolation. Service systems cannot provide the answer. Sometimes it takes family, sometimes friends, always an imaginative, committed person. This wonderful booklet does not pretend community is without risks: it acknowledges that community is "messy." It does, however, make it very clear that when people share "a common humanity," everyone is "changed, softened, enriched." The booklet sells for $4.00. Ask about their other publications.

Center on Human Policy, Research and Training Center on Community Integration. Syracuse University, 200 Huntington Hall, Second Floor, Syracuse, NY 13244.

The Center on Human Policy distributes many excellent and significant resource materials, site visit reports, monographs, and bibliographies about the integration of people with severe disabilities into community life. Send for their complete publication list; it is filled with interesting items available for the cost of reproduction and postage. Among them is a set of **Materials on Integrated School Programs for Students with Severe Disabilities;** it looks at the literature dealing with principles and practices, offers a bibliography on integrated school programs, and lists several existing programs and consultants for integrated school models.

Centre for Integrated Education and Community. 35 Jackes Avenue, Toronto, Ontario M4T 1E2, Canada.

The Centre is a team of educators in Canada who are committed to helping school systems and communities welcome all people. The MAPS planning strategy and the development of Support Circles and Circles of Friends have come from their efforts. **Action for Inclusion: How to Improve Schools by Welcoming Children with Special Needs into Regular Classrooms** describes the process from dream to reality ($10.00).

Communitas, Inc. 73 Indian Drive, Manchester, CT 06040.

Communitas is an international group to help those interested in integrating people with disabilities into community life to network with one another and share information and stories. Two wonderful monographs by Beth Mount, Pat Beeman, and George Ducharme are **What Are We Learning about Circles of Support? A Collection of Tools, Ideas, and Reflections on Building and Facilitating Circles of Support** and **What Are We Learning about Bridge-Building? A Summary of a Dialogue between People Seeking to Build Community for People with Disabilities.** They are $6.00 apiece.

Educational Equity Concepts. 114 East 32nd Street, New York, NY 10016.

Write for their brochure. It lists interesting materials, such as the **Inclusive Resource Packet,** three reprints to facilitate mainstreaming.

ERIC Clearinghouse on Handicapped and Gifted Children. Council for Exceptional Children, 1920 Association Drive, Reston, VA 22091–1589.

Send $1.00 each for **Least Restrictive Environment; Fostering Peer Acceptance of Handicapped Students;** and **Adapting Instructional Materials for Mainstreamed Students.**

Federation for Children with Special Needs, Technical Assistance for Parent Programs (TAPP). 312 Stuart Street, Boston, MA 02116.

Send for **Purposeful Integration . . . Inherently Equal,** by Douglas Biklen, Susan Lehr, Stanford J. Searl, and Steven J. Taylor. It is a clear, common-sense approach to school integration with a wealth of practical guidance, advice for parents, and illustrative examples as well as a discussion of the history of the "least restrictive environment" concept and what current thinking should be. The booklet sells for $5.00. Another important manual is **Least Restrictive Environment: Questions and Answers.**

Institute on Community Integration. University of Minnesota, Pattee Hall, 150 Pillsbury Drive, S.E., Minneapolis, MN 55455.

The Institute has several publications regarding integrated education that will be of real help to parents in designing an educational program in a typical setting for their child. **Learning Together: Stories and Strategies** (first copy free) shares experiences and insights of parents, teachers, and friends of children with disabilities. **Strategies for Full Inclusion** ($10.00) contains seven papers that present examples for designing and implementing educational programs of full inclusion. The Institute also circulates an annotated guide called **Integrated Education for Learners with Severe Disabilities: Print and Media Resources** ($3.00).

The Institute for the Study of Developmental Disabilities. Indiana University, 2853 East Tenth Street, Bloomington, IN 47405.

The Institute offers a number of fine publications regarding public school integration. Titles include **A Catalog of Alternative Performance Systems for High School Students with Severe Handicaps; A New Future for Children with Substantial Handicaps: The Second Wave of 'Least Restrictive Environment';** and **Proceedings of National Leadership Conference 1987: Least Restrictive Environment: Commitment to Implementation.**

LaGrange Area Department of Special Education. 1301 Cossitt Avenue, LaGrange, IL 60525.

A delightful brochure, **Total Integration: Neighborhood Schools,** costs 50 cents.

Mississippi University Affiliated Programs for Persons with Developmental Disabilities. University of Southern Mississippi, Southern Station Box 5163, Hattiesburg, MS 39406–5163.

A series of single-concept fliers designed for both parents and school personnel is called **Providing Services for Students with Moderate and Severe Handicaps.** One title is **How Can Students Be Integrated?**

Montgomery County (Maryland) Public Schools. Division of Supply and Property Management, 550 North Stonestreet Avenue, Rockville, MD 20850.

A useful booklet, **Promoting Successful Mainstreaming: Reasonable Classroom Accommodations for Learning Disabled Students** sells for $7.50.

National Association for the Education of Young Children (NAEYC). 1834 Connecticut Avenue, N.W., Washington, DC 20009–5786.

Write to NAEYC for **Mainstreaming: Ideas for Teaching Young Children.**

PEAK (Parent Education and Assistance for Kids) Parent Center. 6055 Lehman Drive, Suite 101, Colorado Springs, CO 80918.

PEAK's remarkable integration guide, **Discover the Possibilities,** offers ways to train and inform parents, educators, and others about the value of integration in school and community. The guide can be ordered for $14.50 (including handling and shipping charges). Two other fine publications, **Building Integration with the I.E.P.** ($3.00) and **Breaking Ground: Ten Families Building Opportunities through Integration** ($10.00) will help families develop their vision.

Rehabilitation Research and Training Center, Virginia Commonwealth University (RRTC-VCU). 1314 West Main Street, Box 2011, Richmond, VA 23284–2011.

The RRTC-VCU conducts research and training on supported employment for citizens with developmental and other severe disabilities. Their newsletter shares articles of interest about supported employment in the community. Ask to be put on their mailing list.

G. Allan Roeher Institute. Kinsmen Building, York University, 4700 Keele Street, Downsview, Ontario M3J 1P3, Canada.

Write for ordering information for the five-part series, **Making a Difference: What Communities Can Do to Prevent Mental Handicap and Promote Lives of Quality.** The Institute's quarterly magazine, **entourage,** promotes community living for persons with mental handicaps and is written in both French and English.

SAFE (Schools Are For Everyone). P.O. Box 583, Syracuse, NY 13210.

SAFE is a national coalition for integration of all students with disabilities through supported education. Its quarterly newsletter, **The Safety Net,** is free to members. Write for information.

The Association for Persons with Severe Handicaps (TASH). 7010 Roosevelt Way, N.E., Seattle, WA 98115.

TASH materials have long been recognized as state-of-the-art in promoting integrated, community-based services for people who have traditionally been labelled "severely intellectually disabled." Request a sample copy of their newsletter and membership information.

University of Utah. School and Community Integration Products, 1078 Annex, University of Utah, Salt Lake City, UT 84112.

Their materials and information list of reprints and original manuscripts includes **A Different Look for IEPs for Elementary Students with Severe Handicaps** and **The Inclusive Neighborhood School: Educating Students with Severe Disabilities in the Least Restrictive Environment.**

Parent/Professional Partnership

Buscaglia, Leo. **The Disabled and Their Parents: A Counseling Challenge.** Thorofare, N.J.: Slack, 1983. 392 pp. $14.95.

With a well-established reputation for warmth, vitality, and sensitivity among parents of children with disabilities—especially learning disabilities—Leo Buscaglia promises good reading. This older book is a collection of chapters on the challenge of working with families as seen by the researcher, by the family, by the person with a disability, and by the counselor.

Downs-Taylor, Carol; Landon, Eleanor M. **Collaboration in Special Education: Children, Parents, Teachers, and the IEP.** Belmont, Calif: Fearon Education, 1981. 109 pp. $11.95 (Paper).

This easy-to-read, suggestion-packed guide for parents, classroom teachers, and special education teachers describes the need for collaboration to make appropriate public school education work for children with special needs. Public Law 94–142 is spelled out. Common sense prevails.

Lillie, David L.; Place, Patricia A. **Partners: A Guide to Working with Schools for Parents of Children with Special Instructional Needs.** Glenview, Ill.: Scott, Foresman, 1982. 106 pp. $9.95 (Paper).

This helpful, easy-reading workbook/guide, with pages perforated and three-hole punched for easy filing, has nine training sections with clear objectives and exercises; its focus is on helping children with special needs receive the appropriate education that is due them. It stresses the need for a positive attitude on the part of parents in working with a school system.

Luterman, David. **Counseling Parents of Hearing-Impaired Children.** Boston: Little, Brown, 1979. 193 pp. $15.00.

Dr. Luterman, the director of a parent-centered nursery program for children with hearing impairments, draws on his experience in counseling parents to explore their deepest anxieties and concerns about their role in nurturing and educating their children. He urges sympathetic and understanding support from professionals in developing appropriate child-centered programs.

Mittler, Peter; McConachie, Helen, eds. **Parents, Professionals and Mentally Handicapped People: Approaches to Partnership.** Cambridge, Mass.: Brookline Books, 1984. 243 pp. $14.95 (Paper).

A European seminar held at the University of Manchester in 1981 had, as its theme, closer collaboration between professionals and parents of sons and daughters with mental retardation. This book is based on the work of the seminar. It suggests a number of specific ways in which a parent/professional partnership can happen at all stages in a child's development. Particular parent training programs are described. Similar difficulties are reported the world over, although responses to those problems vary. There is much room for reflection in these perceptive and thoughtful writings.

Mulik, James A.; Pueschel, Siegfried, M. **Parent-Professional Partnerships in Developmental Disability Services.** Washington, D.C.: Academic Guild Publishers, 1983. 238 pp. $19.95.

This significant book has much to say to parents and professionals in its examination of what must be a working relationship among those people most important to children with developmental disabilities. Subjects range from the initial diagnosis to societal perspectives on disabilities. Professionals reading this book will gain important insight into parent feelings and what their own role should be; parents will find understanding and respect as well as valuable ideas in its pages.

Ozer, Mark N. **Solving Learning and Behavior Problems of Children.** San Francisco: Jossey-Bass, 1980. 258 pp. $32.95.

The author asks that we abandon the traditional approach to assessment and planning in which professionals had sole responsibility without the involvement of parents or children. He recommends a system in which parents and child team with professionals to identify the child's abilities and needs in real-life terms and then plan services accordingly. Interviews with children and their parents and teachers show how the system can work.

Seligman, Milton, ed. **The Family with a Handicapped Child: Understanding and Treatment.** Orlando, Fla.: Grune & Stratton, 1983. 317 pp. $29.50 (Paper).

Throughout this book, parents will find useful suggestions as well as a tone that is highly understanding of both parent feelings and a family's daily reality. Professionals who work with families in which there is a child with a disability would do well to read this work; it offers important perspectives. In addition to the identification of philosophical, historical, and legislative trends that have shaped our society's attitudes toward families, chapters discuss the parenting contribution of fathers, the sibling role, extended families, and the community service maze.

Seligman, Milton. **Strategies for Helping Parents of Exceptional Children: A Guide for Teachers.** New York: The Free Press, 1979. 240 pp. $18.95.

Parent-educator Seligman has studied the literature on counseling parents of children with disabilities; he also writes from his own personal and professional experience. The book offers practical, sensible guidelines for improving relationships between parents and teachers. The author is unusually sensitive to parents' feelings and needs.

Turnbull, Ann P.; Turnbull, H. Rutherford III. **Families, Professionals, and Exceptionality: A Special Partnership.** Columbus, Ohio: Merrill, 1986. 427 pp. $23.95 (Paper).

If families and professionals are to work together effectively, professionals need to understand family strengths; this important book should help them to view the family in all its diversity. It outlines the evolving history—the "revolution"—of parent roles, discusses family characteristics, interaction, needs, and life cycles, describes positive communication skills and strategies for effective communication, elaborates on the law governing special education and how to make it work, and deals with issues of professional ethics and morals. Parents are quoted throughout.

Webster, Elizabeth J. **Professional Approaches with Parents of Handicapped Children.** Springfield, Ill.: Charles C Thomas, 1976. 268 pp. $34.00.

A number of models for parent-professional dialogue are included in this book for practicing professionals who deal with children with disabilities and their families.

Planning for Your Child's Future

Russell, L. Mark. **Alternatives: A Family Guide to Legal and Financial Planning for the Disabled.** Evanston, Ill.: First Publications, 1983. 194 pp. $18.95 (Paper).

All parents worry about care for their adult son or daughter with mental retardation or mental illness when the parents will no longer be alive; this estate planning sourcebook will help families plan appropriately for the future. Topics include wills, guardianship, trusts, government benefits, taxes, insurance, and financial planning. The basic information can also educate family lawyers not versed in disability law. Changes in information on taxes and government benefits have occurred since the book's publication.

Summers, Jean Ann, ed. **The Right to Grow Up: An Introduction to Adults with Developmental Disabilities.** Baltimore: Paul H. Brookes, 1986. 336 pp. $21.95 (Paper).

This textbook should prove of interest to parents looking ahead. It explores the needs of adults with developmental disabilities, what services are necessary to meet those needs, and the self-advocacy, federal laws, and policies that will ensure that all needs will be met. Chapters include sexuality, marriage and parenthood, maintaining dignity in later years, residential and vocational options and issues, leisure and religious experiences, and independent living programs.

Turnbull, H. Rutherford III; Turnbull, Ann P.; Bronicki, G.J.; Summers, Jean Ann; Roeder-Gordon, Constance. **Disability and the Family: A Guide to Decisions for Adulthood.** Baltimore: Paul H. Brookes, 1989. 417 pp. $29.00 (Paper).

Both as an up-to-date source of information and a thought-organizing guide, this comprehensive work will help families resolve significant issues for the most satisfying adult lives of sons and daughters with disabilities. Topics include who will be responsible for decision making; financial planning; setting up leisure, residential, and vocational opportunities in the community; being an effective parent advocate; and encouraging self-advocacy. Illustrative family stories, guidelines, and strategies for "futures planning" are accompanied by helpful checklists. Appendices include public, national, and professional resources, a bibliography, and even "sample enabling documents for family-directed agencies."

Where to Write for Information

Association for Retarded Citizens of the United States (ARC/US). P.O. Box 6109, 2501 Avenue J, Arlington, TX 76006.

How to Provide for Their Future is for parents concerned with providing lifetime protection for their son or daughter who has mental retardation. The 1989 edition was prepared by the ARC of the United States Insurance Committee. Write for ordering information.

Governor's Planning Council on Developmental Disabilities, 300 Centennial Building, 658 Cedar Street, St. Paul, MN 55155.

It's Never Too Early, It's Never Too Late is a booklet about personal futures planning for people with developmental disabilities, their families and friends, case managers, service providers, and advocates.

148

Maryland State Planning Council on Developmental Disabilities. One Market Center, 300 West Lexington Street, Box 10, Baltimore, MD 21201.

 The Maryland Developmental Disability Council circulates, free of charge, a lengthy handbook entitled **Estate Planning for Families of Persons with Developmental Disabilities.** While estate planning specific to Maryland, Virginia, and the District of Columbia is its concentration, the basic information about wills, trusts, and taxes, as well as discussion of the special problems any family with a son or daughter with a developmental disability faces in planning for that child's future, should prove of considerable help to parents throughout the United States.

New Ways Magazine. P.O. Box 5072, Evanston, IL 60204.

 Future Care Planning Guide: Assuring Future Care for Dependents with Disabilities ($10.00) is a brief but helpful checklist.

Northwestern Mutual Life. 720 East Wisconsin Avenue, Milwaukee, WI 53202.

 A thirty-four-page study titled **Planning for the Disabled Child** was written to acquaint estate planning professionals with the particular concerns of parents with a child with a disability. It presents realistic alternatives in planning for both the personal care and financial assistance of the child after the death of parents. Guardianship, gifts, and trusts are discussed. Send fifty cents.

Parent Resources on Disabilities (PROD). P.O. Box 14391, Portland, OR 97214.

 Send $3.00 for the Spring 1989 issue of **The Bridge;** its article, called "Sorting Out S.S.I.: A Consumer's Guide to Supplemental Security Income," will help you make sense of the way S.S.I. is meant to work.

U.S. Department of Education. Office of Special Education and Rehabilitative Services, Clearinghouse on Disability Information, Room 3132, 330 C Street, S.W., Washington, DC 20202–2524.

 Request a copy of the twenty-six-page guide, **Pocket Guide to Federal Help for Individuals with Disabilities**.

U.S. Department of Health and Human Services. Social Security Administration, Room 45–10, West High Rise Building, 6401 Security Boulevard, Baltimore, MD 21235.

 Write for fact sheets entitled **Disability Reviews.** Titles include **SSI; Medicare;** and **Your Social Security Rights and Responsibilities: Disability Benefits.** Your regional Social Security office should be able to supply a **Summary Guide to Social Security and Supplemental Security Income with Incentives for the Disabled and Blind.**

Prevention

Dorris, Michael. **The Broken Cord.** New York: Harper & Row, 1989. 300 pp. $18.95.

Fetal Alcohol Syndrome (FAS) is a commonplace, preventable birth defect caused solely by alcohol in an unborn baby's developing body and brain—maternal drinking during pregnancy. This extraordinary book tells of a family and a society facing the problems of FAS. Dorris, who was a single parent when he adopted a young Sioux Indian child, writes of the sometimes terrible realities of the subsequent years. Beyond the poignant honesty of a father's discovery is the chilling indictment of the reasons for this lessening of what a life could be. The sad story is marvelous in its telling; Dorris is a critically acclaimed novelist and an anthropologist. The final chapter is "The Adam Dorris Story by Adam Dorris"; it is painful reading.

Milunsky, Aubrey. **Choices Not Chances: Controlling Your Genetic Heritage.** Boston: Little, Brown, 1989. 488 pp. $19.95.

Dr. Milunsky has provided a wealth of information on genetics—the risks, the implications, and the options involved when one is aware of one's family history. Genetic diseases can be prevented through new technologies such as prenatal screening and diagnosis. Chromosomes and genes, birth defects (minor and major, inherited and acquired), ethical issues, and environmental hazards are discussed in nontechnical, readable language.

Where to Write for Information

Association of Birth Defect Children (ABCD). 3526 Emerywood Lane, Orlando, FL 32812.

The purpose of ABCD is to prevent birth defects through education about potential environmental causes. A $12.00 annual donation will buy a subscription to the quarterly newsletter. A sample of a past newsletter can be ordered for $2.00.

Association for Retarded Citizens of the United States (ARC/US). National Headquarters, 2501 Avenue J, Arlington, TX 76005.

Send for their order list; it includes several pamphlets and guides of interest. Titles include **Mental Retardation: The Search for Cures** ($1.25), **Prevention: If Not You, Who? If Not Now, When?** ($1.25), and **Ten Projects for Preventing Fetal Alcohol Syndrome and Other Alcohol-Related Birth Defects** ($2.50).

Channing L. Bete Company. 200 State Road, South Deerfield, MA 01373–0200.

The booklet, **What Everyone Should Know about Fetal Alcohol Effects,** is 79 cents; a minimum of 25 copies must be ordered. It covers basic information in an attractive, easy-to-read format.

Consumer Product Safety Commission. Washington, DC 20207.

Buyer's Guide: The Safe Nursery; For Kids' Sake; Protect Your Child; and **Tips for Your Baby's Safety** are available free of charge.

Cystic Fibrosis Foundation. National Office, 6931 Arlington Road, Bethesda, MD 20814.
Send for **The Genetics of Cystic Fibrosis** and other material for parents.

Food and Drug Administration (FDA). Office of Consumer Affairs, 5600 Fishers Lane, Rockville, MD 20857.
The FDA circulates a brochure called **X-Rays, Pregnancy, and You**.

March of Dimes. Public Health Education and Community Services Department, 1275 Mamaroneck Avenue, White Plains, NY 10605.
Single copies of their current brochures and pamphlets are available while supplies last. They include: **Birth Defects: Tragedy and Hope; Be Good to Your Baby Before It Is Born; Babies Don't Thrive in Smoke-Filled Wombs; Drugs, Alcohol, and Tobacco Abuse During Pregnancy; Genetic Counseling; Will My Drinking Hurt My Baby?** and easy-to-read public health education information sheets on a number of birth defects. Write for ordering information.

National Clearinghouse for Alcohol and Drug Information. P.O. Box 2345, Rockville, MD 20852.
The National Institute on Alcohol Abuse and Alcoholism has produced a number of pamphlets and monographs of interest. Single copies are free. Titles include **Alcohol Topics Fact Sheet: Fetal Alcohol Syndrome; The Fetal Alcohol Syndrome;** and **My Baby . . . Strong and Healthy.** Other titles circulated by the Clearinghouse include the **Surgeon General's Advisory on Alcohol and Pregnancy; Opiates;** and **Sedative-Hypnotics.**

National Hemophilia Foundation. Soho Building, 110 Greene Street, Room 406, New York, NY 10012.
Send for **Inheritance of Hemophilia.**

National Institute of Child Health and Human Development. Office of Research Reporting, Building 31, Room 2A-32, Bethesda, MD 20892.
Send for **Facts about Pregnancy and Smoking.**

National Maternal and Child Health Clearinghouse. 38th & R Streets, N.W., Washington, DC 20057.
A ninety-eight page free publication, **Prenatal Care,** identifies some of the decisions that can increase the chances of having a healthy infant.

National Mental Health Association. 1021 Prince Street, Alexandria, VA 22314.
Write to the Mental Health Association for its publications list. Several items deal directly or tangentially with prevention of mental illness.

National Rural Development Institute. Western Washington University, Miller Hall 359, Bellingham, WA 98225.
Send $4.00 for **Prevention of Mental Retardation in Rural America.**

National Tay-Sachs Foundation and Allied Diseases Association. 385 Elliot Street, Newton, MA 02164.
Send for **What Every Family Should Know.**

Office on Smoking and Health. Technical Information Center, 5600 Fishers Lane, Room 116, Rockville, MD 20857.

    Now You're Smoking for Two: A Guide to Smoking and Pregnancy is free.

G. Allan Roeher Institute. Kinsmen Building, York University, 4700 Keele Street, Downsview, Ontario M3J 1P3, Canada.

    Ask for ordering information for the five-booklet set **Making a Difference: What Communities Can Do to Prevent Mental Handicap and Promote Lives of Quality.** The entire series sells for $20.00.

United States Department of Health and Human Services. National Center for Education in Maternal and Child Health, National Maternal and Child Health Clearinghouse, 38th & R Streets, N.W., Washington, DC 20057.

    Their joint catalog lists **Comprehensive Clinical Genetic Services Centers—A National Listing** and **Learning Together: A Guide for Families with Genetic Disorders.** Both are free.

U.S. Government Printing Office. Superintendent of Documents, Washington, DC 20402.

    Dozen Dangers to Your Baby's Brain and How to Reduce Those Dangers (Stock Number 017–092–00100–2) sells for $1.00.

U.S. Department of Health and Human Services. Public Health Service, National Institute of Neurological and Communicative Disorders and Stroke, National Institutes of Health, 9000 Rockville Pike, Building 31, Room 8A06, Bethesda, MD 20892.

    The **Hope through Research** series gives information about various disabilities and disorders and the progress being made toward cure and prevention through research. Single copies are free. Titles include **Autism; Cerebral Palsy; Epilepsy; Hearing Loss; Spina Bifida;** and **Tourette Syndrome.**

Public Policy and Rights of Individuals with Disabilities

Berkowitz, Edward D. **Disabled Policy: America's Programs for the Handicapped.** New York: Cambridge University Press, 1987. 280 pp. $24.95; $14.95 (Paper).

This Twentieth Century Fund Report is a careful, thoughtful historical description of disability programs in America. It gives some perspective on how and why they are themselves disabling to a surprising degree. The origins of workers' compensation, Social Security Disability Insurance, vocational rehabilitation, civil rights, and independent living programs are examined and the ways in which they fail to meet the needs of today are discussed.

Blatt, Burton; Kaplan, Fred. **Christmas in Purgatory.** Syracuse, N.Y.: Human Policy Press, 1974. 121 pp. $5.25 (Paper).

This practical portrait of life in the back wards of "State Institution, Anywhere, U.S.A." was originally published in 1965. Burton Blatt's exposé led the way for a burgeoning of exposés in newspapers across the nation, which in turn stimulated reform in several institutions.

Bowe, Frank. **Rehabilitating America: Toward Independence for Disabled and Elderly People.** New York: Harper & Row, 1980. 203 pp. $13.45.

Bowe documents the heavy costs spent by our society to keep people dependent, costs we can no longer afford. He makes a compelling argument for a sensible five-step plan to turn tax users into taxpayers.

Children's Defense Fund. **Children Out of School in America.** Washington, D.C.: Children's Defense Fund, 1974. 366 pp. $5.50 (Paper).

The staff of a Children's Defense Fund project conducted a survey to determine how many children in the United States had been excluded from school and for what reasons. The 1974 report presents an eye-opening description of how various social, political, and classroom postures permitted schools of the past to deny children their right to an education. The discussion is interesting both as history and as argument against possible future erosion of the law.

Ennis, Bruce J.; Emery, Richard D. **The Rights of Mental Patients: An American Civil Liberties Union Handbook.** New York: Avon Books, 1981. 220 pp. $2.50 (Paper).

The authors give basic facts about mental illness and psychiatry, present arguments against involuntary hospitalization, define and discuss voluntary hospitalization, discuss standards and procedural rights in the civil commitment process, deal with the rights of people who are mentally ill and in institutions or in the community, and outline the appropriate role for lawyers. Published in 1981, the book is still useful.

Foster, Susan Braverman. **The Politics of Caring.** Philadelphia: The Falmer Press, 1987. 166 pp. $16.00.

This fascinating study examines how thirteen individuals were considered for admission to a particular public residential facility during the deinstitutionalization period of the early 1980s.

The author recognizes the "desperate need and anguish" of the familes as well as the "larger ideological and political issues of institutionalization versus community placement." She argues for essential change: rewriting the role of professionals, government, and consumers. "Resources and status" must be given to families rather than to "the experts." "The growth of specialized, exclusionary services should be arrested" and generic services expanded and modified.

Friedman, Paul R., ed. **The Rights of Mentally Retarded Persons: An American Civil Liberties Union Handbook.** New York: Avon Books, 1981. 186 pp. $2.50 (Paper).

Friedman outlines some of the problems and consequences of classifying people as mentally retarded, and deals with civil commitment, competency, and guardianship proceedings, the rights of people with retardation in institutions and in the community, and the rights of people with retardation in the criminal system. Published in 1981, the book is still helpful.

Goldman, Charles D. **Disability Rights Guide: Practical Solutions to Problems Affecting People with Disabilities.** Lincoln, Nebr.: Media Publishing, 1987. 160 pp. $14.95 (Paper).

The author demystifies federal and state law governing employment, accessibility, housing, education, and transportation, and, in a chapter on attitudinal barriers, makes clear why public policy enacted them. His lively style ensures accessibility to legal safeguards and the ways in which they can be used. A glossary defines the jargon of the disability field; appendices enumerate state laws and federal and state contacts.

Herr, Stanley, S.; Arons, Stephen; Wallace, Richard E., Jr. **Legal Rights and Mental-Health Care.** Lexington, Mass.: Lexington Books, 1983. 180 pp. $29.00.

The basic legal principles underlying the rights of people receiving mental health care are summarized and examined in this articulate work. Its subjects include competency and consent; the right to treatment; the right to refuse treatment; the least restrictive alternative principle; privacy, confidentiality, and access to records; and rights to community services. One chapter deals with the special problems and special rights of children; another with guardianship. Written for clinicians, this book should also prove valuable to sophisticated parents wanting to learn about mental health law.

Hobbs, Nicholas, ed. **The Futures of Children.** San Francisco: Jossey-Bass, 1975. 339 pp. $29.95.

This lucid, thought-provoking report grew out of a massive study on the classification and labeling of exceptional children conducted at Vanderbilt University from 1973 to 1975. It deals with theoretical and practical aspects of labeling and presents recommendations for improving policies, services, and the delivery system so that all children are better served. The report had a major impact on the shape and substance of Public Law 94–142 and is still interesting reading.

Hobbs, Nicholas, ed. **Issues in the Classification of Children: A Sourcebook on Categories, Labels, and Their Consequences.** 2 vols. San Francisco: Jossey-Bass, 1975. 1104 pp. $75.00.

These two volumes contain papers written by the thirty-one task forces participating in the Vanderbilt study described above. Papers on various disabilities, schools, mental health services, experiences of parents, and the perspective of labeled children will be of special interest to parents.

Hull, Kent. **The Rights of Physically Handicapped People: An American Civil Liberties Union Handbook.** New York: Avon Books, 1981. 253 pp. $2.25 (Paper).

This concise, question-and-answer handbook covers the rights to access of people with physical disabilities. Subjects include architectural barriers and transportation, and the rights to education, to employment, and to live in the world.

National Center for Law and the Deaf. **Legal Rights of Hearing-Impaired People.** 3d ed. Washington, D.C.: Gallaudet College Press, 1986. 193 pp. $13.95 (Paper).

This is a comprehensive resource on legal rights and remedies for people of all ages with hearing impairments.

Roth, William. **The Handicapped Speak.** Jefferson, N.C.: McFarland, 1981. 211 pp. $18.95.

In question-and-answer format, the author interviews thirteen people with different disabilities. All of them are articulate and perceptive in sharing their thoughts about themselves, their lives, their reactions, and, in some instances, more global perspectives arising from their experience. The author's comments, indicating the pressing need for changes in public policy, are direct and thoughtful.

Rothman, David J.; Rothman, Sheila M. **The Willowbrook Wars: A Decade of Struggle for Social Justice.** New York: Harper & Row, 1984. 405 pp. $27.95.

An historian and a sociologist write of the court case that resulted in the move of more than five thousand, four hundred residents of the New York Willowbrook State School, a residential facility for people with mental retardation, into community group homes. The barriers to social change in the courts, the legislature, and particularly the state bureaucracy, are exquisitely delineated. So, too, are the difficulties and the triumphs of providing normalization for people who have known no other life than that of an inhumane institution.

Sheehan, Susan. **Is There No Place on Earth for Me?** Boston: Houghton Mifflin, 1982. $14.95. New York: Vintage, 1983. $6.95 (Paper).

Journalist Susan Sheehan's book won the Pulitzer Price for Nonfiction in 1982. It is the detailed history of "Sylvia Frumkin," who was diagnosed as schizophrenic in her late teens and spent her next seventeen years in and out of psychiatric hospitals. Sheehan describes the mediocrity of hospitalization and the lack of appropriate care in the community. This extraordinary chronicle is both a sympathetic and disturbing look at one individual and an indictment of our society's mental health system, no less true today than when it was written.

Stinson, Robert and Peggy. **The Long Dying of Baby Andrew.** Boston: Little, Brown, 1983. 375 pp. $17.95.

Andrew Stinson was born sixteen weeks prematurely, and, through a succession of medical calamities, was kept alive for nearly six months. His parents chronicle the long days and their individual reactions. Brutal, painful, and honest, their book raises important ethical questions about doctor decisions, parent rights, and the routine use of sophisticated neonatal technology.

Sutherland, Allan T. **Disabled We Stand.** Cambridge, Mass.: Brookline Books, 1984. 159 pp. $17.95 (Paper).

    In this thought-provoking work, Sutherland, who has epilepsy, effectively challenges the stereotypes, stigma, and humiliations inflicted by society on people with disabilities. He and others he interviewed articulate convincingly their conviction that people with disabilities should be in charge of decisions affecting their lives. They express their pain and anger at the denial of fundamental human rights to access, employment, and education. (Issues relating to mental disability are not included.)

Torrey, E. Fuller. **Nowhere to Go: The Tragic Odyssey of the Homeless Mentally Ill.** New York: Harper & Row, 1988. 256 pp. $18.95.

    Mental institutions four decades ago were snake pits of horror, but the promise that deinstitutionalization and community mental health centers would solve the lot of people with mental illness did not materialize. **Nowhere to Go** presents the author's view of the background and history as to why this social policy failed. Many of America's homeless today are seriously mentally ill. A final chapter outlines Torrey's recommendations for solving this critical problem. This notable work is direct and impressive.

Turnbull, H. Rutherford III; Turnbull, Ann. **Free Appropriate Public Education: Law and Implementation.** Denver, Colo.: Love, 1986. 309 pp. $29.95.

    The authors define and suggest techniques for school systems to implement the six major principles present in Public Law 94–142, the Education for All Handicapped Children Act: zero reject, guidelines in testing, classification and placement, what constitutes an individualized and appropriate education, what constitutes the least restrictive appropriate placement, procedural due process, and parent participation in decision making.

Veatch, Robert M. **The Foundations of Justice: Why the Retarded and the Rest of Us Have Claims to Equality.** New York: Oxford University Press, 1986. 210 pp. $27.95.

    What is the responsibility, if any, of a community to meet all the extraordinary needs of the most needy of its citizens? **The Foundations of Justice** presents a comprehensive look at the complex moral, legal, philosophical, and ethical questions surrounding the allocation of limited resources to people with severe multiple handicapping conditions. Religious and secular views of equality are explored and implications for public policy are offered.

Wolfensberger, Wolf. **The Origin and Nature of Our Institutional Models.** Syracuse, N.Y.: Human Policy Press, 1975. 88 pp. $5.25 (Paper).

    Originally written in 1968, this history of institutions continues to raise issues of importance today. Wolfensberger's examination of the perceptions of people with mental retardation which led to the justification for their segregation quotes from documents of the past and calls for new attitudes. The author has, of course, long been a distinguished and articulate leader in the march toward "normalization," and, more recently, "social role valorization."

Where to Write for Information

American Association on Mental Retardation. 1719 Kalorama Road, N.W., Washington, DC 20009.

    The **Consent Handbook** outlines the issues central to understanding consent as a legal concept, who may give consent, when it is informed and voluntary, and the application of consent to specific areas such as medical treatment or behavioral treatment programs. The handbook sells for $9.00.

Channing L. Bete Company. 200 State Road, South Deerfield, MA 01373–0200.

    The booklet, **What Everyone Should Know about Educating Handicapped Children,** is 79 cents; a minimum of 25 copies must be ordered. It covers basic information about P.L. 94–142 in an attractive, easy-to-read format.

Children's Defense Fund (CDF). 122 C Street, N.W., Washington, DC 20001.

    CDF has long specialized in advocacy for children's rights, exposing federal and state policies and programs which fail children or put them at risk. Write for information.

The Council for Exceptional Children (CEC). 1920 Association Drive, Reston, VA 22091–1589.

    Send $5.50 for a sixteen-page booklet called **P.L. 94–142, Section 504, and P.L. 99–457— Understanding What They Are and Are Not.** It answers questions about rights and protections, fiscal policy, school management, preschool programs, and early intervention.

Disability Focus, Inc. 1010 Vermont Avenue, N.W., #1100, Washington, DC 20005.

    Focus on Disability is the quarterly newsletter of Disability Focus. This non-profit membership organization defines its mission as providing a "disability perspective on all social policy." Write for information and an impressive packet of previously published articles.

Disability Rights Education and Defense Fund (DREDF). 2112 Sixth Street, Berkeley, CA 94710.

    DREDF, a national law and policy center, publishes the monthly **Disability Rights Education and Defense Fund News.**

The Governor's Planning Council on Developmental Disabilities. State Planning Agency, 201 Capitol Square Building, 550 Cedar Street, St. Paul, MN 55101.

    Write for a free copy of **A New Way of Thinking,** which describes a significant change in the way the service system should be set up to serve people with developmental disabilities. This articulate report describes quality of life needs—having a home, learning, working, and developing and sustaining relationships. Its focus is on Minnesota; its content is universal.

Mental Health Law Project (MHLP). 2021 L Street, N.W., Suite 800, Washington, DC 20036–4909.

    MHLP is a non-profit, public interest law firm devoted to protecting and expanding the rights of people with mental illness and developmental disabilities. Write for information.

National Organization on Disability (NOD). 910 16th Street, N.W., Suite 600, Washington, DC 20006.

      NOD is the only independent federal agency appointed by the President that makes recommendations on issues of public policy affecting Americans with disabilities. Get on its mailing list to receive copies of position papers and its free quarterly newsletter, **Focus.**

The G. Allan Roeher Institute. York University, Kinsmen Building, 4700 Keele Street, Downsview, Ontario M3J 1P3, Canada.

      The G. Allan Roeher Institute is Canada's National Institute for the Study of Public Policy Affecting Persons with an Intellectual Impairment. It publishes material in a wide range of areas, with a major focus on public policy and funding, on studies of innovative social programs, and on the development of policy alternatives. Request a publications list.

U.S. Department of Health and Human Services. National Maternal and Child Health Clearinghouse, 38th & R Streets, N.W., Washington, DC 20057.

      A significant new publication is **The Intent and Spirit of P.L. 99–457: A Sourcebook,** which discusses the law that provides services from birth to infants and toddlers with disabilities and their families.

Young Adult Institute (YAI). 460 West 34th Street, New York, NY 10001.

      In 1984, YAI published an important monograph by Stanley S. Herr, titled **Issues in Human Rights: A Guide for Parents, Professionals, Policymakers and All Those Who Are Concerned about the Rights of Mentally Retarded and Developmentally Disabled People.** The guide sets out the specific rights, human and legal, of "clients in mental disability service systems." Herr speaks of basic rights, using Pennhurst, Willowbrook, Baby Doe, and Phillip Becker as examples; he outlines several Supreme Court decisions—*Romeo, Mills, Rowley*—and their implications. $11.25 includes mailing charges.

Sexuality

Blum, Gloria; Blum, Barry. **Feeling Good about Yourself: A Guide for People Working with People Who Have Disabilities or Low Self-Esteem.** Rev. ed. Kealakekua, Hawaii: Feeling Good Associates, 1986. 80 pp. $9.95 (Paper).

　　The relationship between self-esteem, social skills, and sexuality is discussed in this guide. Group techniques and principles for teaching self-esteem to "slow learners" are shared; many parents will find material they can adapt to home instruction. All areas of sexuality are included.

Duffy, Yvonne. **All Things Are Possible.** Ann Arbor, Mich.: A.J. Garvin & Associates, 1981. 179 pp. $8.95 (Paper).

　　The author, who is herself "differently abled" as a result of polio when she was two years old, interviewed seventy-seven women who have physical disabilities. She shares their honest and intimate thoughts about all phases of sexuality from menstruation and sex education to marriage and lesbianism. Of particular value to parents is the articulate, sensitive discussion of how parents influence their children's self-images.

Edwards, Jean P.; Elkins, Thomas E. **Just Between Us: A Social Sexual Guide for Parents and Professionals with Concerns for Persons with Developmental Disabilities.** Austin: Pro-Ed, 1988. 157 pp. $14.00 (Paper).

　　Written for parents and professionals, this very helpful work is a book on attitudes, human relations, and the social-sexual needs of those with mental retardation. The attitudes include a commitment to heightened expectations, normalization, and human dignity. The authors give specific examples in discussing socialization skills, reproductive health issues, masturbation, self-esteem building, sterilization and contraception, avoiding exploitation, marriage, and parenthood.

Enby, Gunnel. **Let There Be Love: Sex and the Handicapped.** New York: Taplinger, 1975. 65 pp. $7.50.

　　This is a mind-opening account of the author's personal experience with archaic and repressive attitudes toward sex for people with disabilities in institutions. She addresses, also, the isolation experienced by people with disabilities in a society that is not only ignorant of their needs, but often of their capabilities as well. Helpful insights into feelings and ways parents can help their own child with a physical disability are offered. The work was translated from the Swedish.

Hopper, C. Edmund; Allen, William A. **Sex Education for Physically Handicapped Youth.** Springfield, Ill.: Charles C Thomas, 1980. 130 pp. $15.75 (Paper).

　　Written directly to teenagers, this book deals honestly and realistically with all aspects of sexuality as it affects young people with physical disabilities. It could be a valuable resource for parents in helping them discuss issues with their children.

Johnson, Warren R.; Kempton, Winifred. **Sex Education and Counseling of Special Groups.** Springfield, Ill.: Charles C Thomas, 1981. 255 pp. $27.25.

　　Guidelines for the sex education of people with mental and physical disabilities as well as those who are ill or elderly are provided in this direct and honest discussion. Specific behaviors examined include physical contact, nudity, masturbation, sex play, menstruation, nocturnal emissions, "dirty" words, sexual intercourse, homosexuality, contraception, abortion, dating, paid sexual companions, marriage, and parenthood.

Kempton, Winifred. **Sex Education for Persons with Disabilities That Hinder Learning: A Teacher's Guide.** Santa Monica, Calif.: James Stanfield, 1988. 198 pp. $14.95 (Spiral-bound).

   Winifred Kempton is recognized throughout the world as a leading authority on the social-sexual aspects of the lives of people with special needs. This update of the 1975 edition of her book is addressed specifically to teachers of students with learning problems, and many of the situations described refer to school settings. For parents who feel comfortable about advising their adolescent sons and daughters, this book should be of great benefit in helping them explore their own attitudes and develop teaching strategies. Practice exercises with answers and an extensive bibliography are provided.

McKee, Lyn; Blacklidge, Virginia. **An Easy Guide for Caring Parents: Sexuality and Socialization.** Walnut Creek, Calif.: Planned Parenthood Shasta-Diablo, 1986. 56 pp. $5.95 plus $1.50 postage and handling (Paper).

   Written specifically for parents of people with mental handicaps, this excellent overview will help them "guide their sons and daughters toward greater responsibility, sexually and socially." The authors acknowledge parents as the "most influential teachers" and offer them practical suggestions and realistic advice spanning childhood to the adult years.

Stehle, Bernard F. **Incurably Romantic.** Philadelphia: Temple University Press, 1985. 241 pp. $ 29.95.

   Photographs and words of couples at a private, total-care institution, once known as "The Philadelphia Home for Incurables," makes it clear that people with physical disabilities can and do have romantic relationships. Viewing the "profound affirmation of . . . [people's] essential normality" challenges stereotypical thought.

Where to Write for Information

Channing L. Bete Company. 200 State Road, South Deerfield, MA 01373–0200.
   What Everyone Should Know about Sexuality and People with Disabilities, is 79 cents; a minimum of 25 copies must be ordered. It encourages sharing information in an attractive, easy-to-read format.

ETR Associates/Network Publications. P.O. Box 1830, Santa Cruz, CA 95061–1830.
   Write for the excellent booklet, designed for adults with learning disabilities or low level reading skills, called **An Easy Guide to Loving Carefully.** It sells for $5.95.

Planned Parenthood Federation of America. 810 Seventh Avenue, New York, NY 10019.
   Planned Parenthood has offices throughout the United States, and many are good sources of information and counseling for people with disabilities. Call your local office or write to the Federation in New York for information on family planning, on various methods of birth control, including sterilization, and on abortion. Some local Planned Parenthood offices have publications specifically for parents of children with disabilities or for teenagers and adults with dis-

abilities. Planned Parenthood Southeastern Pennsylvania, 1144 Locust Street, Philadelphia, PA 19107 offers the classic booklet, **Love, Sex, and Birth Control for Mentally Handicapped People: A Guide for Parents** by Winifred Kempton, Medora S. Bass, and Sol Gordon. This booklet contains the facts everyone needs to know and advice from experts on how to share them; the cost is $2.95 plus 60 cents postage. Write to Six Rivers Planned Parenthood, 2316 Harrison Avenue, Eureka, CA 95501 for **Sexuality and the Disabled Child** ($1.25).

Public Affairs Committee. 381 Park Avenue South, New York, NY 10016.
    Sex Education for Disabled Persons is $1.00.

Siblings*

Carlisle, Wendy. **Siblings of the Mentally Ill.** Saratoga, Calif.: R & E Publishers, 1984. 190 pp. $8.95 (Paper).

Mental illness profoundly affects an entire family. This book describes the experiences, problems, and special needs of a group of brothers and sisters of people who became mentally ill during adolescence. Relationships with parents, relationships among siblings, relationships outside the home, and contacts with mental health professionals were investigated. Numerous direct quotations share both common trends and individual coping skills. A significant finding points to the almost total lack of mental health services provided to those vulnerable and often needy family members, the siblings.

Levy, Erin Lynn. **Children Are Not Paper Dolls: A Visit with Bereaved Siblings.** Incline Village, Nev.: Publishers Mark, 1982. 121 pp. $8.95 plus $1.25 shipping and handling (Paper).

Children, too, go through a grieving process when a brother or sister dies. Pictures and quotes are offered by six bereaved siblings. They address the subjects of funerals, family, friends, school, feelings, and holidays. Their sharing offers significant and important understanding.

Meyer, Donald J.; Vadasy, Patricia F.; Fewell, Rebecca R. **Living with a Brother or Sister with Special Needs: A Book for Sibs.** Seattle: University of Washington Press, 1985. 110 pp. $20.00; $9.95 (Paper). (Ages 6–11)

The University of Washington's Child Development and Mental Retardation Center has developed workshops for young brothers and sisters of children with handicaps; this book is based on that experience. Written for siblings of elementary school age, the book shares some basic information about a number of handicapping conditions, explores a variety of sibling feelings, and offers strategies for solving everyday problems. It is an easy-to-understand guide book, both reassuring and realistic. Parents will also find this book valuable in learning more about all their children.

Powell, Thomas H.; Ogle, Peggy Ahernhold. **Brothers & Sisters—A Special Part of Exceptional Families.** Baltimore: Paul H. Brookes, 1985. 226 pp. $16.95 (Paper).

Based on research, counseling, and observation, this well-written and valuable book recognizes the unique significance of nondisabled siblings in families in which there is a child with a disability. It suggests a number of strategies for parents and professionals to assist positive sibling relationships and help siblings without handicaps discover their own strengths within the family unit.

---

* Many of the books in the category *Books for the Younger Reader* are told from a sibling's point of view. They offer important insights into the feelings and thoughts of brothers and sisters who grow up with a sibling with a disability. Parents will find them of interest.

Rosenberg, Maxine B. **Finding a Way: Living with Exceptional Brothers and Sisters.** New York: Lothrop, Lee & Shepard, 1988. 48 pp. $11.95.

> This is a book for children. Danielle's brother has diabetes, two of Danny's siblings have asthma, and Rachel's brother has spina bifida. Their account, in words and photographs, confirms that the sibling relationship can be special in many ways. There are feelings of fear, frustration, and anger, as well as pleasure, sensitivity, and caring. The "Afterword" by a psychologist will help parents make the best use of this book.

Where to Write for Information

Minneapolis Children's Medical Center. Exceptional Children with Communication and Interaction Disorders, 2525 Chicago Avenue South, Minneapolis, MN 55404.

> **Having a Brother Like David** is a booklet to share with young children who have a sibling with autism. In simple language, a young boy shares the difficulties and frustrations of not being able to meet David's special needs. There is genuine concern, as well.

National Information Center for Children and Youth with Handicaps (NICHCY). P.O. Box 1492, Washington, DC 20013.

> You will want to request a free copy of their news digest on siblings.

The Ohio State University Nisonger Center. 1581 Dodd Drive, Columbus, OH 43216.

> A brief and helpful guide to the needs of children who live with a brother or sister with a disability and how parents can help is called **Profiles of the Other Child: A Sibling Guide for Parents** ($2.00).

PACER (Parent Advocacy Coalition for Educational Rights) Center. 4876 Chicago Avenue South, Minneapolis, MN 55417–1055.

> **Brothers and Sisters Talk with PACER** ($4.00) are personal accounts of brothers and sisters who range in age from ten to twenty-eight; they offer important insights into what it means to grow up with a sibling who has a disability.

Salem Association for Retarded Citizens. 8 Centerville Drive, Salem, NH 03079.

> Send for **For the Love of Siblings Who Cope with Special Brothers and Sisters.**

Sibling and Adult Children's Network. SAC Network/NAMI, 2101 Wilson Boulevard, Suite 302, Arlington, VA 22201.

> This organization for brothers, sisters, and adult sons and daughters of people with mental illness publishes a newsletter, **The Bond** ($10.00 a year), and circulates resource materials. Write for information.

Sibling Information Network. Connecticut's University Affiliated Program on Developmental Disabilities, 991 Main Street, Suite 3A, East Hartford, CT 06108.

> The Network's quarterly newsletter costs $2.00 yearly; it carries news of special interest to all family members of a person with a disability.

United Cerebral Palsy Association of Western New York. Children's Center, 4635 Union Road, Cheektowaga, NY 14225.

Young brothers and sisters of children with physical or multiple disabilities participated in a workshop led by a social worker and an art therapist. The booklet that shares their thoughts and feelings in words and art is called **Am I the Only One?** Write for ordering information.

BOOKS FOR THE YOUNGER READER

PART IV

Bibliographies

There are several fine resources that either comment on the way in which disability is portrayed in children's literature or that annotate books in which a character with a disability plays a part. Be sure to check publication dates; many of the books reviewed in the listed volumes are no longer in print but may be available in libraries.

Azarnoff, Pat. **Health, Illness, and Disability: A Guide to Books for Children and Young Adults.** New York: R.R. Bowker, 1983. 259 pp. $34.95.

Baskin, Barbara H.; Harris, Karen H. **Notes from a Different Drummer: A Guide to Juvenile Fiction Portraying the Handicapped.** New York: R.R. Bowker, 1977. 375 pp. $29.95.

Baskin, Barbara H.; Harris, Karen H. **More Notes from a Different Drummer: A Guide to Juvenile Fiction Portraying the Handicapped.** New York: R.R. Bowker, 1984. 495 pp. $39.95.

Bracken, Jeanne; Wigutoff, Sharon. **Books for Today's Children: An Annotated Bibliography of Nonstereotyped Picture Books.** Hagerstown, Md.: The Feminist Press, 1979. 42 pp. $4.95 (Paper).

Bracken, Jeanne; Wigutoff, Sharon; Baker, Ilene. **Books for Today's Young Readers: An Annotated Bibliography of Recommended Fiction for Ages 10–14.** Hagerstown, Md.: The Feminist Press, 1981. 64 pp. $4.95 (Paper).

Dreyer, Sharon Spredemann. **The Bookfinder: A Guide to Children's Literature about the Needs and Problems of Youth Aged 2–15.** 3 vols. Circle Pines, Minn.: American Guidance Service, 1981–85. $139.75 (set); $54.95 per volume; $19.95 (Paper).

Friedberg, Joan Brest; Mullins, June B.; Sukiennik, Adelaide Weir. **Accept Me As I Am: Best Books of Juvenile Nonfiction on Impairments and Disabilities.** New York: R.R. Bowker, 1985. 363 pp. $29.95.

Quicke, John. **Disability in Modern Children's Fiction.** Cambridge, Mass.: Brookline Books, 1985. 176 pp. $17.95.

Redburn, Lisa. **Books for Children and Teenagers about Hospitalization, Illness, and Disabling Conditions.** Washington, D.C.: Association for the Care of Children's Health, 1987. 65 pp. $13.50.

All Disabilities*

Hobby, Janice Hale. **Staying Back.** Gainesville, Fla.: Triad, 1982. 96 pp. $6.95 (Paper). (Ages 7–12)

Stories are told from the point of view of seven elementary-school-aged children who are coping with academic failure for a variety of reasons, including hearing loss, sickle cell anemia, and a learning disability. A helpful message to parents suggests concrete ways to support their child.

McConnell, Nancy P. **Different and Alike.** Colorado Springs, Colo.: Current, 1983. 28 pp. Write for ordering information. (Ages 6–10)

"Having different people in the world is what makes it an interesting place to live!" This book of facts will help children understand what it's like to have a disability. A page of sign and a page of Braille are included.

Rosenberg, Maxine B. **My Friend Leslie: The Story of a Handicapped Child.** New York: Lothrop, Lee & Shepard, 1983. Unpaginated. $13.00. (Ages 5–8)

Leslie is a girl with multiple handicaps and several talents. Told from the point of view of the author's daughter, Karin, the book describes in words and photographs how she, her friend Leslie, and their kindergarten classmates spend their days.

Slepian, Jan. **The Alfred Summer.** New York: Macmillan, 1980. 119 pp. $10.95; $2.50 (Paper). (Ages 11–14)

Four teenagers share a summer project. The feelings of a young person with cerebral palsy, reactions of people to someone who is mentally retarded, and the families of these two special people are described with great skill and engaging humor.

Sullivan, Mary Beth; Brightman, Alan J.; Blatt, Joseph. **Feeling Free.** Reading, Mass.: Addison-Wesley, 1979. 192 pp. $10.95. (Ages 8–14)

Activities, short stories, games, and accounts of real children explaining their feelings about their own learning problem or physical disability fill the pages of this book. Many black-and-white photographs of the children who were originally on an award-winning television series, **Feeling Free,** are included.

---

* Please refer to the section on "Attitudes for the Younger Reader" for more books for children.

Autism

Gold, Phyllis. **Please Don't Say Hello: Living with Childhood Autism.** New York: Human Sciences Press, 1975. 47 pp. $14.95; $5.75 (Paper). (Ages 9–12)

This is an absorbing, sensitive introduction to autism. More broadly, it is a book that generates real thinking about people who are "different" and people who are "normal" and how they can find a comfortable meeting ground.

Hyde, Margaret O. **Is This Kid "Crazy?" Understanding Unusual Behavior.** Philadelphia: Westminster Press, 1983. 96 pp. $9.95. (Ages 12–15)

In an attempt to help young people understand mental illness and other reasons for unusual behavior, the author discusses the possible causes, symptoms, and treatments of autism, schizophrenia, depression, eating disorders, and other emotional problems.

Chronic Condition or Illness

Arnold, Katrin. **Anna Joins In.** Nashville: Abingdon, 1982. Unpaginated. $9.95. (Ages 5–9)

Anna is five years old and dealing with the everyday concerns of cystic fibrosis. She has fun in her kindergarten class, she has a loving family, and she has a friend with whom she sometimes argues.

Carter, Sharon; Monnig, Judy. **Coping with a Hospital Stay.** New York: Rosen Publishing Group, 1987. 108 pp. $12.95. (Ages 13–17)

Written in language meant to appeal to an adolescent audience, this book offers tips on handling a hospital stay for someone new to the process. Most reasons given for hospitalization are the results of accidents but one chapter deals with psychiatric problems and another with "When Things Are Not Going to Be 'All Right.'"

Doherty, Berlie. **Granny Was a Buffer Girl.** New York: Franklin Watts, Orchard Books, 1986. 131 pp. $12.95. (Ages 14–17)

The night before Jess leaves her English village for a University year in France, three generations of family gather to share time and stories. One of the memories is of Danny, Jess's brother, who lived his short life in a wheelchair and helped Jess learn about herself and death and life.

Ethridge, Kenneth E. **Toothpick.** New York: Holiday House, 1985. 118 pp. $10.95. (Ages 12–15)

"Toothpick" is the name given to the new girl in the eleventh grade who is painfully thin. She has cystic fibrosis. A classmate, Jamie, gets to know her as someone good in math and easy to talk to.

Frazier, Claude A. **Sniff, Sniff, Al-Er-Gee.** St. Petersburg, Fla.: Johnny Reads, 1978. 36 pp. $6.75; $3.25 (Paper). (Ages 5–9)

Written for children with allergy problems by a specialist in the field, this pleasant story describes what allergies are and how doctors diagnose and treat them. It was published in 1978 but should still prove of interest.

Howe, James. **A Night without Stars.** New York: Atheneum, 1983. 178 pp. $10.95. (Ages 8–12)

Eleven-year-old Maria is in the hospital for surgery to repair the hole in her heart. She needs answers to all her unasked questions and she gets some from Donald, a boy terribly scarred from being burned in a fire. She helps him find some answers, too.

Jones, Rebecca C. **Angie and Me.** New York: Macmillan, 1981. 113 pp. $8.95. (Ages 8–12)

The summer before junior high, Jenna is diagnosed as having juvenile rheumatoid arthritis. Her hospital stay involves therapy, shots, discomfort, learning, and important new friends.

Kipnis, Lynne; Adler, Susan. **You Can't Catch Diabetes from a Friend.** Gainesville, Fla.: Triad, 1979. 62 pp. $9.95. (Ages 9–12)

> Many fine black-and-white photographs of four children at their normal daily activities help the interesting text to explain what diabetes is and its effect on those who have it and their families.

Krementz, Jill. **How It Feels to Fight for Your Life.** Boston: Little, Brown, 1989. 132 pp. $15.95. (Ages 10–16)

> Fourteen children who have faced or are facing serious illnesses and disabilities speak candidly about their very real emotions. Some of the conditions with which they live are cystic fibrosis, diabetes, heart disease, juvenile rheumatoid arthritis, asthma, epilepsy, and spina bifida. Photographs of the young authors are included.

Kuklin, Susan. **Thinking Big: The Story of a Young Dwarf.** New York: Lothrop, Lee & Shepard, 1986. Unpaginated. $10.25. (Ages 6–9)

> An interesting text, an informative epilogue, and many delightful photographs tell the story of eight-year-old Jaime Osborn who is "like everybody else, just little."

Radley, Gail. **CF in His Corner.** New York: Four Winds Press, 1984. 134 pp. $9.95. (Ages 10–14)

> The summer that fourteen-year-old Jeff makes the awful discovery that his younger brother has cystic fibrosis is a time of turmoil and pain, loneliness and dreams, for Jeff, Scott, and their mother.

Rogers, Alison. **Luke Has Asthma, Too.** Burlington, Vt.: Waterfront Books, 1987. 31 pp. $6.95 (Paper). (Ages 4–7)

> It isn't fun to have asthma, but family, doctors, and an older friend named Luke help the young narrator adjust.

Roy, Ron. **Where's Buddy?** New York: Clarion Books, 1982. 95 pp. $11.95. (Ages 8–12)

> It's time for Buddy's shot of insulin but his brother Mike can't find him anywhere. The tension is high as Mike and a friend battle against the clock. A diabetic condition provides the suspense in this well-written story.

Sachs, Marilyn. **It Can't Hurt Forever.** New York: Harper & Row, Harper Trophy Book, 1978. 186 pp. $2.95 (Paper). (Ages 8–12)

> Being in the hospital for the repair of a heart defect is scary but the experience isn't all bad. The author had heart surgery when she was eight and remembers the feelings; through Ellie, her pleasant heroine, she shares solid information and many of the realities of a hospital stay.

Silverstein, Alvin; Silverstein, Virginia B. **Allergies.** New York: Harper & Row, 1977. 128 pp. $12.70. (Ages 9–12)

> In nontechnical language, the authors explain various allergies and how they are diagnosed and treated. The book was published in 1977.

Silverstein, Alvin; Silverstein, Virginia B. **Runaway Sugar: About Diabetes.** New York: Harper & Row, Harper Junior, 1981. 34 pp. $11.70. (Ages 6–10)

    Diabetes may be hard to understand for young children; the Silversteins have done an admirable job in dealing with a difficult subject factually and yet as simply as possible. The possible cause of diabetes, what happens to the body when diabetes occurs, its symptoms, and different treatments are all included. This will be a good book for parents who need to explain diabetes to the young.

Silverstein, Alvin; Silverstein, Virginia B. **The Sugar Disease: Diabetes.** Philadelphia: J.B. Lippincott, 1980. 111 pp. $11.70. (Ages 9–12)

    Diabetes—what it is, what may cause it, how it is diagnosed and treated, and what it means to the individual who lives with it—is explained in this science book for young readers. Its clear explanations may prove helpful to parents, as well.

Epilepsy

Girion, Barbara. **A Handful of Stars.** New York: Charles Scribner's Sons, 1981. 179 pp. $10.95. (Ages 12–15)

    Julie Meyers discovers early in high school that her memory lapses are caused by epilepsy. The problems of adolescence, coupled with having to deal with societal fears and ignorance, are realistically described. A significant amount of information about epilepsy, its diagnosis, and treatment are also shared.

Hermes, Patricia. **What If They Knew?** Orlando, Fla.: Harcourt Brace Jovanovich, 1980. 121 pp. $10.95; New York: Dell, $2.25 (Paper). (Ages 9–12)

    Ten-year-old Jeremy learns what friendship is really all about when she has a seizure in her new school. The author understands Jeremy's feelings and concerns; she, too, kept her epilepsy a secret in her growing-up years.

Kornfield, Elizabeth J. **Dreams Come True.** Boise, Idaho: Rocky Mountain Children's Press, 1986. Unpaginated. $5.95 (Paper). (Ages 6–9)

    Katie Kornfield likes to figure skate "more than anything else in the whole world." She has learned a lot about epilepsy and this book shares what she knows.

Moss, Deborah M. **Lee, the Rabbit with Epilepsy.** Rockville, Md.: Woodbine House, 1989. Unpaginated. $12.95. (Ages 3–7)

    Lee has a seizure when she goes fishing with Grandpa Jake. The doctor explains epilepsy to her and she learns that she still can do everything she wants to do.

Silverstein, Alvin; Silverstein, Virginia B. **Epilepsy.** Philadelphia: J.B. Lippincott, 1975. 64 pp. $12.75. (Ages 9–12)

    This is an objective, readable book, written to tell young people what epilepsy is, and to describe research, treatment, and popular misconceptions. Although its audience is specifically intended to be teenagers, this clear overview should prove of interest to parents as well.

Hearing Impairment

Arthur, Catherine. **My Sister's Silent World.** Chicago: Children's Press, 1979. 32 pp. $11.95. (Ages 5–8)

    Heather, who lives in a world of silence, celebrates her eighth birthday in words and photographs. Her older sister talks about Heather and her hearing impairment.

Aseltine, Lorraine. **I'm Deaf and It's Okay.** Niles, Ill.: Albert Whitman, 1986. Unpaginated. $10.95. (Ages 4–7)

    A young boy feels angry and sad because he can't hear. A teenager who wears hearing aids helps him to "feel good inside."

Charlip, Remy; Miller, Mary Beth; Ancona, George. **Handtalk: An ABC of Finger Spelling and Sign Language.** New York: Four Winds Press, 1974. Unpaginated. $13.95. (Ages 5–10)

    Actors from the National Theatre of the Deaf illustrate in charming photographs signing and finger spelling for the letters of the alphabet.

Charlip, Remy; Miller, Mary Beth; Ancona, George. **Handtalk Birthday.** New York: Four Winds Press, 1987. Unpaginated. $14.95 (All ages)

    In this delightful companion volume to **Handtalk,** Mary Beth celebrates a surprise birthday party with her friends. Signing and fingerspelling illustrate words and numbers.

Greenberg, Judith E. **What is the Sign for Friend?** New York: Franklin Watts, 1985. 30 pp. $9.40. (Ages 5–8)

    Shane cannot hear. He goes to a typical elementary school and he can do almost everything his hearing friends can. Black-and-white photographs and single word signs accompany the story.

LaMore, Gregory S. **Now I Understand.** Washington, D.C.: Gallaudet College Press, 1986. 48 pp. $8.95. (Ages 9–12)

    When a student who has a hearing impairment joins the class, his teacher helps his classmates to learn all about the condition. The story is incidental; the factual information includes the anatomy of the ear, hearing tests, hearing aids, and communication methods.

Peterson, Jeanne Whitehouse. **I Have a Sister, My Sister is Deaf.** New York: Harper & Row, 1977. Unpaginated. $11.75; $3.95 (Paper). (Ages 5–9)

    A young girl describes what her little sister who is deaf can and cannot do in this gentle, feeling story.

Riskind, Mary. **Apple is My Sign.** Boston: Houghton Mifflin, 1982. 146 pp. $12.95. (Ages 8–12)

    It is the turn of the century and Harry Berger, a spirited ten-year-old who, like everyone else in his family, was born deaf, is attending a special boarding school in Philadelphia and learning about the world and himself. The author is a hearing person who grew up with deaf parents. She writes in a way that helps to make the language of signing real to her reader.

Starowitz, Anne Marie. **The Day We Met Cindy.** Washington, D.C.: Gallaudet University Press, Kendall Publications, 1988. Unpaginated. $9.95. (Ages 4–7)

This is a pleasant picture storybook about a first grade's reaction when a student's aunt, who was deaf, came to their classroom. It outlines in brief description and in pictures created by the students how and why they went about learning sign language.

Sullivan, Mary Beth; Bourke, Linda. **A Show of Hands.** New York: Harper & Row, Harper Junior, 1980. 96 pp. $12.70. (Ages 9–13)

This introduction to sign language will also help readers to understand what it is like to be deaf in a hearing world.

Walker, Lou Ann. **Amy: The Story of a Deaf Child.** New York: E.P. Dutton, Lodestar Books, 1985. Unpaginated. $14.95. (Ages 7–10)

Amy Rowley, who is the only person in her school who is deaf, talks about her interests, her family, her friends, her pets, and adaptations she uses at home and in school. Many charming photographs show Amy at her many activities and signing selected words.

Zelonky, Joy. **I Can't Always Hear You.** Milwaukee: Raintree, 1980. 31 pp. $15.50. Elgin, Ill.: David C. Cook, 1986. $4.95 (Paper). (Ages 5–8)

After some initial difficulties with her classmates and with some help from adults, Kim adjusts to being the only student in her classroom who has a hearing impairment.

Learning Disabilities, Hyperactivity, and/or Attention Deficit Disorder

Aiello, Barbara; Shulman, Jeffrey. **Secrets (Aren't) Always for Keeps.** Frederick, Md.: Twenty-First Century Books; distributed by Paul H. Brookes, 1988. 48 pp. $12.95. (Ages 8–12)

The upbeat "Kids on the Block" puppets have long been effective in introducing young audiences to individual differences through presentations and question-and-answer sessions. Now the "Kids on the Block" characters appear in stories, along with representative questions and answers. In this book, Jennifer meets her pen pal from Australia and finds out that a learning disability doesn't need to be a secret.

DeClements, Barthe. **Sixth Grade Can Really Kill You.** New York: Viking Kestrel, 1985. 146 pp. $11.95. New York: Scholastic, Apple Paperback. $2.50. (Ages 9–12)

Helen is great in P.E., music, math, and making mischief, but she's in danger of failing sixth grade because of a reading problem. Working with her mother hasn't helped; working with a teacher in a special education room does.

Galvin, Matthew. **Otto Learns about His Medicine: A Story about Medication for Hyperactive Children.** New York: Brunner/Mazel, Magination Press, 1988. Unpaginated. $14.95; $5.95 (Paper). (Ages 7–11)

Otto is a young car who has problems paying attention and doing his homework and staying still. A mechanic helps his motor slow down with "a special car medicine."

Gilson, Jamie. **Do Bananas Chew Gum?** New York: Lothrop, Lee & Shepard, 1980. 158 pp. $10.95. (Ages 9–12)

Sam has "this learning disability thing"; in a new town and a new school, he hopes to overcome the old "Dumbhead Sam" image. With the help of a baby-sitting job, a couple of new friends, a tornado, and a special test, he's on his way.

Hansen, Joyce. **Yellow Bird and Me.** New York: Ticknor & Fields, 1986. 155 pp. $12.95. (Ages 9–12)

Doris is the smartest girl in her sixth grade class; James Towers, alias "Yellow Bird," isn't just clowning when he can't read or write. This interesting story of today, set in an inner-city New York school, is about friendship.

Lasker, Joe. **He's My Brother.** Niles, Ill.: Albert Whitman, 1974. 36 pp. $10.95. (Ages 3–8)

An older brother talks realistically, yet empathetically, about Jamie, a boy whose physical and mental development are uneven —a boy with "the invisible handicap."

Levinson, Marilyn. **And Don't Bring Jeremy.** New York: Holt, Rinehart and Winston, 1985. 122 pp. $10.95. (Ages 10–14)

Sixth grader Adam wants to fit into the new neighborhood but his older brother complicates things. Jeremy is different—clumsy, not good at sports, friendly with younger children, "neurologically impaired." Adam learns that friendship with peers is not always as one would wish and that it is possible for brothers who are very different from one another to be friends.

Martin, Ann M. **Yours Turly, Shirley.** New York: Holiday House, 1988. 133 pp. $12.95. (Ages 8–12)
    Shirley's learning disability is making school more miserable than ever for her. To add to her difficulties, her parents adopt a child from Vietnam who proves, with Shirley's help, to be super-smart. And then fourth grade turns out to be not so bad, after all.

Moss, Deborah. **Shelley, the Hyperactive Turtle**. Rockville, Md.: Woodbine House, 1989. Un-paginated. $12.95. (Ages 4–7)
    Shelley is wiggly and squirmy and moves like a rocket. A doctor helps Shelley and his family understand hyperactivity and gives Shelley special medicine to control that wiggly feeling.

Pevsner, Stella. **Keep Stompin' Till the Music Stops.** Boston: Houghton Mifflin, 1976. 136 pp. $10.95. (Ages 9–12)
    Richard, a twelve year old with learning disabilities, gains in self-esteem and understanding during a family reunion at the home of his great-grandfather. Richard's perceptual problems are described with sensitivity.

Rabe, Berniece. **Tall Enough to Own the World.** New York: Franklin Watts, 1989. 160 pp. $12.90. (Ages 9–12)
    Ten-year-old Joey Caruba can't read and that makes him wild and rebellious, always in trouble. A secret club and a determined volunteer teacher change his life.

Smith, Doris Buchanan. **Kelly's Creek.** New York: Harper & Row, Harper Junior, 1975. 69 pp. $13.75. (Ages 9–12)
    The thoughts and feelings of nine-year-old Kelly, a boy with motor and perceptual problems, are explored with insight and understanding; the teaching techniques used to help him are clearly described. How Kelly gains more self-confidence and approval from others through his interest in a Georgia marsh and with the help of a college student makes an interesting story.

Swenson, Judy Harris; Kunz, Roxane Brown. **Learning My Way: I'm a Winner!** Minneapolis: Dillon, 1986. 39 pp. $8.95. (Ages 7–10)
    In this informational book, Dan talks about his trouble at school, how his learning disability and hyperactivity were diagnosed, and the ways in which his Individualized Education Plan helped to make learning easier. An adult resource guide, including ideas for discussion and "Fun-work Activities," is appended.

Wolff, Virginia Euwer. **Probably Still Nick Swansen.** New York: Henry Holt and Company, 1988. 144 pp. $13.95. (Ages 12–15)
    This well-written and sympathetic story is about Nick, a student in special education. Told from Nick's point of view, the book relates some events in Nick's sixteenth year: inviting newly mainstreamed Shana to the prom and waiting when she doesn't arrive, dealing with his dog being hit by a car, still having the dream about his older sister's death some years earlier.

Mental Illness and Behavior Disorders

Dinner, Sherry H. **Nothing to Be Ashamed Of: Growing Up with Mental Illness in Your Family.** New York: Lothrop, Lee & Shepard, 1989. 212 pp. $7.95. (Ages 12–15)

Written to help young people who are growing up with a family member who is mentally ill, this book offers information about the symptoms and treatments of the major mental illnesses and coping strategies for the reader. The author is a child psychologist and her tone is reassuring and helpful. She uses real-life descriptions and anticipates the questions a young person trying to deal with a "jumble of mixed-up reactions" might ask.

Galvin, Matthew. **Robby Really Transforms: A Story about Grown-Ups Helping Children.** New York: Brunner/Mazel, Magination Press, 1988. Unpaginated. $4.95 (Paper). (Ages 10–13)

Robby is almost nine years old and living in a foster home. He is obsessed by robots. A case worker, his foster parents, and a therapist help Robby understand more of the real world around him.

Johnson, Julie Tallard. **Understanding Mental Illness: For Teens Who Care about Someone with Mental Illness.** Minneapolis: Lerner Publications, 1989. 72 pp. $9.95. (Ages 12–15)

This slim book will help adolescents understand serious mental illness—depression, manic depression, and schizophrenia—and the ways in which they affect all members of a family. Appropriate ways to cope are suggested.

Hamilton-Paterson, James. **The House in the Waves.** Chatham, N.Y.: S.G. Phillips, 1970. 157 pp. $14.95. (Ages 12–15)

The struggle of a severely withdrawn fourteen-year-old boy to regain contact with reality is described in this sensitive story. Although the boy is not necessarily developmentally disabled (his past history includes a mother who died early and an abusive father), the book is well worth reading for its knowledgeable account of hospital life, staff, and therapy.

Hyde, Margaret O. **Is This Kid "Crazy?" Understanding Unusual Behavior.** Philadelphia: Westminster Press, 1983. 96 pp. $9.95. (Ages 12–15)

In an attempt to help young people understand mental illness and other reasons for unusual behavior, the author discusses the possible causes, symptoms, and treatments of schizophrenia, depression, eating disorders, and other emotional problems.

Hyland, Betty. **The Girl with the Crazy Brother.** New York: Franklin Watts, 1987. 137 pp. $12.90. (Ages 12–15).

Dana's family has moved from Boston to California and she is adjusting to a new high school and new friends when her older brother is diagnosed as schizophrenic. Dana, her brother, and her parents must make further adjustments.

Mental Retardation

Baldwin, Anne Norris. **A Little Time.** New York: Viking, 1978. 96 pp. $8.95. (Ages 8–12)

From the point of view of ten-year-old Sara, life in a family which includes a four year old with Down syndrome is described. The reactions of others, the long-term issues, as well as the daily problems and rewards of living with a brother who is retarded, are simply and honestly presented.

Cairo, Shelley. **Our Brother Has Down's Syndrome: An Introduction for Children.** Willowdale, Ontario: Annick Press, 1985. Unpaginated. $6.00. (Ages 5–8)

Two sisters share what it's like to live with their younger brother, Jai, who has Down syndrome. Charming color photographs help to tell their loving story.

Carrick, Carol. **Stay Away from Simon.** New York: Clarion Books, 1985. 63 pp. $10.95. (Ages 8–12)

The story takes place on Martha's Vineyard in the 1830s. Simon, the miller's son, has a mind "too slow for schooling," and some of the children are afraid of him. Lucy learns something about Simon and herself when she and her younger brother get lost in a snowstorm; it is Simon who saves them.

Cassedy, Sylvia. **M.E. and Morton.** New York: Thomas Y. Crowell, 1987. 312 pp. $12.95. (Ages 12–15)

Eleven-year-old Mary Ella really wants a friend. She would also like to be an only child; Morton, her older brother, is slow to learn and an embarrassment. What happens one summer comprises this story of Mary Ella, Morton, and the new girl, Polly, who likes both of them.

Cohen, Floreva. **My Special Friend.** New York: Board of Jewish Education, 1986. Unpaginated. $10.95; $5.95 (Paper). (Ages 5–8)

Doron shares, in words and photographs, his friendship with Jonathan, who has mental retardation. Every Sabbath morning they are together for the services at the synagogue.

Cohen, Miriam. **It's George!** New York: Greenwillow Books, 1988. Unpaginated. $11.95. (Ages 4–8)

George may not be the smartest first grader but there are some very special and important things that he can do well.

Hasler, Eveline. **Martin is Our Friend.** Nashville: Abingdon, 1981. Unpaginated. $7.75. (Ages 4–7)

Martin has mental retardation and cannot do easily what the other children do. He can, however, learn to ride a horse and eventually share that ability with others.

Hunt, Irene. **The Everlasting Hills.** New York: Charles Scribner's Sons, 1985. 184 pp. $12.95. (Ages 10–14)

Newberry Medalist Irene Hunt portrays Jeremy Tydings as a sympathetic young character with mental retardation. His older sister tries to shield him from their father's cruel contempt; Jeremy grows in maturity and understanding during one fateful summer.

Litchfield, Ada B. **Making Room for Uncle Joe.** Niles, Ill.: Albert Whitman, 1984. Unpaginated. $10.25. (Ages 7–10)

> Uncle Joe moves from a "state hospital school" to live with his sister and her family; his nephew describes the adjustments they all have to make. Uncle Joe has Down syndrome.

Rabe, Berniece. **Where's Chimpy?** Niles, Ill.: Albert Whitman, 1988. Unpaginated. $11.95. (Ages 4–8)

> This utterly charming book tells the delightful story of Misty and her Daddy at bedtime when she discovers her favorite stuffed monkey is missing. The story is simple and very real; the color photographs are extraordinary. Down syndrome is incidentally described in an introductory page.

Shalom, Debra Buchbinder. **Special Kids Make Special Friends.** Bellmore, N.Y.: Association for Children with Down Syndrome, 1984. 43 pp. $5.00 (Paper). (Ages 3–6)

> Written to educate the very young about Down syndrome, this engaging booklet illustrates, in photographs and text, students learning and playing in their special preschool class. Its emphasis is on their similarities with typical children.

Shyer, Marlene Fanta. **Welcome Home, Jellybean.** New York: Macmillan, Aladdin Books, 1978. 152 pp. $3.95 (Paper). (Ages 12–15)

> Twelve-year-old Neil writes of the drastic changes faced by his family when his sister, who has spent nearly all of her thirteen years in institutions, comes home to live. The events are sometimes amusing and usually believable; this older book is honest and important.

Sobol, Harriet Langsman. **My Brother Steven is Retarded.** New York: Macmillan, 1977. 26 pp. $8.95. (Ages 6–10)

> Eleven-year-old Beth talks frankly about life with her older brother Steven, who was brain-damaged during the birth process. Black-and-white photographs illustrate the simple, truthful text.

Stefanik, Alfred T. **Copycat Sam: Developing Ties with a Special Child.** New York: Human Sciences Press, 1982. Unpaginated. $13.95. (Ages 6–10)

> Freddie's new neighbor, Sam, looks strange, talks like a baby, and imitates everything Freddie does. Freddie feels uncomfortable and exasperated until he learns that Sam can be a friend.

Wright, Betty Ren. **My Sister Is Different.** Milwaukee: Raintree, 1981. 31 pp. $15.35. (Ages 5–8)

> Carlo discovers some important truths about all his feelings toward his older sister Terry when he loses her in a department store. Terry has mental retardation.

Multiple Disabilities

Emmert, Michelle. **I'm the Big Sister Now.** Niles, Ill.: Albert Whitman, 1989. Unpaginated. $12.95. (Ages 7–10)

    Michelle and Amy Emmert are actual sisters. Nine-year-old Michelle talks about living with a sibling who has cerebral palsy and is severely disabled. Even though Amy is five years older, Michelle is "the big sister now." Lovely drawings illustrate the text.

Prall, Jo. **My Sister's Special.** Chicago: Children's Press, 1985. 31 pp. $4.95. (Ages 4–8)

    Fine black-and-white photographs help Angie's brother tell her story. Angie can't walk or talk or use her arms. She can, however, laugh and go to school and be a real and important part of her family.

Physical Disabilities

Aiello, Barbara; Shulman, Jeffrey. **It's Your Turn at Bat.** Frederick, Md.: Twenty-First Century Books; distributed by Paul H. Brookes, 1988. 48 pp. $12.95. (Ages 8–12)

The upbeat "Kids on the Block" puppets have long been effective in introducing young audiences to individual differences through presentations and question-and-answer sessions. Now the "Kids on the Block" characters appear in stories, along with representative questions and answers. In this book, Mark Riley's interest in sports and a writing assignment cause and resolve a problem. Mark has cerebral palsy.

Allen, Anne. **Sports for the Handicapped.** New York: Walker, 1981. 80 pp. $10.85. (Ages 8–12)

The author tells the real stories of real people with disabilities who have become winners in a variety of adapted sports—skiing, wheelchair basketball, swimming, track and field, football, and horseback riding. The book includes a number of black-and-white photographs.

Blos, Joan W. **Brothers of the Heart.** New York: Charles Scribner's Sons, 1985. 162 pp. $12.95. (Ages 13–17)

The year is 1837 when fourteen-year-old Shem and his family make their way to a far-away village. Shem's crippled leg causes him anguish, estrangement from his family, and isolation with an old Indian woman in the Michigan wilderness. This is a beautifully written survival novel of love and growth in life and spirit.

Blume, Judy. **Deenie.** New York: Macmillan, Bradbury Press, 1973. 159 pp. $11.95. (Ages 10–14)

A young teenager confronts her feelings about disability when scoliosis (curvature of the spine) is diagnosed. This temporary but serious orthopedic disability interferes with her mother's plans for a modeling career for Deenie and allows the reader to watch an adolescent cope with typical social and emotional fears, along with family pressures.

Fassler, Joan. **Howie Helps Himself.** Niles, Ill.: Albert Whitman, 1975. 32 pp. $11.95. (Ages 4–8)

Howie, who uses a wheelchair, makes his wish come true. This is a story for the very young that deals with the frustration—and the triumph—of coming to terms with a disability.

Gould, Marilyn. **Golden Daffodils.** Reading, Mass.: Addison-Wesley, 1982. 172 pp. $10.95. (Ages 9–12)

The fifth-grade heroine of **Golden Daffodils** has cerebral palsy. When she transfers from her special school to her neighborhood school, she meets challenges, problems, and new friends and comes to some important understandings.

Gould, Marilyn. **The Twelfth of June.** New York: J.B. Lippincott, 1986. 183 pp. $11.70. (Ages 9–12)

The feisty heroine of **Golden Daffodils** is now in junior high and her friend Barney wants to make the day of his bar mitzvah their secret betrothal day as well. Living with cerebral palsy is treated frankly and openly.

Greenfield, Eloise. **Darlene.** New York: Routledge, Chapman & Hall, 1980. Unpaginated. $8.95. (Ages 4–7)

Darlene really doesn't want to continue her visit; her uncle and her cousin help to change her mind. Darlene just happens to use a wheelchair.

Howard, Ellen. **Circle of Giving.** New York: Atheneum, 1984. 99 pp. $10.95. (Ages 8–12)

It is California in the late 1920s and the First Annual Stanley Avenue Christmas Eve Party brings neighbors of many different backgrounds together. Francie, the "poor, little paralyzed girl," helps them all to share some very special gifts in this well-written story.

Kaufman, Curt; Kaufman, Gita. **Rajesh.** New York: Atheneum, 1985. 32 pp. $8.95. (Ages 4–7)

When Rajesh was born, his legs and one hand "weren't all there." This story shares, in words and photographs, what it was like in his kindergarten class. The author was his teacher.

Lasker, Joe. **Nick Joins In.** Niles, Ill.: Albert Whitman, 1980. Unpaginated. $12.95. (Ages 6–9)

Nick is starting school and he is worried; how will other children react to him and to his wheelchair? School turns out to be a good place for everyone to be together.

Muldoon, Kathleen M. **Princess Pooh.** Niles, Ill.: Albert Whitman, 1989. Unpaginated. $12.95. (Ages 7–10)

Patty Jean thinks of her older sister as "Princess Pooh" who uses "a throne with wheels" and gets lots of special attention. One day, Patty Jean tries out her sister's wheelchair and begins to understand what living with a disability is really like.

Nadas, Betsy P. **Danny's Song.** Northbrook, Ill.: Hubbard Scientific, 1975. Unpaginated. $4.95. (Ages 4–8)

Danny Mason is slow to do some things because of his leg braces and crutches, but there are many things he can do—and do well. This is a colorful story for very young children—one of the **I Am, I Can, I Will** series of video, audio, and print materials developed by the producers of "Mister Roger's Neighborhood."

Perske, Robert. **Don't Stop the Music.** Nashville: Abingdon, 1986. 140 pp. $7.95 (Paper). (Ages 13–17)

Two teenagers with cerebral palsy crack an auto-theft ring and teach the journalist-narrator about a different lifestyle.

Rabe, Berniece. **The Balancing Girl.** New York: E.P. Dutton, 1981. 29 pp. $11.95; $3.95 (Paper). (Ages 4–7)

Margaret uses a wheelchair and sometimes crutches at school, has a problem getting along with Tommy, and is quite adept at balancing things. She and her classmates work together to make a successful school carnival; even Tommy can share in the triumph.

Rabe, Berniece. **Margaret's Moves.** New York: E.P. Dutton, 1987. 105 pp. $10.95. (Ages 9–12)

    The heroine of **The Balancing Girl** is now nine years old and determined to get a sports-model wheelchair so that she can be as fast as her younger brother, Rusty. The summer is a busy one.

Robinet, Harriette Gillem. **Ride the Red Cycle.** Boston: Houghton Mifflin, 1980. 34 pp. $6.95. (Ages 7–10)

    Jerome has a dream—he wants to ride a red cycle. But Jerome can't even walk. Making his dream come true takes courage, pride, and a stubborn determination.

Roy, Ron. **Move Over, Wheelchairs Coming Through!** New York: Clarion Books, 1985. 83 pp. $12.95. (Ages 9–12)

    The author has interviewed young people who use wheelchairs for a variety of reasons: arthrogryposis, hemolymphangioma, cerebral palsy, spina bifida, and muscular dystrophy. Excellent photographs and interesting text introduce us to seven individuals who lead active lives and have found adaptive ways to be part of the mainstream.

Sallis, Susan. **An Open Mind.** New York: Harper & Row, Harper Junior, 1978. 139 pp. $12.25. (Ages 12–15)

    David must adjust to his divorced father's intention to remarry. His new brother will be a boy with cerebral palsy who lives at an English school where David is doing volunteer work. The plot is not wholly credible but the book deals in an interesting way with a teenager learning about himself and his reactions to others.

Savitz, Harriet May. **Run, Don't Walk.** New York: New American Library, Signet, 1979. 132 pp. $2.25 (Paper). (Ages 12–15)

    This fictional account follows two teenagers who use wheelchairs in their struggles with personal, social, and political barriers. Putting laws to work at an immediate level, opening doors—both literally and figuratively—and finding out about oneself and others, make a gripping, contemporary story.

Seuling, Barbara. **I'm Not So Different.** Racine, Wis.: Western Publishing, A Golden Learn about Living Book, 1986. Unpaginated. $4.95. (Ages 5–8)

    Kit uses a wheelchair, goes to her neighborhood school, fights with her brother, and likes rock concerts. This book offers the pleasant reminder that children with disabilities feel the same as everyone else.

Southall, Ivan. **Let the Balloon Go.** New York: Bradbury Press, 1968. 136 pp. $10.95. (Ages 9–14)

    This story portrays the tensions, frustrations, and need for freedom of an intelligent, imaginative boy with a physical disability. All family members are dealt with honestly, sympathetically, and nonjudgmentally.

Stein, Sara Bonnett. **About Handicaps: An Open Family Book for Parents and Children Together.** New York: Walker, 1974. 47 pp. $10.95; $6.95 (Paper). (Ages 4–8)

This unique book has separate texts for adults and children. Vivid photographs and a reassuring, honest story explore the relationship between two young boys, one of whom has cerebral palsy. The text for parents provides specific detail and is designed to help adults prepare their children for the realities of the world about them.

Whinston, Joan Lenett. **I'm Joshua and "Yes I Can."** New York: Vantage Press, 1989. 34 pp. $6.95. (Ages 6–9)

Joshua is starting regular first grade and he is afraid of "the scariest day of his life." Joshua has cerebral palsy. His family and teachers help him to realize that there are things he can't do and things he can. The author is the real-life Joshua's mother.

Wolf, Bernard. **Don't Feel Sorry for Paul.** New York: Harper & Row, Harper Junior, 1974. 96 pp. $18.50. (Ages 5–8)

Good photographs illustrate the true story of two weeks in the life of seven-year-old Paul, born with his hands and feet incompletely formed. Paul and his family have adapted well to his physical differences; his experiences indicate the need for changes in the attitudes of outsiders.

Speech and Language Disabilities

Lee, Mildred. **The Skating Rink**. Boston: Houghton Mifflin, 1969. 126 pp. $10.95. (Ages 10–14)
  Fifteen-year-old Tuck Faraday has locked himself into a silent and isolated world because of his stammering; the understanding owner of a new skating rink helps him break out.

White, E.B. **The Trumpet of the Swan.** New York: Harper & Row, Harper Junior, 1970. 210 pp. $10.95; $2.95 (Paper). (All ages)
  Real facts of wildlife and nature blend with delightful fantasy in the charming story of Louis, a trumpeter swan who came into the world lacking a voice and learned to play a trumpet. This is a touching and inspiring story for all ages about adaptation and triumph.

Visual Disabilities

Aiello, Barbara; Shulman, Jeffrey. **Business is Looking Up.** Frederick, Md.: Twenty-First Century Books; distributed by Paul H. Brookes, 1988. 48 pp. $12.95. (Ages 8–12)

The upbeat "Kids on the Block" puppets have long been effective in introducing young audiences to individual differences through presentations and question-and-answer sessions. Now the "Kids on the Block" characters appear in stories, along with representative questions and answers. In this book, Renaldo's visual impairment doesn't get in the way of trying out a business venture with his friend, Jinx.

Cohen, Miriam. **See You Tomorrow, Charles.** New York: Greenwillow Books, 1983. Unpaginated. $2.95 (Paper). (Ages 4–7)

One of Miriam Cohen's delightful stories of a first grade class, **See You Tomorrow, Charles** introduces a new student. Charles is blind. The plot is simple and the unstated message will help develop a young child's appreciation of all people.

Delaney, Ned. **Two Strikes, Four Eyes.** Boston: Houghton Mifflin, 1976. 32 pp. $11.95. (Ages 4–8)

Toby is a mouse who loves baseball but cannot see without his glasses. This is a fantasy for young children that deals with the problems of teasing and social fears.

Dickerson, Peter. **Annerton Pit.** Boston: Little, Brown, 1977. 175 pp. $14.95. (Ages 12–15)

This is a lively, contemporary adventure story of two brothers who set off to find their grandfather who is investigating reports of ghosts in Northern England. Jake's blindness is not emphasized but fits naturally into the telling of this exciting tale.

Eyerly, Jeannette. **The Seeing Summer.** New York: Harper & Row, Harper Junior, 1981. 153 pp. $12.70. (Ages 10–14)

Ten-year-old Carey learns much about adaptations and friendship when a girl who is blind moves in next door. The story includes a kidnapping adventure.

Giff, Patricia Reilly. **Watch Out, Ronald Morgan!** New York: Viking Kestrel, 1985. $9.95. (Ages 4–7)

Ronald learns that glasses can't change everything but they can help him see things more clearly.

Hall, Lynn. **Half the Battle.** New York: Charles Scribner's Sons, 1982. 151 pp. $10.95. (Ages 12–15)

Two teenage brothers realize important things about one another and about themselves on a hundred-mile endurance ride on horseback. One of the brothers is blind.

Herman, Helen; Herman, Bill. **Jenny's Magic Wand.** New York: Franklin Watts, 1988. 32 pp. $9.90. (Ages 5–8)

After going to a school for children who are blind, Jenny moves to a school with children who can see. Her cane is her magic wand. Fine black-and-white photographs help to tell Jenny's story.

Kent, Deborah. **Belonging.** New York: Ace Books, 1979. 100 pp. $2.25 (Paper). (Ages 12–15)

Fifteen-year-old Meg has chosen to go to a regular high school rather than the special school for students who are blind. The difficulties and challenges she encounters in her desire for acceptance and her relationships with peers and teachers are described convincingly; the author was herself the only student who was blind in a regular public school.

Kuklin, Susan. **Mine for a Year.** New York: Coward-McCann, 1984. 77 pp. $10.95. (Ages 9–12)

This is the true account of twelve-year-old George and the dog he prepares for training as a guide dog for someone who is blind. George has an eye problem and thinks it may be possible that he will one day need a dog guide himself. Nice black-and-white photographs accompany the text.

McPhee, Richard. **Tom & Bear.** New York: Harper & Row, Harper Junior, 1981. 149 pp. $12.70. (Ages 10–14)

A factual account of the complete, twenty-six-day training process of a guide dog team by Guiding Eyes for the Blind is detailed. The author-photographer provides much additional information about blindness, the people being trained, and the early history of one guide dog.

Martin, Bill, Jr.; Archambault, John. **Knots on a Counting Rope.** New York: Henry Holt, 1987. Unpaginated. $14.95. (Ages 7–11).

An American Indian boy and his grandfather share memories of the past. The boy, "born with a dark curtain in front of [his] eyes," has dreams "more beautiful than rainbows and sunsets."

Newth, Philip. **Roly Goes Exploring.** New York: G.P. Putnam, 1981. 24 pp. $13.99 (Paper). (Ages 5–8)

Roly explores the geometric shapes in the pages of this unusual book. The unique format is described as a "book for blind and sighted children, in Braille and standard type, with pictures to feel as well as to see."

Sargent, Susan; Wirt, Donna Aaron. **My Favorite Place.** Nashville: Abingdon, 1983. Unpaginated. $4.35 (Paper). (Ages 6–9)

A young girl visits the seashore with her parents. She describes what she hears and feels, smells and tastes. The only thing she cannot do is see.

Wolf, Bernard. **Connie's New Eyes.** New York: Harper & Row, Harper Junior, 1976. 96 pp. $12.70. (Ages 10–14)

A photographic essay details both the training of Blythe, a Seeing-Eye dog, and that of her new mistress, Connie, who has been blind for all of her twenty-two years. Connie and Blythe are also shown together in the school for children with handicaps where Connie is a new teacher.

Yolen, Jane. **The Seeing Stick.** New York: Thomas Y. Crowell, 1977. Unpaginated. $13.89. (Ages 5–9)

This gentle tale, set in long-ago China, tells the story of an emperor's daughter who is saddened by the beauty around her because she is blind. And then one day an old man arrives to help the princess learn a different way to see.

JOURNALS, MAGAZINES, NEWSLETTERS, AND DIRECTORIES

PART V

Journals, Magazines, and Newsletters

For All Disabilities

American Rehabilitation. Rehabilitation Services Administration. (Send payment to Superintendent of Documents, U.S. Government Printing Office, Washington, DC 20402.) 4 issues a year, $5.00.

Children Today. U.S. Department of Health and Human Services, Office of Human Development Services, Administration for Children, Youth, and Families, Children's Bureau. (Send payment to the Superintendent of Documents, U.S. Government Printing Office, Washington, DC 20402.) 6 issues a year, $16.00.

Closing the Gap. P.O. Box 68, Henderson, MN 56044. (The focus of this newsletter is on practical use of technology in special education and rehabilitation.) 6 issues a year, $26.00.

Disability Rag. Box 145, Louisville, KY 40201. (The **Rag** offers an honest and often irreverent look at disability issues.) 6 issues a year, $12.00.

Disability Studies Quarterly. Department of Sociology, Brandeis University, Waltham, MA 02254. 4 issues a year, $10.00.

Especially Grandparents. ARC (Advocates, Resources and Counseling for Persons with Developmental Disabilities) of King County, 2230 Eighth Avenue, Seattle, WA 98121. 4 issues a year, $10.00.

Exceptional Children. Council for Exceptional Children, 1920 Association Drive, Reston, VA 22091–1589. 6 issues a year, $25.00, or with membership.

Exceptional Parent. P.O. Box 3000, Department EP, Denville, NJ 07834. 8 issues a year, $18.00.

Focus on Exceptional Children. Love Publishing Company, 1777 South Bellaire Street, Denver, CO 80222. (The subject of this newsletter is special education for children with special needs.) 9 issues a year, $24.00.

Focus on Fathers. Fathers' Outreach Project, Experimental Education Unit WJ-10, University of Washington, Seattle, WA 98195. 4 issues a year, no charge.

Journal of Disability Policy Studies. The University of Arkansas Press, Fayetteville, AR 72701. 4 issues a year, $24.50.

Kaleidoscope: International Magazine of Literature, Fine Arts, and Disability. Kaleidoscope Press, 326 Locust Street, Akron, OH 44310–0202. 4 issues a year, $9.00.

Special Parent/Special Child. Lindell Press, P.O. Box 462, South Salem, NY 10590. (The focus of this newsletter is on helping young children to learn developmental skills.) 6 issues a year, $18.00.

Teaching Exceptional Children. Council for Exceptional Children, 1920 Association Drive, Reston, VA 22091–1589. 4 issues a year, with membership.

Worklife: A Publication on Employment and Persons with Disabilities. The President's Committee on Employment of Persons with Disabilities, Suite 636, 1111 20th Street, N.W., Washington, DC 20036. 4 issues a year; limited number of complimentary subscriptions.

For Autism

Advocate. Autism Society of America, Suite 1017, 1234 Massachusetts Avenue, N.W., Washington, DC 20005. 4 issues a year, $30.00.

Focus on Autistic Behavior. Pro-Ed Journals, 8700 Shoal Creek Boulevard, Austin, TX 78758–6897. 6 issues a year, $20.00 (for individual).

Journal of Autism and Developmental Disorders. Plenum Publishing Corporation, 233 Spring Street, New York, NY 10013. 4 times a year, $25.00.

For Hearing Impairment

The Deaf American. National Association of the Deaf, 814 Thayer Avenue, Silver Spring, MD 20910. 4 issues a year, $10.00.

The Volta Review. Alexander Graham Bell Association for the Deaf, 3417 Volta Place, N.W., Washington, DC 20007. 7 issues a year, $35.00 with membership.

For Learning Disabilities

Academic Therapy. Pro-Ed Journals, 8700 Shoal Boulevard, Austin, TX 78758–6897. 5 issues a year, $26.00 (for individual).

Journal of Learning Disabilities. Pro-Ed Journals, 8700 Shoal Boulevard, Austin, TX 78758–6897. 10 issues a year, $45.00 (for individual).

Learning Disabilities Quarterly. Council for Learning Disabilities, Box 40303, Overland Park, KS 66204. 4 issues a year, $40.00.

For Mental Illness and Behavior Disorders

Claiming Children. The Federation of Families for Children's Mental Health, 1021 Prince Street, Alexandria, VA 22314–2971. 4 issues a year, $15.

For Mental Retardation

American Journal on Mental Retardation. American Association on Mental Retardation, 1719 Kalorama Road, N.W., Washington, DC 20009–2684. 6 issues a year, $60.00.

Down Syndrome: Papers and Abstracts for Professionals. 2525 Belmont Road, N.W., Washington, DC 20008. 4 issues a year, $10.00.

Education and Training in Mental Retardation. Council for Exceptional Children, 1920 Association Drive, Reston, VA 22091–1589. 4 issues a year, $28.00; $4.50 with membership.

Journal of Special Education. Pro-Ed Journals, 8700 Shoal Boulevard, Austin, TX 78758–6897. 4 issues a year, $55.00.

Mental Retardation. American Association on Mental Retardation, 1719 Kalorama Road, N.W., Washington, DC 20009–2684. 6 issues a year, $50.00; $13.00 with membership.

New Ways. P.O. Box 5072, Evanston, IL 60204. (This parent-friendly magazine shares articles on current trends and thinking.) 4 issues a year, $23.95.

Sharing Our Caring. P.O. Box 400, Milton, WA 98354. (Articles, parent sharing, and pictures are all about children with Down syndrome.) 5 issues a year, $12.00.

For Physical Disabilities

Accent on Living Magazine. P.O. Box 700, Gillum Road and High Drive, Bloomington, IL 61702–0700. 4 issues a year, $8.00.

Computer-Disability News. c/o National Easter Seal Society, 70 East Lake Street, Chicago, IL 60601. 4 issues a year, $15.00.

Journal of Rehabilitation. National Rehabilitation Association, 633 South Washington, Alexandria, VA 22314. 4 issues a year, $35.00 for nonmembers.

Mainstream. P.O. Box 370598, San Diego, CA 92137–0598. 10 issues a year, $16.98; 2 years, $32.00.

Spinal Network Extra. P.O. Box 4162, Boulder, CO 80306. 4 issues a year, $12.00.

For Speech and Language Disabilities

Augmentative Communication News. c/o Sunset Enterprises, One Surf Way, Suite 215, Monterey, CA 93940. 6 issues a year, $24.00 for families.

For Visual Impairments

Journal of Vision Impairment and Blindness. American Foundation for the Blind, 15 West 16th Street, New York, NY 10011. 10 issues a year, $25.00.

For Severe and Multiple Disabilities

JASH: The Journal of the Association for Persons with Severe Handicaps. The Association for Persons with Severe Handicaps, 7010 Roosevelt Way, N.E., Seattle, WA 98116. 4 issues a year, $30.00; or with membership.

Additional Resource

For journals and magazines throughout the world dealing with disability issues, see A Readers'/Writers' Guide to Periodicals in the Disability Field. The Committee to Promote Writing in Disability Studies, c/o Joseph L. Baird, English Department, Kent State University, Kent, OH 44242. $10.00.

Directories

For All Disabilities

College Guide for Students with Disabilities. $40.00. Abt Books, 140 Mt. Auburn Street, Cambridge, MA 02138.

Comprehensive Clinical Genetic Services Centers—A National Listing. Free. National Center for Education in Maternal and Child Health and National Maternal and Child Health Clearinghouse, 38th & R Streets, N.W., Washington, DC 20057.

Directory for Exceptional Children: A List of Educational and Training Facilities. 11th ed. $45.00. Porter Sargent, 11 Beacon Street, Boston, MA 02108.

Directory of College Facilities and Services for the Disabled. 2d ed. $95.00. Oryx Press, 2214 North Central at Encanto, Phoenix, AZ 85004–1483.

Directory of National Information Sources on Handicapping Conditions and Related Services. $17.00. U.S. Department of Education. Order from Superintendent of Documents, U.S. Government Printing Office, Washington, DC 20402.

Directory of Organizations Interested in the Handicapped. Free. People-to-People Committee for the Handicapped, 1111 20th Street, N.W., Suite 660, Washington, DC 20036–3470.

Directory of Private Schools for Exceptional Children. Free. National Association of Private Schools for Exceptional Children, 1625 Eye Street, N.W., Suite 50 C, Washington, DC 20006.

Directory of Travel Agencies for the Disabled. $21.95. Order from The Disability Bookshop, P.O. Box 129, Vancouver, WA 98666.

Disability and Rehabilitation Handbook. $52.95. McGraw-Hill, 11 West 19th St., New York, NY 10011.

Getting through College with a Disability: A Summary of Services Available on 5500 Campuses for Students with Handicapping Conditions. Limited quantities free. The President's Committee on Employment of Persons with Disabilities, Suite 636, 1111 20th Street, N.W., Washington, DC 20036.

The Guide to Recreation, Leisure, and Travel for the Handicapped. Volume 1: Recreation and Sports. Volume 2: Travel and Transportation. $59.95 each; $109.00 per set. Resource Directories, 3103 Executive Parkway, Toledo, OH 43606.

Handbook of Private Schools. $45.00. Porter Sargent, 11 Beacon Street, Boston, Massachusetts 02108.

Handicapped Funding Directory. $32.50. Research Grant Guides, P.O. Box 4979, Margate FL 33063.

Health Care U.S.A. $19.95. Prentice Hall, Simon & Schuster, 1230 Avenue of the Americas, New York, NY 10020.

The Illustrated Directory of Handicapped Products. $12.95. 497 Cameron Way, Buffalo Grove, IL 60089.

International Directory: Birth Defects, Genetic Services. $2.00. March of Dimes, 1275 Mamaroneck Avenue, White Plains, NY 10605.

The International Directory of Recreation-Oriented Assistive Device Sources. $36.95. Lifeboat Press, P.O. Box 11782, Marina del Rey, California 90295.

National Rural Parent Resource Directory. $7.50. American Council on Rural Special Education (ACRES), Western Washington University, Bellingham, WA 98225.

Parent's Guide to Accredited Camps. $9.95. American Camping Association, 5000 State Road, Martinsville, IN 46151.

Private Independent Schools. $75.00. Bunting & Lyon, 238 North Main Street, Wallingford, CT 06492.

Reaching Out: A Directory of National Organizations Related to Maternal and Child Health. 3d ed. Free. National Center for Education in Maternal and Child Health, 38th & R Streets, N.W., Washington, DC 20057.

The Self-Help Sourcebook: A Comprehensive National Guide to Finding and Forming Mutual and Self-Help Groups. 2d ed. $9.00. Self-Help Clearinghouse, Saint Clares-Riverside Medical Center, Pocono Road, Denville, NJ 07834.

Services for Women and Girls with Disabilities: A National Directory. $12.00. Educational Equity Concepts, 114 East 32nd Street, New York, NY 10016.

Starting Early: A Guide to Federal Resources in Maternal and Child Health. 2d ed. Free. National Center for Education in Maternal and Child Health, 38th & R Streets, N.W., Washington, DC 20057.

A World of Options: Guide to International Educational Exchange, Community Service, and Travel for Persons with Disabilities. $13.00. Mobility International USA, P.O. Box 3551, Eugene, OR 97403.

For Hearing and Speech Impairment

College and Career Programs for Deaf Students. $12.95 plus postage. Gallaudet University, Center for Assessment and Demographic Studies, Kendall Green, 800 Florida Avenue, N.E., Washington, DC 20002.

Guide to Professional Services. $28.00. American Speech-Language-Hearing Association, 10801 Rockville Pike, Rockville, MD 20852.

For Learning Disabilities

BOSC Directory: Facilities for Learning Disabled People. $25.00. BOSC Publishers, Box 305, Congers, NY 10920.

Directory of Facilities and Services for the Learning Disabled. 13th ed. $3.00. Academic Therapy Publications, 20 Commercial Boulevard, Novato, CA 95947–6191.

Directory of Summer Camps for Children with Learning Disabilities. $3.00. Association for Children and Adults with Learning Disabilities, 4156 Library Road, Pittsburgh, PA 14234.

HEATH Resource Directory. 6th ed. Free. HEATH (Higher Education and Adult Training for People with Handicaps), One Dupont Circle, Suite 800, Washington, D.C. 20036–1193.

National Directory of Four Year Colleges, Two Year Colleges, and Post High School Training Programs for Young People with Learning Disabilities. $21.95. Partners in Publishing, P.O. Box 713, Carmel, CA 93921.

What Do You Do after High School? The Nationwide Guide to Residential, Vocational, Social, and Collegiate Programs Serving the Adolescent, Young Adult, and Adult with Learning Disabilities. $29.95. Skyer Consultation Center, Inc., P.O. Box 121, Rockaway Park, NY 11694.

For Mental Illness and Behavior Disorders

Directory of Public and Private Programs for Emotionally Disturbed Children and Youth. $74.50. Oryx Press, 2214 North Central at Encanto, Phoenix, AZ 85004–1483.

Directory of Residential Facilities for Emotionally Handicapped Children and Youth. $74.50. Oryx Press, 2214 North Central at Encanto, Phoenix, AZ 85004–1483.

Mental Health Directory. $9.00. U.S. Department of Health and Human Services, National Clearinghouse for Mental Health Information, National Institute of Mental Health, 200 Independence Avenue, S.W., Washington, DC 20201.

For Mental Retardation

Clinical Programs for Mentally Retarded Children. Free. National Center for Education in Maternal and Child Health and National Maternal and Child Health Clearinghouse, 38th & R Streets, N.W., Washington, DC 20057.

Directory of Residential Centers for Adults with Developmental Disabilities. $75.00. Oryx Press, 2214 North Central at Encanto, Phoenix, AZ 85004–1483.

International Directory of Mental Retardation Resources. Free. President's Committee on Mental Retardation and the International League of Societies for the Mentally Handicapped. 330 Independence Avenue, S.W., Washington, DC 20201.

For Physical Disabilities

Accent on Living Buyer's Guide: Your Number One Source of Information on Products for the Disabled. $6.00. Cheever Publishing, P.O. Box 700, Bloomington, IL 61702.

Colleges That Enable: A Guide to Support Services Offered to Physically Disabled Students on 40 U.S. Campuses. $14.45. Park Avenue Press, 401 Park Avenue, Oil City, PA 16301.

For Visual Disabilities

Directory of Camps for Blind and Visually Impaired Children, Youths, and Adults. $7.95. American Foundation for the Blind, 15 West 16th Street, New York, NY 10011.

Directory of Services for Blind and Visually Impaired Persons in the United States. $39.95. American Foundation for the Blind, 15 West 16th Street, New York, NY 10011.

APPENDIX AND
INDEXES

PART VI

Appendix: Publishers' Addresses

Abbey Press, Hill Dr., St. Meinard, IN 47577. 812/357–8011.

Abingdon Press, 201 Eighth Ave. South, Nashville, TN 37202. 800/251–3320; 615/749–6000.

Ablenet, 1081 10th Ave., S.E., Minneapolis, MN 55414–1312. 800/322–0956.

Abt Books, 140 Mt. Auburn St., Cambridge, MA 02138. 617/661–1300.

Academic Guild Publishers, Child Welfare League of America, 440 First St., NW, Ste. 301, Washington, D.C. 20001–2085. 202/638–2952.

Academic Therapy Publications, 20 Commercial Blvd., Novato, CA 94949. 415/883–3314.

Academy Chicago Publishers, 213 W. Institute Place, Chicago, IL 60610. 800/248–READ; 312/644–1723.

Accent Books, 12100 W. Sixth Ave., Denver, CO 80215. 800/525–5550; 303/988–5300.

Ace Books, Berkley Publishing Group, 200 Madison Ave., New York, NY 10016. 212/686–9820.

Adama Books, 306 W. 38th St., New York, NY 10018. 800/672–6672; 212/594–5770.

Addison-Wesley, Rte. 128, Reading, MA 01867. 800/447–2226; 617/944–3700.

Adler & Adler, c/o Woodbine House, 5615 Fishers Lane, Rockville, MD 20852. 800/843–7323; 301–468–8800.

Aladdin Books, Macmillan Publishing Co., 866 Third Ave., New York, NY 10022. 800/257–5755; 212/702–2000.

American Association on Mental Retardation, 1719 Kalorama Rd., N.W., Washington, DC 20009. 202/387–1968.

American Foundation for the Blind, 15 W. 16th St., New York, NY 10011. 800/232–5463; 212/620–2000.

American Guidance Service, Publishers' Building, Circle Pines, MN 55014/1796.

Annick Press, 15 Patricia Ave., Willowdale, Ontario M2M 1H9, Canada. 416/221–4802.

Apple Paperback, Scholastic, 730 Broadway, New York, NY 10003. 800/392–2179; 212/505–3000.

Arco Publishing Co., Simon & Schuster, 1230 Ave. of the Americas, New York, NY 10020. 800/223–2336; 212/698–7000.

Arena Press, Academic Therapy Publications, 20 Commercial Blvd., Novato, CA 94949. 415/883–3314.

Jason Aronson, 230 Livingston St., Northvale, NJ 07647. 201/767–4093.

Association for the Care of Children's Health, 3615 Wisconsin Avenue, N.W., Washington, DC 20016

Atlantic-Little, Brown. See Little, Brown.

Atheneum, 866 Third Ave., New York, NY 10022. 212/614–1300.

Augsburg Publishing House, P.O. Box 1209, 426 S. Fifth St., Minneapolis, MN 55440. 800/328–4648; 612/330–3300.

Avon Books, 105 Madison Ave., New York, NY 10016. 800/654–5888; 212/481–5600.

Ballantine, 201 E. 50th St., New York, NY 10022. 800/638–6460; 212/751–2600.

Bantam Books, 666 Fifth Ave., New York, NY 10103. 800/223–6834; 212/765–6500.

Basic Books, 10 E. 53rd St., New York, NY 10022. 800/638–3030; 212/207–7057.

Beacon Press, 25 Beacon St., Boston, MA 02108. 617/742–2110.

Alexander Graham Bell Association for the Deaf, 3417 Volta Place, Washington, D.C. 20007. 202/337–5220.

Berkley Publishing Group, 200 Madison Ave., New York, NY 10016. 800/223–0510; 212/951–8800.

Betterway Publications, P.O. Box 219, Crozet, VA 22932. 804/823–5661.

John F. Blair, 1406 Plaza Dr., Winston-Salem, NC 27103. 800/222–9796; 919/768–1374.

Board of Jewish Education, 426 W. 58th St., New York, NY 10019.

R.R. Bowker, 245 W. 17th St., New York, NY 10011. 800/521–8110; 212/645–9700.

Bradbury Press, Macmillan Publishing Co., 866 Third Ave., New York, NY 10022. 800/257–5755; 212/702–2000.

Brian's House, 1300 S. Concord Rd., West Chester, PA 19382. 215/399–1175.

Paul H. Brookes, P.O. Box 10624, Baltimore, MD 21285. 800/638–3775; 301/337–9580.

Brookline Books, P.O. Box 1046, Cambridge, MA 02238. 617/868–0360.

William C. Brown, 2460 Kerper Blvd., Dubuque, IA 52001. 800/338–5578; 319/588–1451.

Brunner/Mazel, 19 Union Square West, New York, NY 10003. 212/924–3344.

Bubba Press, 2100 Cactus Court, No. 2, Walnut Creek, CA 94595. 415/943–5340.

Bull Publishing Co., P.O. Box 208, Palo Alto, CA 94302. 415/322–2855.

Cambridge University Press, 32 E. 57th St., New York, NY 10022. 800/221–4512; 212/688–8885.

Caring, Inc., P.O. Box 400, Milton, WA 98354. 206/922–8607.

Center for Thanatology Research and Education, 391 Atlantic Ave., Brooklyn, NY 11217–1701. 718/858–3026.

Children's Defense Fund, 122 C St., NW, Washington, D.C. 20001.

Children's Press, 5440 N. Cumberland Ave., Chicago, IL 60656. 800/621–1115; 312/693–0800.

Citadel Press, 120 Enterprise Ave., Secaucus, NJ 07094. 800/LS-BOOKS; 201/866–4199.

Clarion Books, Ticknor & Fields, 52 Vanderbilt Ave., New York, NY 10017. 212/972–1190.

Cleis Press, P.O. Box 8933, Pittsburgh, PA 15221. 412/731–3863.

College-Hill Press, 4284 41st St., San Diego, CA 92105. 617/227–0730.

Colwell Press, 500 S. Seventh St., Minneapolis, MN 55415.

CompCare Publishers, 18551 Von Karman, Irving, CA 92715. 800/328–3330; 612/559–4800.

Contemporary Books, 180 N. Michigan Ave., Chicago, IL 60601. 312/782–9181.

David C. Cook, 850 N. Grove Ave., Elgin, IL 60120. 800/323–7543; 708/741–0800.

Coordinating Council for Handicapped Children, 20 E. Jackson Blvd., Room 900, Chicago, IL 60604. 312/939–3513.

Council for Exceptional Children, 1920 Association Dr., Reston, VA 22091–1589. 703/620–3660.

Coward-McCann. See Coward, McCann & Geoghegan

Coward, McCann & Geoghegan, Putnam Publishing Group, 200 Madison Ave., New York, NY 10016.

Thomas Y. Crowell, Harper & Row, 10 E. 53rd St., New York, NY 10022. 800/242–7737; 212/207–7000.

Crown Publishers, 225 Park Ave. South, New York, NY 10002. 800/526–4264; 212/254–1600.

Current, Inc., P.O. Box 2559, Colorado Springs, CO 80901. 719/594–4100.

David & Charles, North Pomfret, VT 05053. 802/457–1911.

Delacorte Press, 1 Dag Hammarskjold Plaza, 245 E. 47th St., New York, NY 10017. 800/221–4676; 212/605–3000.

Dell Publishing Co., 666 5th Ave., New York, NY 10103. 800/223–6834; 212/765–6500.

Delta Books, 1 Dag Hammarskjold Plaza, 245 E. 47th St., New York, NY 10017. 800/255–4133/212–765–6500.

Demos, 156 5th Ave., Ste. 1018, New York, NY 10016. 212/255–8768.

Dillon Press, 242 Portland Ave. South, Minneapolis, MN 55415. 612/333–2691.

Dodd, Mead and Co., 6 Ram Ridge Rd., Spring Valley, NY 10977. 800/237–3255; 800/544–4463 (in NY).

Doubleday, 666 Fifth Ave., New York, NY 10103. 800/223–6834; 212/765–6500.

E.P. Dutton, 2 Park Ave., New York, NY 10016. 800/526–0275; 212/725–1818.

Ed-U Press, P.O. Box 583, Fayetteville, NY 13066. 315/637–9524.

Education Equity Concepts, 440 Park Avenue South, New York, NY 10016.

EPM Publications, 1003 Turkey Run Rd., McLean, VA 22101. 703/442–7810.

Exceptional Parent Press, 605 Commonwealth Ave., Boston, MA 02215. 617/536–8961.

Faber & Faber, 50 Cross St., Winchester, MA 01890. 617/721–1427.

Faith and Life Press, P.O. Box 347, Newton, KS 67114–0347. 316/283–5100.

Falmer Press, Taylor and Francis, Inc., 242 Cherry St., Philadelphia, PA 19106–1906.

Fearon Education, 500 Harbor Blvd., Belmont, CA 94002. 800/877–4283; 415/592–7810.

Feeling Good Associates, P.O. Box S, Kealakekua, HI 96750.

The Feminist Press, Box 1654, Hagerstown, MD 21741.

First Publications, P.O. Box 1832, Evanston, IL 60204. 708/869–7210.

Four Winds Press, Macmillan Publishing Co., 866 Third Ave., New York, NY 10022. 800/257–5755; 212/702–2000.

Free Press, Macmillan Publishing Co., 866 Third Ave., New York, NY 10022. 800/257–5755; 212/702–2000.

Friendship Press, 475 Riverside Dr., New York, NY 10115. 212/870–2586.

Gallaudet College Press. See Gallaudet University Press.

Gallaudet University Press, 800 Florida Ave. NE, Washington, D.C. 20002. 800/451–1073; 202/651–5488.

MIA.J. Garvin & Associates, P.O. Box 7525, Ann Arbor, MI 48107. 313/662–2734.

Golden Books, 850 Third Ave., New York, NY 10022. 212/753–8500.

Gollancz, St. Edmundsbury Press, Bury St. Edmunds, Suffolk, England.

Greenbaum & Markel Associates, 374 Hilldale Dr., Ann Arbor, MI 48105.

Greenwillow Books, 105 Madison Ave., New York, NY 10016. 800/631–1199; 212/889–3050.

Grune & Stratton, Harcourt Brace Jovanovich, Promotion Department, Orlando, FL 32887–0018. 800/782–4479; 407/345–2525.

Gryphon House, P.O. Box 275, Mt. Ranier, MD 20712.

Guilford Press, 72 Spring St., New York, NY 10012. 800/221–3966; 212/431–9800.

Harcourt Brace Jovanovich, 6277 Sea Harbor Dr., Orlando, FL 32821. 407/345–2000.

Harper & Row, 10 E. 53rd St., New York, NY 10022. 800/242–7737; 212/207–7000.

Harvard University Press, 79 Garden St., Cambridge, MA 02138. 617/495–2600.

Herald Press, 616 Walnut Ave., Scottdale, PA 15683. 800/245–7894; 412/887–8500.

Holiday House, 18 E. 53rd St., New York, NY 10022. 212/688–0085.

Henry Holt & Co., 115 W. 18th St., New York, NY 10011. 800/247–3912; 212/886–9200.

Holt, Rinehart and Winston. See Henry Holt & Co.

The Horn Book, 31 St. James Ave., Park Square Bldg., Boston, MA 02116. 800/325–1170; 617/482–5198.

Houghton Mifflin, 1 Beacon St., Boston, MA 02108. 800/225–3362; 617/725–5000.

Hubbard Scientific, P.O. Box 104, 1946 Raymond Dr., Northbrook, IL 60065–9976. 800/323–8368; 708/272–7810.

Human Kinetics Publishers, P.O. Box 5076, Champaign, IL 61820. 800/342–5457; 800/324–3665 (in IL).

Human Policy Press, P.O. Box 127, Syracuse, NY 13210. 315/423–3851.

Human Sciences Press, 72 Fifth Ave., New York, NY 10011. 212/243–6000.

Human Services Press, P.O. Box 421, Richmond Hill, Ontario, L4C 4Y8, Canada.

Susan Hunter Publishing, 1447 Peachtree St., NE, Ste. 807, Atlanta, GA 30309.

International Universities Press, 59 Boston Post Rd., Madison, CT 06443–1524. 203/245–4000.

Interstate Printers and Publishers, 19 N. Jackson St., P.O. Box 50, Danville, IL 61834–0050. 800/843–4774; 217/446–0500.

Jalmar Press, 45 Hitching Post Dr., Bldg. 2, Rolling Hills Estates, CA 90274–4297. 800/662–9662; 213/547–1240.

Johnny Reads, P.O. Box 12834, St. Petersburg, FL 33733. 813/867–7647.

Jossey-Bass, 350 Sansome St., San Francisco, CA 94104. 415/433–1767.

La Leche League International, 9619 Minneapolis Ave., P.O. Box 1209, Franklin Park, IL 60131.

Lea & Febiger, 600 Washington Square, Philadelphia, PA 19106. 800/433–3850; 215/922–1330.

Leisure Press, P.O. Box 5076, Champaign, IL 61820. 800/334–3665; 217/351–5076.

Lerner Publications, 241 First Ave., N. Minneapolis, MN 55401.

Lexington Books, D.C. Heath & Co., 125 Spring St., Lexington, MA 02173. 800/235–3565; 617/862–6650.

LINC Associates, 3857 North High St., Columbus, OH 43214.

J.B. Lippincott, E. Washington Square, Philadelphia, PA 19105. 215/238–4200.

Little, Brown, 34 Beacon St., Boston, MA 02108. 800/343–9204; 617/227–0730.

Lodestar Books, 2 Park Ave., New York, NY 10016. 800/526–0275; 212/725–1818.

Lothrop, Lee & Shepard, 105 Madison Ave., New York, NY 10016. 800/631–1199; 212/889–3050.

Love Publishing Co., 1777 S. Bellaire St., Denver, CO 80222. 303/757–2579.

Carol L. Lutey Publishing, Carol L. Lutey Publishing, North Star Rte., Lyons, CO 80540.

Longman, Longman Building, 95 Church St., White Plains, NY 10601. 914/993–5000.

McFarland & Co., P.O. Box 611, Jefferson, NC 28640. 919/246–4460.

McGraw-Hill, 11 W. 19th St., New York, NY 10011. 212/512–2000.

Macmillan Publishing Co., 866 Third Ave., New York, NY 10022. 800/257–5755; 212/702–2000.

Magination Press, Brunner/Mazel, 19 Union Square West, New York, NY 10003. 212/924–3344.

Media Productions & Marketing, 2440 O St., Ste. 202, Lincoln, NE 68510. 402/474–2676.

Memphis State University Press, Memphis, TN 38152. 901/454–2752.

Merrill Publishing Co., 1300 Alum Creek Dr., Columbus, OH 43216. 800/848–6205; 614/258–8441.

MIT Press, 55 Hayward St., Cambridge, MA 02142. 617/253–5646.

William Morrow, 105 Madison Ave., New York, NY 10016. 800/843–9389; 212/889–3050.

Mosaic Press, c/o Riverrun Press, 1170 Broadway, Ste. 804, New York, NY 10001.

C.V. Mosby Co., 11830 Westline Industrial Dr., St. Louis, MO 63146. 800/325–4177; 314/872–8370.

National Association for the Education of Young Children, 1834 Connecticut Ave., N.W., Washington, D.C. 20009–5786.

National Association of the Deaf, 814 Thayer Ave., Silver Spring, MD 20910.

Nelson-Hall Publishers, 111 N. Canal St., Chicago, IL 60606. 312/930–9446.

New American Library, 1633 Broadway, New York, NY 10019. 212/397–8000.

New Idea Press, P.O. Box 13683, Boulder, CO 80308–3683.

Newmarket Press, 18 E. 48th St., New York, NY 10017. 212/832–3575.

W.W. Norton, 500 Fifth Ave., New York, NY 10110. 800/223–2584; 212/354–5500.

Ohio University Press, Scott Quadrangle 220, Athens, OH 45701. 800/666–2211; 614/593–1155.

Orchard Books, Franklin Watts, 387 Park Ave. South, New York, NY 10016. 212/686–7070.

Oxford University Press, 200 Madison Ave., New York, NY 10016. 212/679–7300.

Padre Publications, Box 3113, Pismo Beach, CA 93449. 805/473–1947.

Pantheon Books, 201 E. 50th St., New York, NY 10022. 800/638–6460; 212/751–2600.

Parent/Professional Publications, P.O. Box 59730, Chicago, IL 60645.

Parenting Press, P.O. Box 15163, 7744 31st Ave. NE, Seattle, WA 98115. 800/99–BOOKS; 206/527–2900.

Penguin, 1633 Broadway, New York, NY 10019. 212/397–8000.

Perinatal Loss, 2116 N.E. 18th Ave., Portland, OR 97212. 503/284–7426.

Pharos Books, 200 Park Ave., New York, NY 10166.

S.G. Phillips, P.O. Box 83, Chatham, NY 12037. 518/392–3068.

Planned Parenthood Federation of America, 810 Seventh Ave., New York, NY 10019.

Planned Parenthood Shasta-Diablo, 1291 Oakland Blvd., Walnut Creek, CA 94596.

Plenum Publishing Corp., 233 Spring St., New York, NY 10013. 800/221–9369; 212/620–8000.

Pocket Books, Simon & Schuster, 1230 Ave. of the Americas, New York, NY 10020. 800/223–2336; 212/698–7000.

Practical Allergy Research Foundation, P.O. Box 60, Buffalo, NY 14223–0060. 716/875–5578.

Praeger Publishers, 1 Madison Ave., New York, NY 10010. 212/685–5300.

Prentice Hall, Simon & Schuster, 1230 Ave. of the Americas, New York, NY 10020. 800/223–2348; 212/698–7000.

Pro-Ed, 8700 Shoal Creek Blvd., Austin, TX 78758. 512/451–3246.

PST Educational Consultants, P.O. Box 620492, Littleton, CO 80162.

Publishers Mark, P.O. Box 6939, Incline Village, NV 89450. 702/831–5139.

Puffin Books, Viking Penguin, 40 W. 23rd St., New York, NY 10010. 212/337–5200.

G.P. Putnam's Sons, 51 Madison Ave., New York, NY 10010. 212/951–8700.

John Racila Associates, 2820 Oak Brook Rd., Oak Brook, IL 60521.

R & E Publishers, P.O. Box 2008, Saratoga, CA 95070. 408/866–6303. 408/866–6303.

Raintree Publishers, 310 Wisconsin Ave., Milwaukee, WI 53203. 800/558–7264; 414/273–0873.

Random House, 201 E. 50th St., New York, NY 10022. 800/638–6460; 212/751–2600.

Reality Productions, 9978 Holder St., Buena Park, CA 90620. 714/828–2199.

Research Press, 2612 N. Mattis Ave., Champaign, IL 61821. 217/352–3273.

Rocky Mountain Children's Press, 1520 Shaw Mountain Rd., Boise, ID 83712.

G. Allen Roeher Institute, c/o Fitzhenry & Whiteside, 195 Allstate Parkway, Markham, Ontario L3R 4T8, Canada. 800/387–9776; 416/477–0030.

Rosen Publishing Group, 29 E. 21st St., New York, NY 10010. 800/237–9932; 212/777–3017.

Routledge, Chapman & Hall, 29 W. 35th St., New York, NY 10001. 212/244–3336.

Routledge & Kegan Paul. See Routledge, Chapman & Hall.

St. Edmundsbury Press, Bury St., Edmunds, Suffolk, England.

St. Martin's Press, 175 5th Ave., New York, NY 10010. 800/221–7945; 212/674–5151.

Scholastic, 730 Broadway, New York, NY 10003. 800/392–2179; 212/505–3000.

Science and Behavior Books, P.O. Box 60519, Palo Alto, CA 94306. 415/965–0954.

Scott, Foresman, 1900 E. Lake Ave., Glenview, IL 60025. 708/729–3000.

Charles Scribner's Sons, Macmillan Publishing Co., 866 Third Ave., New York, NY 10022. 800/257–5755; 212/702–2000.

Seven Locks Press, P.O. Box 27, Cabin John, MD 20818. 301/320–2130.

Signet, New American Library, 1633 Broadway, New York, NY 10019. 212/397–8000.

Simon & Schuster, 1230 Ave. of the Americas, New York, NY 10020. 800/223–2336; 212/698–7000.

Slack Incorporated, 6900 Grove Rd., Thorofare, NJ 08086–9447. 800/257–8290; 609/848–1000.

Southern Illinois University Press, P.O. Box 3697, Carbondale, IL 62901. 618/453–2281.

Spinal Network, P.O. Box 4162, Boulder, CO 80306.

Springer Publishing Co., 536 Broadway, New York, NY 10012. 212/431–4370.

James Stanfield, P.O. Box 1983, Santa Monica, CA 90406.

Stanford University Press, Stanford, CA 94305. 415/723–9434.

State University of New York Press, State University Plaza, Albany, NY 12246. 800/252–3206; 518/472–5000.

Syracuse University Press, 1600 Jamesville Ave., Syracuse, NY 13244–5160.

Taplinger Publishing Co., 132 W. 22nd St., New York, NY 10011. 212/741–0801.

Teachers College Press, 1234 Amsterdam Ave., New York, NY 10027. 800/356–0409; 212/678–3929.

Teaching Research Publishers, 345 N. Monmouth Ave., Monmouth, OR 97361. 503/838–1220.

Temple University Press, 1601 N. Broad St., USB 306, Philadelphia, PA 19122. 215/787–8787.

Charles C Thomas, 2600 S. First St., Springfield, IL 62794–9265. 217/789–8980.

Ticknor & Fields, 52 Vanderbilt Ave., New York, NY 10017. 212/687–8996.

T.J. Publishers, 817 Silver Spring Ave., Silver Spring, MD 20910. 301/585–4440.

Triad Publishing Co., 1110 N.W. Eighth Ave., Gainesville, FL 32601. 800/874–7777, ext. 10; 904/373–5800.

Twenty-First Century Books, 44 N. Market St., Frederick, MD 21701. 800/692–6300; 301/694–0100.

Twin Peaks Press, P.O. Box 129, Vancouver, WA 98666.

University of California Press, 2120 Berkeley Way, Berkeley, CA 94720. 800/822–6657; 415/642–4247.

University of Michigan Press, P.O. Box 1104, 839 Greene St., Ann Arbor, MI 48106. 313/764–4394.

University of Minnesota Press, 2037 University Ave. SE, Minneapolis, MN 55414. 612/624–2516.

University of Toronto Press, 63A St. George St., Toronto, ON M5S 1A6. 416/978–2239.

University of Washington Press, P.O. Box 50096, Seattle, WA 98145–5096. 800/441–4115; 206/543–4050.

University Press of America, 4720 Boston Way, Lanham, MD 20706. 301/459–3366.

Van Nostrand Reinhold, 115 Fifth Ave., New York, NY 10003. 212/254–3232.

Vantage Press, 516 W. 34th St., New York, NY 10001. 212/736–1767.

Viking Kestral, 40 W. 23rd St., New York, NY 10010. 212/337–5200.

Viking Penguin, 40 W. 23rd St., New York, NY 10010. 212/337–5200.

Vintage Books, Random House, 201 E. 50th St., New York, NY 10022. 800/638–6460; 212/751–2600.

Walker & Co., 720 Fifth Ave., New York, NY 10019. 800/AT-WALKER; 212/265–3632.

Warner Books, 666 5th Ave., New York, NY 10103. 800/638–6460; 212/484–2900.

Washington Square Press, 1230 Avenue of the Americas, New York, NY 10020. 800/223–2336/212/698–7000.

Waterfront Books, 98 Brookes Ave., Burlington, VT 05401. 800/456–7500, ext. 2000; 802/658–7477.

Franklin Watts, 387 Park Ave., New York, NY 10016. 800/672–6672; 212/686–7070.

Western Psychological Services, 12031 Wilshire Blvd., Los Angeles, CA 90025. 800/222–2670; 213/478–2061.

Western Publishing Co., 1120 Mound Ave., Racine, WI 53404. 800/235–3089.

Westminster Press, 925 Chestnut St., Philadelphia, PA 19107. 800/523–1631; 215/928–2700.

Westview Press, 5500 Central Ave., Boulder, CO 80301. 303/444–3541.

Albert Whitman, 5747 W. Howard St., Niles, IL 60648. 800/255–7675; 708/647–1355.

B.L. Winch & Associates, 45 Hitching Post Dr., Rolling Hills Estates, CA 90274.

Woodbine House, 5615 Fishers Lane, Rockville, MD 20852. 800/843–7323; 301/468–8800.

World Rehabilitation Fund, 400 E. 34th St., New York, NY 10016.

Yale University Press, 302 Temple St., New Haven, CT 06511. 203/432–0960.

Young Adult Institute Press, 460 W. 34th St., New York, NY 10001.

Zigler Keyes Associates, P.O. Box 6394, Peace River, Alberta, Canada.

Index of Organizations and Agencies

Index of Authors and Editors

Index of Titles

Index of Subjects

ABOUT THE AUTHOR

Cory Moore's experience as the mother of a child with multiple disabilities influences her both personally and professionally. Since 1974, she has worked tirelessly for the Association for Retarded Citizens in Montgomery County, Maryland as a consultant and a parent information specialist. She also acts as Community Organizer for the Maryland Coalition for Integrated Education. In addition, she is a frequent speaker on disability issues throughout the United States and abroad. With **A READER'S GUIDE** now in its third edition, Cory Moore is a well respected critic of literature on disabilities and a dedicated advocate for people with special needs.